The Ambitious Elementary School

The Ambitious Elementary School

Its Conception, Design, and
Implications for Educational Equality

Elizabeth McGhee Hassrick, Stephen W. Raudenbush,
and Lisa Rosen

The University of Chicago Press Chicago and London

The University of Chicago Press, Chicago 60637
The University of Chicago Press, Ltd., London
© 2017 by The University of Chicago
All rights reserved. No part of this book may be used or
reproduced in any manner whatsoever without written
permission, except in the case of brief quotations in critical
articles and reviews. For more information, contact the
University of Chicago Press, 1427 E. 60th St., Chicago, IL
60637.
Published 2017
Printed in the United States of America

26 25 24 23 22 21 20 19 18 17   1 2 3 4 5

ISBN-13: 978-0-226-45651-5   (cloth)
ISBN-13: 978-0-226-45665-2   (paper)
ISBN-13: 978-0-226-45679-9   (e-book)
DOI: 10.7208/chicago/9780226456799.001.0001

Library of Congress Cataloging-in-Publication Data

Names: Hassrick, Elizabeth McGhee, author. | Raudenbush,
    Stephen W., author. | Rosen, Lisa Stefanie, author.
Title: The ambitious elementary school : its conception,
    design, and implications for educational equality /
    Elizabeth McGhee Hassrick, Stephen W. Raudenbush, and
    Lisa Rosen.
Description: Chicago ; London : The University of Chicago
    Press, 2017. | Includes bibliographical references and
    index.
Identifiers: LCCN 2016046171 | ISBN 9780226456515 (cloth :
    alk. paper) | ISBN 9780226456652 (pbk. : alk. paper) |
    ISBN 9780226456799 (e-book)
Subjects: LCSH: Education, Primary—United States. |
    Educational change—United States. | Educational
    equalization—United States.
Classification: LCC LA219 .H388 2017 | DDC 372—dc23
LC record available at https://lccn.loc.gov/2016046171

♾ This paper meets the requirements of ANSI/a Z39.48–1992
(Permanence of Paper).

CONTENTS

ACKNOWLEDGMENTS

For essential help obtaining information about the University of Chicago Charter School (UCCS), providing data support for the lottery study, and facilitating access to the school to conduct our research, we are grateful to our colleagues at the University of Chicago Urban Education Institute (UEI): Timothy Knowles, Linda Wing, Shayne Evans, Sara Ray Stoelinga, Ursula Mardyla, Penny Bender Sebring, Paul Goren, Julia Gwynne, and Sue Sporte. Diane Schanzenbach and Jonah Deutsch were also key in providing preliminary analyses of the school lottery data. Finally, we thank school founders Anthony S. Bryk, Sara Spurlark, and Sharon Greenberg for sharing archival documents and personal reflections related to the founding of the school that greatly assisted our historical analysis in chapter 3.

We are likewise thankful to the directors, instructional leaders, teachers, and students of the two UCCS elementary campuses that were the focus of this study. Campus directors, instructional coaches, and teachers found time away from their demanding work to meet with our research team. Students welcomed us during our observations. School staff members quickly responded to our questions and requests for data, invited us to observe their practice, and participated in interviews and focus groups. We are especially grateful to campus directors Nicole Woodard-Iliev, Stacy Beardsley, and Tanika Island; family and community engagement directors Todd Barnett and Rodney Brown; lead social workers Elizabeth Brown and Lo Patrick; family center director Danyelle Martin; family support counselor LaTonya Maxwell; literacy leaders Rosemary Baker, Michelle Cooney, Teyona James, Claudine Randolph, Dale Ray, Chris Vega, and Whitney Wall; math instructional leaders Claudine Randolph and Toi Smith; science instructional leader Jeanne Mills; arts coordinator Lauren

Lauter; technology coordinator Cindy Newton; cluster leaders Tina Keller and Kellie Washington; and classroom teachers Karishma Desai, Amanda Djikas, Erica Emmendorfer, Ali Ferguson, Larney Frazier, Shannon Justice, Trish Leslie, Kellie Moss, Sarah Nowak, LeAnita Randolph, Yvette Smith, Aurelia Spurlark, Stephanie Swanlund, Carrie Walsh, and Kandice Washington. Without their extraordinary cooperation and participation, this book would not have been possible. In particular, chapters 3 through 7—describing the history of the development of the elementary school model and the underlying principles of the model in reading, math, and school organization during the 2008–2012 study period—reflect our best attempt to summarize individual interviews, focus group interviews, observations, and feedback sessions between ourselves and these educators. We also wish to thank the following individuals for granting permission to use their photograph on the cover of the book: Tanika Island, Kandice Washington, and the parents of Crystal Rayford and Jaylen McDonald. We are grateful to UEI for permission to reproduce the photograph on the cover.

We also extend our sincere thanks to the many colleagues who offered helpful feedback on our ideas and arguments as they developed, commenting on numerous versions of the manuscript over time. We gratefully acknowledge the thoughtful and rigorous feedback provided by Anthony Bryk, Sharon Greenberg, Micere Keels, Timothy Knowles, Shayne Evans, Linda Wing, Marv Hoffman, Irving Levin, Susan Levine, Charles Lewis, Sybil Madison-Boyd, Michael McPherson, Charles Milgrom, Richard Murnane, Charles Payne, Nichole Pinkard, April Porter, Nancy Rion, Penny Bender Sebring, Ruby Takanishi, and Alex Vance. Terese Schwartzman, Kavita Kapadia Matsko, David Kerbow, Dale Ray, Kimberly Austin, and Emily Art patiently engaged in this project over a seven-year span, participating in workshops, multiple chapter feedback sessions, and ongoing discussions; analyzing the underlying organizing principles of the model; and linking the practice to broader theories about urban education. Elizabeth Branch Dyson, our editor at the University of Chicago Press, provided key editorial guidance, and our anonymous reviewers informed our revisions in thoughtful ways that greatly improved our book.

Others provided vital research assistance and support, including Katie Bennett, Robert Eschmann, Robert Hanna, Sanja Jagesic, Alex Kreuger, and Helen Zhang. Beverly Levy provided essential administrative support throughout every stage of the project. We thank them all sincerely.

We are likewise grateful for the generous support of our funders. Research reported in this book was supported by the Foundation for Child

Development, the William T. Grant Foundation, Irving Levin, the Lewis-Sebring Family Foundation, the Spencer Foundation, and the H. A. Vance Foundation. We are also grateful to Tom Wick for his assistance coordinating this support.

Some of the ideas in this book were articulated in S. W. Raudenbush's 2009 article, "The *Brown* Legacy and the O'Connor Challenge: Transforming Schools in the Images of Children's Potential," published in *Educational Researcher* 38 (3): 169–80. We are grateful to the American Educational Research Association for permission to reprint portions of this work.

Finally, we express deepest gratitude to our spouses—Charles McGhee Hassrick, Guanglei Hong, and Steven Fram—for their patience, support, and encouragement throughout the many years in which we worked on this project.

PART I

LESSONS FROM RESEARCH AND PRACTICE

CHAPTER 1 INTRODUCTION

The premise of our book is that increasing the amount and quality of schooling can substantially reduce economic and racial inequality in children's educational outcomes. We don't make this claim lightly, because the root causes of inequality lie largely outside the school walls. Indeed, it may seem naive to suppose that schooling can help us overcome problems it did not create.

However, considerable empirical evidence, reviewed in the next chapter, supports this claim. Research suggests that increasing access to early childhood education, increasing the amount of instructional time during the school day, and increasing the length of the school year have potential to boost the educational outcomes of the most-disadvantaged children and thereby reduce inequality in educational outcomes. Similarly, increasing the quality of schooling by reducing class size, improving teachers' knowledge and skill, tailoring instruction to students' varied needs, making instruction more coherent and explicit, and systematically supporting children's social and emotional development all have potential to improve achievement, on average, and to reduce inequality.

Encouraging this hopeful view, recent studies identify schools that are remarkably effective for disadvantaged children. These studies use a random lottery system to compare children attending new schools to statistically similar children who did not.[1] Many of the most-effective schools provide extra instructional time for all students and intense tutoring for children who are behind. All of them set high expectations for students. Some emphasize the centrality of a schoolwide culture that allows "no excuses" for failure: the school leaders, the staff, and the students themselves do not tolerate the argument that family difficulties or neighborhood disadvantage prohibit success in school. The most-effective schools typically use assessments of students' skill to guide instruction.[2] Certain comprehensive school reform programs—particularly Success for All, America's Choice, and Core Knowledge—have exhibited significant potential to increase the learning of students attending comparatively disadvantaged elementary schools.[3] This emerging body of research has generated considerable optimism about the notion that school improvement can reduce inequality in educational outcomes.

Unanswered Questions

In contrast to this optimistic view, however, is a history of failed attempts to improve elementary schooling for the children in greatest need, which Charles M. Payne analyzes well in his book *So Much Reform, So Little Change.*[4] For fifty years, overcoming economic inequality in educational achievement has been the central aim of federal education policy. That goal has gone unfulfilled.[5] Indeed, recent research suggests that economic inequality in educational attainment is increasing.[6] Moreover, a century-long march toward racial equality in educational outcomes stalled around 1990.[7] The current reality is that less than two-thirds of all poor minority children in the United States ever earn a regular high school diploma; a minority of those ever attend a four-year college; and a fraction of those attending such a college ever receive a college diploma.[8] These facts would perhaps have been less troubling in past times, when unskilled laborers often earned sufficient wages to support a family. Given the importance of educational credentials and cognitive skills in the current labor market, the dismal results of urban schooling constitute a crisis. We can't say that school reform over the past fifty years hasn't made a positive difference, because we don't know how bad things would be had the country not engaged in school reform. But there is no doubt that school reform has not been sufficient to help low-income children gain the skills they need to be successful.

If school improvement holds great potential for reducing educational inequality, why have forty-five years of sustained and varied attempts to improve schools been so unsuccessful in achieving their goals? And why are the schools that produce excellent results for low-income minority children so exceptional?

The studies reviewed in chapter 2 examine the impact of particular interventions holding constant all other factors, but they don't tell us how to combine knowledge from the entire body of research to create powerful schools. We have discovered, for example, that when we randomly assign teachers and students to small versus large classes, the students attending the smaller classes learn more than do the students attending the large classes. And we have discovered that students exposed to summer instruction learn more than do similar children who stay on summer recess. Similarly, we've seen the isolated effects of particular approaches to reading or science instruction or tutoring. In principle, a school that simultaneously enacts a list of such interventions might produce large gains for students. But effectively implementing a series of interventions in the daily life of a school is not like plugging new appliances into an electrical outlet. New interventions have to be integrated together and meshed with current teaching practice to improve the overall life of a school. Achieving such integration is a problem of school organization about which the research has comparatively little to say. Hence, although the research findings we summarize have potential to substantially improve student learning, the question of how to realize this potential by transforming the daily life of students and teachers within particular schools remains unanswered.

Studies of highly effective elementary schools tend to emphasize the importance of particular school characteristics. But for anyone who wants to create an effective school—or to improve the effectiveness of an existing school—large questions remain unanswered: What are the most important academic skills for children to acquire starting in preschool through the elementary years? What kinds of instruction are needed to ensure that children from varied backgrounds obtain these skills? How can we organize the schoolhouse to make sure that such instruction occurs reliably, so that the vast majority of children become skilled readers and mathematical problem–solvers by grade 3? Specifically, what kinds of skills and practices do teachers need to provide such instruction? How can school leaders help teachers gain the skills they need and support them to work in new ways? How can they assure that skilled teachers are encouraged and promoted while persistently ineffective teachers find other lines of work? What strategies can school principals and teachers use to engage parents productively in this enterprise? How do school leaders identify children and families who need supplementary academic and or social support—and ensure that such support is forthcoming in time to prevent school failure and to prevent unaddressed problems from undermining the broader instructional enterprise?

The answers to these questions lie scattered in the archives of research and in the minds of expert practitioners. Developmental scientists know a lot about the skills students need to gain and in what sequence, but they know little about how to organize instruction to ensure that these skills emerge. Economists know that teachers vary considerably in skill; they have ideas about how to hire the best teachers, but know little about how to improve the skill of practicing teachers. Sociologists have learned a great deal about how schools manage and coordinate teachers' work, but not so much about how the work of teaching most efficiently produces student learning. Research on clinical practice tells us a lot about how to train social workers, but little about how social workers and teachers should coordinate their efforts. Unfortunately, social scientists in these disciplines interact rarely with one another and virtually never discuss how to mobilize their collective knowledge to ensure excellent schooling for the children who need it most.

Similarly, expert practitioners have devised working solutions to many of these problems. Some teachers are masterful at teaching early reading, some at teaching early math. Some principals are powerful instructional leaders, and some social workers take a comprehensive approach with troubled children and families. However, their knowledge is often implicit in practice and is rarely coordinated deliberately to shape the school as an organization. Even more fundamentally, scholars and practitioners rarely engage in the sustained interaction required to clarify and integrate what they know and test it in practice.

Our Research Project

In this book we describe a concerted effort to enact a coherent model of effective elementary schooling rooted in knowledge about learning, teaching, and school organization derived from both scholarly research and expert practice. The founders and subsequent leaders at the University of Chicago Charter School (UCCS) developed this model. UCCS consists of four campuses: two elementary, one middle, and one high school campus on the South Side of Chicago. These are public schools operated by the University of Chicago's Urban Education Institute (UEI) and serve African American children. Our book focuses solely on the two elementary school campuses, North Kenwood/Oakland (NKO) and Donoghue. During the time we collected data at the elementary campuses, from 2008 to 2012, about 80 percent[9] of these children were low income as defined by eligibility for the federally subsidized lunch program.

We knew that the designers of the school had sought to integrate the best available research on reading instruction, math instruction, and school organization in order to create a coherent model of school prac-

tice, and that these designers had worked to hire skilled leaders to help
refine and implement that model. So we launched a research project that
aimed to make the elements of the model explicit and to test the impact
of the school on its students. Over a period of five years, we interviewed
school leaders, teachers, and social workers at the two campuses to clarify the aims and design of their practice. We gathered documents and
visited classrooms to discover visible traces of the model in practice. We
used the random assignment of students by means of an annual lottery to
evaluate the impact of the school on reading and math achievement. This
book describes what we learned and explores implications for reducing
educational inequality.

High dropout rates and low levels of literacy among low-income, minority youth in US schools are intolerable. But the aims of those who
created the school we describe went far beyond correcting this problem.
Our book is about the conception and design of the school they created,
and the implications of their experience for anyone who wants to tackle
educational inequality.

Those who designed and ran this school reasoned that being committed to children's success, adopting good curricula, and hiring good teachers were essential but not sufficient to achieve their ambitious aims. One
needed also to know what children need to know, when, and in what sequence, and what kinds of teaching are required to generate the requisite
learning opportunities. But even with that knowledge, a complex engineering problem emerged because children come to school with remarkably heterogeneous skills. Tailoring instruction to those varied children is
challenging work, requiring considerable collaboration and professional
development. In the view of those we interviewed and observed, solving
this problem required a new conception of teachers' work and a fairly
radical reorganization of the school and its leadership. It required new
tools and practices, new relationships among teachers, new partnerships
with parents, and mobilizing time in highly strategic ways. Above all it
meant keeping close track of every child's progress and taking pains to
ensure that every child got on track for academic success. If this was a "no
excuses" school, it's the adults who refused to make excuses.

A powerful instructional system is not, however, constituted merely
by a list of tools such as textbooks, assessments, teaching strategies, or
summer school schedules; or by a set of new professional roles—though
new roles prove essential in the work we describe later in this book. Also
essential are a set of norms within a culture of commitment to ambitious
learning, a culture that motivates the invention and use of such tools and

roles to serve collective purposes. And knowledge is required to use these tools and roles well. For example, educators at UCCS would hold that one has to assess every child frequently, evaluate each child's recent progress, then set a new instructional plan for every child; otherwise some children will fall through the cracks. The specific tools—that is, the assessment instruments and the instructional plans—do not themselves constitute the model we describe apart from the school culture that compels their invention and use. But a school culture without such tools would not likely produce ambitious learning or be sustained. Using the tools well promotes teacher learning and builds the culture. The culture, the knowledge, and the tools stand in dynamic relation, and together produce evidence day by day that the children can indeed rise to the high level of the adults' expectations. Adults use this evidence to reinforce their efforts.

Emerging from our research project is the sense that instructional improvement within conventional schools is extraordinarily difficult work and that schools that are reliably effective for low-income children look remarkably different from conventional schools. These insights suggest that school reform has failed because it has not been powerful enough, by itself, to transform the core work of teaching and school organization in ways that are essential if we are to reduce socioeconomic and racial inequality in educational outcomes.

Origins of the Model

Our story begins by gauging just how difficult it is to significantly improve fairly typical inner-city schools. In chapter 3, we trace efforts of a team of highly committed and deeply knowledgeable researchers and practitioners from the University of Chicago—led by Anthony S. Bryk, Sharon Greenberg, and Sara Spurlark—to improve literacy instruction in a network of South Side Chicago schools during the early 1990s. Theirs was a sustained effort with many small successes and many lessons learned. The most important lesson they drew from this endeavor, however, was that the organizational structure and culture of these schools posed formidable barriers to schoolwide instructional improvement. The school day was too short to provide the instructional time the children needed to catch up, and too short to enable teachers to collaborate to solve the daunting problems they faced. Teachers' work was so individualized that it was difficult to create a coherent schoolwide instructional program or a schoolwide system of assessing children's skills. As a result, teachers lacked objective evidence of students' skills, and each teacher tended to struggle alone to solve instructional dilemmas that many shared. Because many urban schools have large numbers of inexperienced teachers and high teacher turnover, teacher skills varied enormously. However, these differences were hard to discern because each teacher worked alone with little support. These conditions made it difficult to sustain hard-won gains and in some cases generated low staff expectations for children's learning.

These experiences seemed to suggest that if the aim was to put an ambitious instructional program in place, it would make sense to start a new elementary school free of the organizational and cultural constraints described above. This realization inspired Bryk, Greenberg, Spurlark, Marvin Hoffman, and their colleagues to create the North Kenwood/Oakland (NKO) campus of UCCS in 1998. In 2005, Timothy Knowles, Linda Wing, Nicole Woodard-Iliev, Todd Barnett, and their colleagues established the Donoghue campus.[10] UEI now operates both campuses for Chicago Public Schools (CPS). Chapter 4 tells the story of how efforts to ensure that every child in those schools had the opportunity to succeed in reading and math led to the model we examine in this book.

Key Elements of the Model and Impact on Student Learning

The model we describe in this book entails new conceptions of teachers' work, an expansion of instructional time, a redesign of school leadership, and new strategies for allying with parents. As a result, daily life in the school looks quite different from life in not only most schools on the South Side of Chicago, but also most elementary schools in the United States.

The Organization of Teachers' Work

Teachers in the United States generally conceive their work as highly personalized. They exercise considerable autonomy as they privately pursue their favored approaches to instruction behind a classroom door that is rarely opened to outside visitation.[11] Textbooks and other materials provide some general guidance about what to teach, but teachers rarely have access to frequent, timely, objective assessments of what their students know and need to learn next. This state of affairs, reinforced by traditional professional norms, encourages enormous variability in the quality of instruction. For the most-skilled teachers, this laissez-faire approach to the organization of teachers' work may produce good results within the course of a given year. However, even for the best teachers, this situation makes coordination across years difficult. More significantly, this approach offers precious little guidance to inexperienced teachers and provides little assistance to those teachers who hope to improve their practice. The laissez-faire approach does not encourage the best teachers to share what they know with newer and less-skilled teachers. This generates large variability in the quality of instruction, the results of which are evident in value-added studies reviewed in chapter 2, in which we also explain why this large variation works against the most disadvantaged children.

Those who founded UCCS envisioned an alternative approach that became available when all teachers in a building shared a coherent system of instruction. We call this alternative the "shared, systematic" approach to organizing instruction, as contrasted with the dominant "private, autonomous" approach. In characterizing the UCCS model as shared and systematic, we invoke two senses of the verb form of the word "share": (1) to possess in common; and (2) to reveal something to others, especially something considered personal or private. In the model we describe, teachers, tutors, school leaders, and parents not only possessed a system of instruction in common, but also used this system to reveal or make public aspects of teaching and learning traditionally considered personal or private.

The aim was to engage every child in ambitious intellectual work starting at school entry with the prospect that, by the end of grade 3, all children would read with high levels of comprehension and be able to solve reasonably sophisticated math problems. The school's designers reasoned that early inequality in academic skills was not a problem that a collection of independently operating teachers could solve. Rather, they envisioned for each child a sequence of instructional experiences, unfolding, say, from age three until age eight, that would ensure that this child got on track and stayed on track for success in mathematical reasoning and reading comprehension over the course of these years. To envision and enact such coherent sequences in light of the remarkable heterogeneity in children's skills when they enter school was an extraordinarily challenging engineering problem, the solution of which required sustained, collaborative effort and a schoolwide instructional system. The school's designers reasoned that one needs frequent, objective assessments of children's skills to know whether they are on track, to guide next instructional steps, and to evaluate past instructional interventions. The aim was to build an assessment system that is coherent across multiple grades.

Such a system included frequent assessments of student learning, producing child-specific diagnostic data revealing what each child needed to learn to move to the next level. The shared expectations, the shared assessments, and the common language enabled teachers to collaborate within and across grades. The aim was to ensure that all students make adequate progress in their academic learning and the social and behavioral skills needed to support their ongoing progress. Teachers met to analyze student progress, identify subsets of children who seemed stalled, and generate new strategies for these children, including academic and social supports for those who needed them.

Within such a system, teacher expertise took on a clear definition. Rather than referring to generic traits such as verbal ability or the ability to get along with children, expertise involved skill and knowledge in using this well-defined instructional system to reliably produce good student-learning results. The model defined teacher expertise, at the most elementary level, as an understanding of the tools used to assess students and how the results of those assessments were linked to the required instruction. At a more advanced level, the designers expected the developmental theory behind the assessments and their relationship to instruction to become internalized such that teachers would be able to skillfully "assess and instruct" moment by moment. At a still more advanced level, teachers whose students had reliably progressed to high levels would have gained expertise about how to help other teachers improve their practice. These advanced teachers would then become instructional leaders, with formalized leadership roles and appropriate increases in compensation. At the highest level, expert teachers would be able to revise the instructional system to promote higher levels of student learning.

Because the results of the assessment system were open for all teachers to see, variation in teacher expertise became public knowledge. While perhaps putting inordinate pressure on less effective teachers, UCCS's designers reasoned that it could also motivate those who were more expert to assume responsibility for sharing what they knew. Holding all teachers accountable for schoolwide results had potential to promote this collaborative learning, particularly if more expert teachers could advance their careers by helping their colleagues. The formative assessment of student progress became the backbone of a system of pedagogical guidance and accountability, with the aim of motivating teachers to gain expertise and to seek help from the most expert.

Ideally, this "internal accountability"[12] system would be closely aligned with an external accountability system that used annual statewide tests and other measures to evaluate a school's leadership. External accountability would motivate the school director to select the most expert teachers as instructional leaders. In this way, the school leaders' incentives would be aligned with those of both the novice and expert teacher. The designers of UCCS conjectured that these aligned internal and external accountability systems could become a powerful force for effective schooling. The aim was to make differences in teacher expertise apparent and to enable teachers to learn how to advance their expertise with collegial support and appropriate incentives. At the same time, school leaders would seek to refine their models of school organization and practice.

Extending Instructional Time

These are bold changes in the aims and organization of classroom instruction. However, the designers of UCCS reasoned that even these changes would not be sufficient to ensure that every child would be on track for high levels of reading comprehension and mathematical problem-solving by grade 3. Rather, children who started school farthest behind would need extra instructional time—during the school day, after school, and during the summer. It would be essential to closely coordinate this extra effort with the regular program of instruction, imposing upon teachers and school leaders organizational responsibilities not typically observed in elementary schools (see chapter 7).

Providing Social and Emotional Support

The designers further reasoned that dramatically accelerating the academic achievement of disadvantaged students would require a shared, schoolwide system of academic and social supports tailored to the needs of each student and aimed at reducing or eliminating barriers to learning (for example, tutoring for academic difficulties and/or counseling for social and emotional issues). This, in turn, would require schoolwide strategies for routinely gathering and analyzing evidence of each child's academic and social development and using an array of resources and services to address children's emergent needs.

Allying with Parents

Finally, continually monitoring and supporting each child's academic and social and emotional development required a much closer working relationship with parents than is the norm in urban schools. The idea was to cultivate an authentic partnership with every family rather than waiting to reach out to parents when a child experienced serious difficulties. Instead of limiting parental engagement to formal and sometimes superficial events such as open houses or parent-teacher conferences, parents and school staff would need to be in constant communication about each child's progress and how to support it. The school's shared system of assessments and instruction would create a common language that parents and school personnel could use to coordinate their efforts. The designers of this school reasoned that most parents would embrace their roles in this mission.

Impact on Student Learning

To develop a causal analysis, we have conducted a study that exploits the fact that more families apply to the school than can be admitted and that most UCCS students are offered admission based on a random lottery. The random lottery ensures that children attending the school can be compared to statistically equivalent children who did not. The results are notable. We find that those who "win" the lottery score substantially higher in reading and math than those who lose the lottery. However, these numbers underestimate the effect of actually attending the school. The reason is that some students who win the lottery do not attend and some who lose the lottery end up attending because seats open up when some lottery winners decide not to attend. On average, winning the lottery increases the probability of attending UCCS by about 50 percent. Using now-conventional methods of statistical analysis,[13] we focus on those students whose attendance at UCCS was made possible by winning the lottery. We estimate that, without the benefit of attending UCCS, the students in our study would achieve significantly more than the typical low-income African American student in Chicago, but still very substantially less than the typical white student in the city. We find that attendance at UCCS enabled these students to achieve at nearly the same level as white students, who are on average far more advantaged economically. So the impacts of the school are large and quite similar to effects reported for the most effective charter schools.[14] However, our aim in this book is not simply to report these results but rather to describe in detail the life of the school that produced them and the theory of schooling upon which this practice depended.[15]

A Partnership between Practitioners and Researchers

A fundamental problem with the conventional "private, autonomous" approach is its limited capacity to make use of advances in developmental and organizational science. When each teacher invents his or her own instructional system, the only way research can influence practice is if teachers read research articles or otherwise become familiar with research findings through contacts with professional associations or informal conversations with colleagues. Even then, each teacher would be required to individually engineer an appropriate use of new research findings. Research suggests that such a strategy for mobilizing new evidence to improve practice will not work.[16] So it is hard to imagine evidence-based practice emerging from the private, autonomous organization of teaching.

In contrast, a coherent schoolwide system of student assessment and instruction can be based on what we know from developmental science about what children need to know, when they need to know it, and how they learn. Such a system makes the theoretical and empirical assumptions underlying practice explicit and open to criticism and revision based on new scientific findings. To the extent this scientific knowledge is limited—which it typically is—the system must instead be based on expert judgments under uncertainty. But even then, these judgments, when represented explicitly within the instructional system, become accessible to scrutiny and revision. Instructional leaders can also take advantage of new research findings as they arise by incorporating them within the shared instructional system.

By making visible what we don't know, the shared, systematic, schoolwide approach to instruction also enhances practitioners' opportunities to contribute to research on teaching, learning, and school organization. The attempt to enact an explicit schoolwide approach inevitably generates specific, new questions about how to help children progress. When university researchers and practitioners work together, these new questions become apparent and can potentially shape the agenda for future research. Universities committed to advancing knowledge about schooling can organize these connections to shared, systematic practice, using what they learn not only to drive new research efforts, but also to train new teachers. We consider the importance of researcher-practitioner partnerships in chapter 9.

Organization of This Book

Our book begins by summarizing lessons from research and practice that inform the model for effective schooling we describe and test. The chapters that follow elaborate the various components of this model in detail.

Next, we examine evidence of the model's effectiveness. We conclude by summarizing elements of the model that appear sufficient for enhancing achievement of children like those served by UCCS, and considering the role research universities might play in supporting school improvement.

Part I: Lessons from Research and Practice

In the next chapter (chapter 2), we make the case that increasing the amount and quality of schooling can sharply reduce educational inequality. Research provides a list of interventions and investments that have been found to make a real difference in the lives of children. Yet research cannot answer the question of how to effectively incorporate a new intervention into daily practice or how to combine multiple interventions into a coherent, schoolwide instructional program. Answering these questions requires the judgment of expert practitioners. Chapter 3 describes how a committed team of researchers and practitioners sought to improve reading instruction in conventional CPS schools. What they learned together led to the founding of UCCS, the focus of our book.

Part II: A Model of Instructional Practice and School Organization

In part II, we examine UCCS's approach to classroom teaching and the distinctive approach to school leadership it entailed. In chapter 4, we summarize the model the school's founders created in response to the challenges they encountered working in conventionally organized CPS schools, as described in chapter 3. We further specify this model in two subsequent chapters devoted to instruction (chapters 5 and 6), in which we review research on how children develop high levels of reading comprehension and mathematical reasoning, respectively, and describe in detail the strategies adopted by UCCS to ensure that children achieve these goals. This research shows that, in both reading and mathematics, the complex skills we expect children to demonstrate by roughly ages eight to nine emerge from developmental processes that unfold in early childhood. Because parents vary dramatically in their own educational backgrounds and in skill at promoting their children's academic development, these early childhood differences predict the emergence of later inequality in educational outcomes—unless schools intervene in concerted ways beginning in pre-K and extending after kindergarten. Overcoming such inequality poses a strong challenge to elementary schools as currently organized, requiring a fairly radical redefinition of teachers' work.

The leaders we interviewed suggested that enacting the instruction we describe in chapters 5 and 6 required reorganizing the schoolhouse to enable coordinated action by all educators in the school, including administrators, parents, and social workers as well as teachers. We describe this reorganization in chapter 7. The school director's job was to make certain that this coordination occurred and to promote a school culture that fostered a relentless commitment to ensuring that every student was on a trajectory toward successful preparation for college work. The director worked closely with a broader leadership team, which included individuals in novel leadership roles. The team monitored student learning and promoted teacher expertise in the school's instructional systems. It sought to marshal academic and social resources to ensure the adequate academic progress of every child and to engage parents as vital partners in this endeavor. We provide estimates of how much money was required to sustain such a school. While the price per pupil of the model we examine roughly equaled that spent by Chicago Public Schools, it was significantly less than many other urban school systems, most notably Baltimore, Boston, Milwaukee, Washington DC, and New York City.

Part III: Evidence and Implications

The evidence presented in chapter 8 suggests that these approaches to reading and mathematics instruction were remarkably effective. While these results are extremely encouraging, chapter 9 considers the implications of these findings, not only for the design of elementary schools, but also for the role of research universities in the work of school improvement. We conclude that new collaborations between researchers and practitioners are essential to clarify, improve, and disseminate powerful approaches to schooling for the nation's most disadvantaged children.

Universities will never run more than a tiny fraction of all schools. Yet without highly determined, sustained, and well-orchestrated partnerships between university researchers and practitioners, we don't see how the knowledge needed to produce highly effective schooling for the nation's most disadvantaged children will emerge. It is crucial to explicate the theory underlying expert practice and evaluate it critically using rigorous empirical methods.

All the key elements of "shared, systematic" practice this book describes—the theory of student learning, the design of the assessments that guide instruction, the reorganization of the schoolhouse to support ambitious intellectual work, the new definitions of teacher expertise, and the implications for teacher learning—are products of intense and sustained collaboration between practitioners and scholars. Some key ideas and practices derived from prior research, while others have emerged as school leaders and teachers pursued their practice. This partnership aimed to define exemplary school practice and to put such practice in place at a scale that is convincing. Finally, this partnership exploited a stream of research findings on student learning, school governance, organization, and instruction in order to generate new ideas for instructional improvement. We describe the resulting model of schooling, rigorously evaluate the impact of this practice on student learning, and share these results with a broad community of practitioners, social scientists, and interested citizens. The dynamic interplay between practice and research has profound implications, we believe, for how universities might organize efforts to produce knowledge about schooling.

While collaboration between researchers and practitioners is essential to produce the necessary knowledge about learning, teaching, and school organization, we conclude by agreeing with Cohen and Moffitt that "infrastructure" is needed to support the creation of effective new schools and the improvement of existing ones. Powerful infrastructure involves institutional support that allows educators to use the relevant knowledge. By supplying knowledge, resources, and tools, infrastructure is the antidote to a decentralized system in which each school creates its own organizational model from scratch and each autonomous teacher invents his or her own idiosyncratic approach to teaching math or reading. Nations can supply infrastructure through coherent curricula and exams; districts can do so through common curricula, assessments, and strategies for professional development. According to Cohen and Moffitt, effective school districts and effective charter school management organizations can supply infrastructure, and so can thoughtful comprehensive school organization programs.[17] In our view, universities can play a vital role in helping supply infrastructure, as occurred for the school described in our book. The question of how to supply powerful infrastructure for creating new schools and improving existing ones is, however, beyond the scope of our book, which focuses on how the adults in a building who share a deep commitment to the success of every child can organize themselves to fulfill that commitment.

Our book might be regarded as a companion to *Organizing Schools for Improvement* by Bryk, Sebring, Allensworth, et al.[18] That book considers the problem of improving existing public schools, focusing on the essential conditions required for making these schools more effective within the context of their existing organizational constraints. Our book considers what is possible for students when these constraints no longer hold. By focusing on the creation of a new school, our book asks how, in detail, one can organize teaching and learning in reading and mathematics to dramatically reduce economic and racial inequality in student achievement, and how one can then reorganize the schoolhouse to support such instruction.[19]

Qualitative Consultation Methods

Few studies describe in detail the components of promising school models, rigorously test their effects on student learning, and provide convincing theoretical explanations for these effects.[20] Our primary goal for the qualitative data collection and analysis for this book was consequently to articulate the UCCS model with sufficient specificity to develop a detailed theoretical argument to account for its effects. We worked closely with practitioners at the two campuses to identify the underlying principles of the model. We did not have the resources to examine in detail the fidelity with which the model was being implemented at the two campuses. However, we believe that simply articulating the UCCS model in greater detail than other causal studies is an important contribution to the literature on the design of effective schools for disadvantaged students. Moreover, there was enough consistency in practitioners' accounts of their practices, as well as our observations of them, to let us assert with confidence that the school's effects on student learning are causally related to the principles and practices we elaborate in the chapters that follow.

To accomplish our goals of articulating and testing the UCCS model, we interviewed practitioners, observed instructional activities and leadership practices, and conducted focus groups with teams at the two campuses. We also shared memos and chapter drafts with practitioners and research colleagues to obtain their feedback on our emerging interpretations of their work and to confirm that our descriptions represented this work and their understandings of it accurately.[21] We conducted these activities in three phases. In the first phase, we mapped out our preliminary interpretation of the model. In phase two, we worked with study participants to confirm our interpretation of the principles we identified in the first phase and to refine these in response to their feedback. In the third phase, we shared drafts of the manuscript with a broad range of colleagues and study participants to obtain additional feedback on aspects of the model that were still unclear or underspecified.[22] We looked for patterns that appeared in interviews, documents, workshops, and feedback meetings and confirmed our descriptions of these in phases two and three. We used these methods to develop a sense of the underlying principles that guided school organization and instruction at the UCCS elementary campuses.

CHAPTER 2

**CAN SCHOOL IMPROVEMENT
REDUCE INEQUALITY?
LESSONS FROM RESEARCH**

Since passage of the landmark Elementary and Secondary Education Act of 1965 (ESEA), federal investments in education have focused on improving opportunities for low-income children. As President Johnson said in his 1964 "Great Society" speech, "Poverty must not be a bar to learning, and learning must offer an escape from poverty."[1] Renewals of this legislation have for decades expressed the goal of reducing or eliminating achievement gaps based on economic background, race, and ethnicity. A sobering fact, however, is that social class differences in educational achievement have remained remarkably stable over the last century.[2] More recently, Reardon shows that these differences have actually increased over the past forty years.[3]

It is perhaps surprising that, while social class inequality in education has increased, racial inequality in years of schooling and attained degrees has declined dramatically during the last century, and racial inequality in academic achievement as measured by cognitive test scores declined substantially between 1960 and about 1990.[4] The mass migration of African Americans from the rural South to industrial cities and increasing educational opportunities resulting from the civil rights struggle help explain this convergence.

Unfortunately, this convergence of black-white gaps in test scores stalled around 1990. While many factors may have contributed to this reduction in racial progress, the most convincing explanation involves deep structural changes in the economy. Rapid de-industrialization and job loss in the inner city during the 1970s led to low family income and family disruption among many African Americans who depended on factory jobs.[5] At the same time, other well-educated African Americans, taking advantage of new opportunities resulting from civil rights legislation, moved out of segregated inner-city communities, leaving behind a large number of less-educated African Americans in resource-deprived, racially segregated communities characterized by high unemployment, persistent poverty, family disruption, high crime, and ineffective schools.

In sum, powerful economic and social forces outside the walls of the school have intensified inequality in academic achievement. Given this, perhaps the only plausible way to improve the academic achievement of low-income and minority youth is to alleviate these economic and social conditions. Is it then reasonable to believe that school improvement can significantly reduce inequality in educational outcomes, even in the absence of large-scale social change? We answer this question affirmatively. Although efforts to improve economic and social conditions are essential to the well-being of families and children, we are convinced that increasing the amount and quality of schooling can significantly reduce inequality in educational outcomes. If this is correct, changing schools can help overcome inequalities caused largely by conditions outside of the schoolhouse.

In this chapter we review research indicating that, in the early years of life, schooling reduces inequality in academic skills. Put simply, the most disadvantaged children have the most to gain from attending school. Expanding preprimary schooling helps all children but is particularly effective for low-income children. Expanding the school day and lengthening the school year tend to reduce inequality in academic learning. Improving instruction by increasing the knowledge and skill of teachers, reducing class size, improving curricula, and making instruction more explicit also promise to reduce inequality.

The research we review in this chapter has stirred hopes that research can become a guide to school improvement, with particularly beneficial consequences for low-income and ethnic minority children. The idea is to embrace policies that show evidence of boosting learning and discard policies that don't. For this purpose, the US Department of Education has created the What Works Clearinghouse, which highlights particular interventions found effective in rigorous scientific studies. The aim is to encourage states, school districts, and schools to adopt interventions that are known to work. The underlying assumption is that teaching and learning will incrementally improve as evidence-based interventions gain traction and ineffective policies and practices fall by the wayside.

While recent research inspires optimism, we reason that the adoption of discrete, incremental improvements validated by research is unlikely to make a big difference in children's outcomes or to significantly reduce inequality. Research thrives on focus, enabling us to identify the impact of a clearly defined intervention, holding other things constant. Unfortunately, however, the scientific literature by itself does not explain how practitioners might integrate such promising interventions into a coherent design of school organization and instruction. As a result, we are convinced that the cumulative effect of adding research-based interventions will tend to be less than the sum of the effects of each reported in the literature.

Our conclusion is not founded on philosophical assumptions. Rather, it follows from our reading of the research. As we shall see, every study revealing the promise of a particular intervention raises new questions about how to improve practice. Well-designed studies rarely clarify the conditions under which the intervention becomes effective, and virtually never explain how implementing one intervention might influence attempts to use other interventions or how we can organize instruction later on to capitalize on interventions staged earlier in life.

In other words, a particular research finding does not tell us what to do. Practice is based on expert judgment that is open to influence by new evidence. We reason that collaboration between practitioners and researchers is required to use science to improve schooling. This reasoning lays the basis for subsequent chapters of this book, where we investigate the emergence, design, and effects of an approach to elementary schooling that is grounded on evolving expert judgment informed by scientific evidence.

We do think that anyone who wants to improve schools and reduce inequality should pay attention to the research we review in this chapter. However, every study that answers an empirical question raises new questions about how to use the empirical evidence to improve practice. We'll highlight those unanswered questions. Later chapters will trace how the designers and leaders of UCCS have attempted to answer them.

Early Schooling Reduces Inequality

Evidence strongly supports the claim that increasing the amount and quality of pre-K and elementary schooling can reduce economic and racial inequality in academic outcomes—despite other social forces sustaining inequality. While all children benefit from more and better instruction, the most-disadvantaged children stand to benefit more than others.

The Impact of School Attendance

One set of studies we review below shows that attending school dramatically increases children's academic achievement. The simplest explanation for these findings is that most children receive more effective academic instruction when they are in school than when they are not in school. This finding may seem so obvious that it is hardly worth mentioning, but it is essential for understanding why schools have great potential to reduce inequality.

Parents provide academic instruction, typically informally, by teaching their children to speak, reading to them, discussing experiences, and even playing with puzzles and board games. However, parents vary dramatically in their capacity and opportunity to do so.[6]

For any child at any moment in time, we can conceptualize the schooling effect on academic achievement as the difference between what a child would learn if in school and what that child would learn if at home (or in some other nonschool environment, such as home day care). It follows that, for any child, the schooling effect will be greatest when the contrast between the effectiveness of the academic instruction in school and in the home is greatest.[7]

School Attendance and Inequality

Decades of research show that the effectiveness of the academic instruction parents provide at home in academic English varies enormously from family to family. To some considerable extent, this variation is associated with variation in parent use of academic language at home,[8] parent teaching of reading, and parent provision of school-related general academic knowledge.[9] Moreover, recent research suggests that parent language use predicts early mathematical reasoning—particularly number sense[10]—while games, puzzles, and toys found most frequently in middle-class homes help facilitate the growth of spatial reasoning.[11] Such differences are correlated with socioeconomic status (SES)—particularly maternal education—as well as with ethnicity, and in particular with race.

In contrast, schools, while far from equal in their instructional effectiveness, are much less variable in effectiveness than are homes. The seminal work of James Coleman and colleagues brought this fact to light,[12] which came as a shock to those who believed that variation in children's academic achievement resulted primarily from variation in school quality. However, every assessment of educational attainment since 1966 has replicated this finding.

If school instructional quality varies less than home instructional quality, and if home instructional quality is strongly associated with parents' social and educational background, it follows that, for children of low SES, the contrast between the quality of instruction they receive in school and the quality of instruction they receive at home is, on average, larger than the same contrast for high-SES children. This would imply that low-SES children stand to gain more from attending school than do high-SES children, particularly if educational policy reduces the correlation between student SES and school quality.

This argument is subject to a caveat, however. It assumes that low- and high-SES children have equal capacity to benefit from a given "dose" of instruction. Carneiro and Heckman hypothesize that, as children's academic skill grows early in life, their capacity to benefit from instruction expands. In their words, "skills beget skills."[13] If high-SES parents are especially effective in teaching academic skills to very young children, these children might benefit more, on average, than low-SES children from the same "dose" of instruction they receive at school. It might then be that social and racial inequality in academic learning opportunities early in life creates a basis for increasing inequality later on. This reasoning supports an argument for especially intense schooling interventions early in life, before large skill differences between more- and less-advantaged children have emerged. It follows that one of the most important ways to increase the amount and quality of schooling is to provide more and better schooling for very young children, and, in particular, for low-SES children.

Yet continued exposure to high-quality instruction during the K–12 years would be required to sustain any gains achieved through early childhood intervention. This is partly because high-SES children would tend to experience more favorable academic instruction at home—especially during the summer recess—while in kindergarten through grade 12. Such reasoning may help explain the "fade-out" of the effects of early intervention on low-SES children's cognitive skills after those children enter elementary school.[14] Similarly, high-SES children, on average, attend classrooms with other high-SES children whose school readiness skills are, on average, high. This enables their teachers to peg instruction at a comparatively high level. In contrast, low-SES children typically attend classrooms with other low-SES children; and the conventional teacher response is to peg instruction at a lower level.[15] Hence, even if a low-income child had attended a particularly effective preschool, that child would tend to progress comparatively slowly if attending a class with other low-income children who had not had favorable preschool opportunities.

This reasoning lays the basis for education policy that aims quite dramatically to improve the amount, quality, and equity of schooling to which low-SES students have access as a strategy for reducing inequality in academic skills. Doing so would disproportionately benefit African American children, who are far more often exposed to severe socioeconomic disadvantage than are white children.[16]

In addition, we know that low-income children—who are disproportionately minority—encounter lower-quality schooling experiences than do high-income children, as we elaborate below. Eliminating these disparities can be expected to reduce social inequality in outcomes, which would tend also to close black-white gaps in outcomes. In the next two sections, we review recent research suggesting that increases in the amount, quality, and equity of schooling can reduce social and racial inequality. However, we emphasize that particular interventions on their own are likely to have a limited effect. We therefore emphasize that a stream of research findings, no matter how encouraging, provides just the starting point for our story of how a committed group of practitioners and scholars constructed a novel approach to elementary schooling.

Increasing the Amount of Schooling

Three recent sets of studies reveal powerful effects of schooling: studies that use the age-cutoff method to identify the impact of attending school; early childhood intervention studies; and studies of academic-year versus summer learning. In each case we see that schools have large effects, especially for low-SES students, with the suggestion that expanding schooling can reduce inequality.

Age-Cutoff Studies

Powerful evidence about schooling effects comes from studies that exploit the cutoff age for enrollment. Frederick J. Morrison pioneered this method and replicated it on a number of samples.[17] Morrison and colleagues compared children who were legally too young to enter kindergarten with those who just barely met the legal cutoff age for attending school. The researchers then followed these two samples over the first few years of school. At the outset of these studies, the two groups appeared statistically equivalent except for a trivial difference in age. These studies reveal dramatic effects of schooling on math and literacy skills. It is clear from the results that many children who were regarded as too young for compulsory schooling and therefore stayed home would have benefited from schooling.[18] The benefits presumably would be larger for the children whose home environments are least conducive to literacy acquisition. This simple insight helps explain why early childhood education, discussed briefly below, has been found so important for low-income children, who are least likely to receive effective academic instruction at home. However, the samples followed by Morrison and colleagues were not sufficiently diverse in social background to test the hypothesis that low-income children benefit more from school than do high-income children.

Early Childhood Schooling

Perhaps the most dramatic evidence of the potential long-term impact of formal schooling comes from research on early childhood schooling.[19] The most famous study is the Perry Preschool study,[20] in which children were randomly assigned to receive an intensive program of instruction in school readiness skills. Exposure to the intervention produced immediate effects on children's cognitive test scores, although the effects faded during the early elementary years. The long-term results were remarkable: children assigned to the preschool intervention were found to have higher educational attainment, lower rates of special education placement, lower propensities to commit crimes, and higher earnings as adults. Encouraging as these results are, generalizations from a single, small-sample study are unwarranted. However, since then, several additional randomized studies have essentially replicated the results.[21]

The Perry Preschool study and several related studies show powerful short- and long-term effects on African American children from low-income families. The implication is that similar interventions would tend to reduce educational inequality. Yet a key question remained unanswered: Do socially disadvantaged children gain more from schooling than do more advantaged children? To answer this question, Raudenbush and Eschmann recently reviewed fifteen studies conducted in eight nations that expanded universal schooling to kindergarten and prekindergarten children. Many of these studies used the age-cutoff method described above, and all used comparatively convincing methods for obtaining valid causal inferences. Results were remarkably convergent: socially disadvantaged students gained significantly more than advantaged students on a wide range of outcomes from participation in early schooling.[22]

A troubling finding in many studies, however, is that the large gains in academic skill that disadvantaged children receive from preprimary schooling tend to fade during the first years of elementary school,[23] raising the question of whether early interventions are truly effective. The most plausible conclusion, in our view, is that elementary schools are not designed to capitalize on the early gains provided by effective preprimary schooling. As we'll see when we consider instruction in reading (chapter 5) and mathematics (chapter 6), a key challenge facing elementary schools is to cope effectively with the large heterogeneity of skill that children bring to the classroom. It may be that the benefits of preprimary interventions will be sustained only to the extent educators organize elementary instruction to exploit these benefits. In sum, while preprimary studies document remarkable results, they also raise crucial questions about how to coordinate instruction across the divide of preprimary and primary schooling.

Extending the School Day

A recent large-scale study found that children assigned at random to full-day kindergarten gained significantly more in early literacy skill than did those assigned to half-day kindergarten, and these effects were most pronounced for low-income minority children,[24] again suggesting that increasing the amount of schooling can reduce inequality. However, the evidence in support of extending the school day is, overall, uncertain. Many schools around the nation now offer after-school programs, but schools as currently organized rarely integrate the activities of their after-school programs with the regular instruction carried out during the day. Instead, after-school staff members typically have comparatively little training, little contact with the school's teaching staff, and scant instructional coordination with the regular school program. The evaluations of such programs provide mixed results.[25] Chapter 7 in this book examines how leaders at the University of Chicago Charter School (UCCS) strove to enhance the impact of extending the school day by integrating the after-school program with the regular school-day program.

Academic-Year versus Summer Learning

Striking evidence of the impact of attending elementary schools comes from a series of studies that test children twice annually: in the fall near the beginning of school year, and in the spring at the end of the school year.[26] Such studies allow us to compare children's learning rates during the summer and the academic year. Growth rates are dramatically higher during the school year than during the summer, especially in math, for which summer growth rates are effectively nil. In reading, children do make gains during the summer—not surprisingly, because they encounter text at home from a variety of sources and because they continue to develop oral language skills that are essential for reading comprehension. However, growth rates in reading comprehension are far greater during the academic year than during the summer.

Moreover, there is strong evidence that low-income children benefit more from schooling than do other children. High-income children gain more (or lose less), on average, in the summer than do low-income children, especially in literacy skills.[27] In contrast, academic-year growth rates are similar. So if we define the impact of attending school as the difference between the growth rate while in school and the growth rate during the summer, we see that school effects are greatest for the lowest-income children. Indeed, there is good evidence that socioeconomic differences in summer learning rates account for a substantial fraction of socioeconomic inequality in reading and math skills during the primary years.[28] And this is true despite the current ineffectiveness of many schools serving many low-income and minority children.

Although supporting the hypothesis that schooling reduces inequality, studies of summer learning rates don't tell us how to effectively extend the school year. Two well-designed studies provide strong evidence that even modest summer school programs can boost the math and reading achievement of low-income students.[29] Nevertheless, the key question for practice is how to incorporate summer instruction with instruction during the school year. We'll see in chapter 7 how UCCS used frequent assessments of student skills to tailor summer programming to meet the varied needs of children, with a special focus on ensuring that all children would be on track for success.

In sum, increasing instructional time seems essential to any school reform effort that aims to reduce educational inequality. As we'll see in later chapters, the leaders of UCCS expanded instructional time during the day, after school, on weekends, and in the summer as a strategy to reduce inequality in achievement. However, we have emphasized that increased time is not sufficient. It is also essential to improve instructional quality, and recent research suggests the potential for dramatic quality improvements in this vein, particularly for the most-disadvantaged children.

Increasing the Quality of Schooling

It makes sense to think that spending more money on schools will increase student learning. However, this idea is surprisingly controversial among social scientists. Their skepticism is rooted in almost fifty years of research showing mostly weak effects of improving conventional resources, such as per-pupil spending, school facilities, and teacher credentials.[30] Recent new evidence, however, demonstrates that teachers vary substantially in their effectiveness. Moreover, there is new evidence that three kinds of conventional resources do make a difference: small class size, teacher experience, and teacher knowledge. Taken as a whole, a reasonably coherent picture emerges: the conventional resources that appear to matter most for student learning are those that are most proximally linked to the quality of instruction in the classroom. Low-income children have less access to these resources than do high-income children, so increasing their access to these resources can be expected to reduce social inequality in outcomes. Finally, and even more important, recent research on subject-matter instruction reveals specific ways in which changing instruction can reliably increase student learning, particularly for low-income children.

In reviewing this evidence, we find strong support for the proposition that increasing the quality of schooling overall and equalizing access to high-quality schooling can reduce economic and racial inequality in outcomes. However, we shall also find that, although instructional quality matters, schools are not currently organized well to mobilize effective instruction. This insight leads us to infer that changes in school organization are essential to realize the full potential for increasing the quality of schooling to reduce social inequality in student achievement.

Value-Added Studies of Teacher Effectiveness

We now have good evidence that teachers vary dramatically in their effectiveness. Many "value-added" studies work as follows: identify children who look similar at the beginning of a study in terms of prior outcomes and social origins, and take note of which teachers they are assigned to; next, follow those children for a year, test the children again, and compute, for each teacher, the average gain. The average gain is called the *value added* for that teacher, after correcting for the inevitable errors of measurement and sampling. If value added varies a lot, then the impact of teacher assignment must be substantial. And that is just what researchers from a variety of disciplines using a variety of tests have found. The approach can be made more efficient by following children over multiple years and multiple teachers, and then comparing multiple cohorts.[31]

A criticism of this method is that children are not assigned to teachers at random, and it may well be that controlling for prior test scores and social background is not adequate to remove what statisticians call unobserved selection bias. For example, it may be that highly motivated parents work especially hard to ensure that their children are assigned to the best teachers and that parent motivation is actually driving part or even most of the apparent teacher effect. It's hard for researchers to measure and control for such motivation, so the results of value-added studies may be biased.

To overcome this problem, Nye, Konstantopoulos, and Hedges reanalyzed data from the Tennessee Student-Teacher Achievement Ratio (STAR) study, where teachers were assigned at random to large or small classes, and children were assigned at random to teachers.[32] The researchers compared the value added of teachers, controlling for the assignment to large or small classes. Because the children were randomly assigned to teachers, concerns about selection bias were eliminated. These researchers found very large differences in classroom effects—differences, in fact, that were very similar in size to those found in the earlier, nonrandomized value-added studies. This study shows that which classroom a child attends makes a difference. However, the study could not separate the effect of teacher skill from other possible aspects of classroom life, including idiosyncratic impacts of how particular children get along with one another. To address this problem, Gordon, Kane, and Staiger randomly assigned teachers to classes within each of a large number of schools in California.[33] They found that differences in value-added statistics between teachers in the same school quite strongly predicted the test scores of children attending those teachers' classrooms later on. This study revealed persistent and quite large differences between teachers in their effectiveness. A massive project known as the Measures of Effective Teaching (MET) study used a similar design, effectively replicating these findings.[34]

So value-added studies clearly reveal that the teacher to whom a child is assigned matters a great deal. Indeed, more recent studies show quite convincingly that effective classrooms and teachers improve key lifelong outcomes such as educational attainment and earnings.[35] The clear implication is that exposing children to better teachers holds promise for increasing learning. But these studies tell us little or nothing about how to ensure that children get excellent instruction. There is an irony here.

Value-added studies show dramatic differences in teacher effectiveness, and we know from careful surveys of instruction[36] that elementary teachers vary remarkably in such basic features of their work as the amount of time they devote to literacy instruction, the amount of time they devote to math instruction, whether they group children for instruction, and whether and how they use diagnostic assessments to gauge their children's progress. Teachers' effectiveness appears to be related to their ability to individualize instruction for their students. But with some exceptions that we will mention, we have precious little knowledge about how these core elements of instructional practice are linked to outcomes—or, more important, how these core elements can be combined to produce a coherent instructional system that we can train teachers to enact reliably in order to optimize the impact of schooling.

Why do educators tolerate dramatic, unexplained differences in the effectiveness of teaching practice while physicians insist that medical practice be subject to rigorous research and conform to common standards? In part, the difference reflects differences in the knowledge base that underlies practice. Vastly more money is spent to study cell biology, disease transmission, and trials of the efficacy of new drugs and surgical procedures than is spent to understand how children learn, how they respond to instruction, or how well new models of instruction work. Perhaps for this reason, contradictory notions of professionalism have evolved in the two domains. In medical practice, professionalism requires that practitioners know the science underlying practice and that their decisions are guided by shared, explicit notions of best practice. Autonomy is not the highest virtue; attending physicians scrutinize the practice of residents, and decisions are open to professional and legal challenge.

In contrast, teachers tend to work quite independently in the privacy of their classrooms, with little support or guidance and without objective evidence of their children's progress. In this setting, an effective teacher is one who can mobilize commitment and personal knowledge to respond flexibly and expertly to the high levels of uncertainty that arise in day-to-day interactions with heterogeneous students. While some teachers are quite skilled in managing this challenging project, the collective effect of such private, autonomous, and idiosyncratic practice is largely unexplained variation in teaching effectiveness, leading to amplified inequality in student outcomes. So the system of private, autonomous instruction that is pervasive in most schools generates enormous variation in classroom quality. But this variation is clearly not entirely random. Rather, it works to the disadvantage of low-income minority students, who are the least likely to encounter experienced, well-trained teachers, as we shall discuss below.

It follows that an instructional system that aims to reduce educational inequality would reduce the variation in teaching effectiveness that our system currently tolerates. This means finding ways to compensate for the lack of skill of novice teachers while helping those teachers improve their skills. It means rigorously evaluating instruction, providing incentives for teachers to improve, and retaining only those teachers who develop high levels of proficiency. Yet because many teachers experience common challenges in their classrooms, an effective system would presumably foster collaborative problem-solving and collective learning. Aligning higher expectations, providing support, and fostering collaboration would plausibly improve instruction overall and reduce teacher variability. It was the express intent of the designers of UCCS to create such a system, as later chapters will show.

Class-Size Reduction

The late Frederick Mosteller, a revered statistician and a leader in the movement to use randomized clinical trials in medicine, regarded the Tennessee class-size experiment as the most important study in the history of educational research.[37] Teachers and children in seventy-nine school districts in Tennessee were assigned at random to small or large classes. The results settled one of the most enduring questions in education: Can the reduction of classroom sizes in elementary schools significantly improve educational achievement? The answer was a definitive yes. The effects on test scores appeared modest in magnitude, but they were sustained and led to significant long-term differences in college attendance. Moreover, African American children especially benefited. Indeed, a sophisticated analysis by Krueger and Whitmore suggested that class-size reduction can significantly reduce the black-white gap in college attendance.[38] Perhaps even more remarkable, this result was achieved with no deliberate attempt to modify instruction to capitalize on the reduced class size. It makes sense to conjecture that the impact could have been much larger if teaching practice had fully capitalized on the smaller classes.[39]

The major limitation of the Tennessee study is that, without knowing anything about how class size influenced instruction—or how to tailor instruction to benefit from reduced class size—it is hard to know whether the benefits of class-size reduction found in Tennessee would be reproduced elsewhere. When California invested massive amounts of money in class-size reduction, school districts competed for a limited pool of teachers, and many perceived a rather substantial deterioration in the quality of classroom instruction, particularly in hard-pressed districts. Observers concluded that, perhaps because of this resulting shortage of effective teachers, California failed to reap the benefits of reduced class size achieved in Tennessee.[40]

Class-size reduction can work only if it leads to better interactions between teachers and students around the subject matter.[41] Without knowing the other resources required to make better interactions occur (e.g., teacher knowledge), and without in fact ensuring that these instructional changes do happen, it is simply an educated guess as to whether reducing class size will boost achievement in any particular setting. In a schooling system that emphasizes teacher autonomy, each teacher uses a small class size to do what that teacher thinks is best. Class-size reduction is an innovation without a known technology, and therefore without a strategy for quality control. Moreover, it's a rather expensive innovation. To make such an expensive innovation without any handle on quality control risks wasting the investment.

Given current resources available for schooling, the model we investigate in this book operated with class sizes that ranged from twenty-two at the beginning of the study in 2008 to twenty-seven by its conclusion in 2012. This is smaller than often observed in many elementary schools but not as small as we would wish. If greater resources were available for schooling, we would recommend yet smaller classes. However, situating students in smaller classes is not enough. The model we evaluate uses an explicit instructional system shared by the entire staff that helps teachers make strategic decisions about how to target instruction for each child. Using shared formative assessments to determine which skills or concepts students need to master next in order to continually advance their reading and mathematics achievement can help streamline schoolwide efforts to support students' learning. This can potentially take the guesswork out of how to gain from small classes and ensure careful use of the resources required to achieve small class size.

Teacher Experience

There is growing evidence that teachers with two or more years of experience are, on average, more effective than teachers with one year of experience or less.[42] Low-income children are less likely than high-income children to have access to such experienced teachers, as experienced teachers frequently use their seniority to transfer out of challenging schools. Taken together, these findings suggest that creating incentives for experienced teachers to stay in high-poverty schools would reduce social and ethnic inequality in outcomes.

Obtaining an equitable social distribution of teacher experience is fair and just. But if inexperienced teachers are ineffective, perhaps no children should simply be left alone with them! Changes in school organization would plausibly reduce the inequality in student learning generated by variation in teacher experience. An emphasis on a common system of instruction and mutual observation and feedback, and on-the-job training would plausibly help compensate for teacher inexperience and advance the rate at which teachers learn. The aim would be to reduce or even eliminate the statistical association between teacher inexperience and poor teaching rather than to distribute inexperience and poor teaching more equitably. As we shall see in chapter 7, UCCS leaders organized the school precisely to provide such on-the-job training and support.

Teacher Knowledge

There is likewise evidence that teacher knowledge also affects achievement, especially in mathematics,[43] and that low-income children are less likely than high-income children to have access to teachers with high levels of knowledge.[44] The implication is that a policy that creates incentives for well-prepared teachers to take jobs in high-poverty schools will increase equity in outcomes. So it makes great sense to recruit knowledgeable teachers and to ensure that low-income children have equal access to such teachers. Once again, however, how schools are organized would plausibly modify the association between teacher knowledge and student outcomes.

Consider an extreme example of teacher autonomy in which every elementary school teacher is required to invent his or her textbook, assessments, and instructional strategies in mathematics. Clearly, only the most knowledgeable teachers could produce decent instruction. The association between teacher subject-matter knowledge and student achievement would be extraordinarily high; and given the current level of mathematical knowledge of most elementary school teachers in the United States, most students would suffer a terrible mathematical fate.[45]

In contrast, consider Liping Ma's study of elementary mathematics instruction in China.[46] The teachers she studied did not have four-year college degrees, but they had a good working knowledge of the mathematics they needed to teach, and somewhat beyond. They had a common curriculum, common assessments, common instructional strategies—a shared instructional system. They collaborated closely, sharing knowledge, expertise, and teaching plans. They tested their students frequently and generated common strategies to overcome student misconceptions and to drive instruction to the next level. Their students displayed uniformly high levels of achievement. The accessibility of expert teachers supported the least expert teachers and developed the leadership capacities of the most expert.

Increasing the subject-matter knowledge of those who enter teaching would surely benefit all students, and if those highly knowledgeable teachers were dispatched preferentially to low-income schools—where teacher knowledge is currently lowest—the effect would be especially pronounced. However, the capacity of the schooling system in the United States to recruit a better-trained teaching force is constrained not only by available funding but also by the fact that prospective teachers are themselves the product of an ineffective educational system, particularly in the mathematical sciences. As a result, a model of effective schooling would presumably incorporate strategies for enabling incumbent teachers to build their subject-matter knowledge as well as their pedagogical skill. Alternatively, flexibly organized schools can impose specialization when needed, such that the teachers with the highest levels of mathematical knowledge do most of the math teaching. The private, autonomous model of teaching works against the school's capacity to strongly influence knowledge or to reorganize instruction adaptively to incorporate variation in teacher expertise. Within such a system, teacher professional development is effective only to the extent it influences the private decisions about instruction made by individual teachers, and only then to the extent that those teachers are able to monitor their own practice and learn from it. UCCS educators aimed to encourage on-the-job advancement of teacher knowledge as well as flexible reallocation of teachers based on differences in expertise.

Studies of Instruction

Studies of instruction reveal enormous potential to improve school quality because they focus on the proximal cause of student learning in schools. Moreover, there have been major advances in research on instruction in recent years. However, schools are not currently organized well to capitalize on this work, as is clear in a brief review of studies of instruction in reading, science, and mathematics.

Early reading instruction. For years, researchers battled over whether to emphasize phonics versus "whole language" in elementary school reading instruction. However, a series of careful studies in the 1990s, many funded by the National Reading Panel, have led to a consensus.[47] There is now broad agreement that explicit instruction in phonemic awareness and word decoding is essential to achieve high levels of reading literacy, especially for disadvantaged children. The operative word "essential," however, does not imply sufficiency. We have known for many years that the ability to decode familiar text (in grades 1 and 2) is foundational for learning to read new text.[48] We also know, however, that children with parents of modest educational attainment generally come to school behind in terms of academic English vocabulary, syntax, and narrative skill. In contrast, children who come to school with strong oral language skills, well-established word decoding skills, and familiarity with academic knowledge can read new text with high comprehension by grades 3 and 4. The implication is that early elementary instruction must aspire much higher than simply to teach decoding skills. Thus much more instructional time in reading is required to bolster these skills early on than is generally observed in US elementary schools, particularly if the most disadvantaged children are to read with high comprehension by grade 3.

We mentioned earlier the findings of Frederick J. Morrison.[49] Using the age-cutoff method, he has repeatedly found that although children typically learn a great deal about word decoding during the early elementary years, they appear to learn very little vocabulary. Why is this so? A plausible explanation lies with the fact that early elementary instruction is commonly focused on teaching children the decoding of familiar text—one of the foundations of successful reading instruction. Morrison's findings suggest that this common focus comes at the expense of sufficient emphasis on the acquisition of oral language, which would drive the acquisition of vocabulary—an essential component of reading comprehension that is often lacking among the most disadvantaged children.

To capitalize on the best available research on reading instruction calls for, we think, a coherent schoolwide instructional system. First, such a system can ensure that all teachers in the early grades carry out the explicit instruction in word analysis that we know is required to support high levels of reading fluency, particularly among the most disadvantaged students. Second, we know from research mentioned above (and which we review in greater detail in chapter 5) that pre-K, kindergarten, and first-grade teachers must help their children develop powerful syntax and vocabulary even as those students are in the early stages of learning to decode familiar text. However, the results of such an innovation will not likely show up until grade 2 and beyond. Essentially, the early teaching must make investments that will not immediately pay off. This requires strategic coordination of instruction across the grade levels, with early emphasis on oral language skills. We describe how educators at UCCS attempted to do this.

Early mathematics instruction. There are fewer rigorous studies of mathematics instruction than of reading instruction. Nevertheless, a National Academy of Sciences report summarized reasonably convincing evidence from a series of studies that new, conceptually driven early mathematics curricula produce, on average, better math learning than do more traditional curricula.[50] A limitation of such programs is that they generally provide a curriculum alone rather than a systematic approach to instruction. Such an approach would include not only a curriculum but also formative assessments and shared approaches for using the assessments in instruction.[51] In short, these curricula are developed for dissemination within a paradigm of private, idiosyncratic instruction, constraining the potential power of the approach.

As is true for literacy, cognitive skills developed early in childhood lay the foundation for the later emergence of higher-order thinking in math. For example, key mathematical ideas such as the cardinality of a set and distances on a number line will become crucial later and must be taught earlier to ensure that students are on the path to the powerful mathematical knowledge needed in the sciences.[52] Moreover, early instruction can ensure that all children develop the spatial reasoning skills required for the later emergence of mathematical reasoning. We describe in chapter 5 how such a model can work to ensure procedural fluency along with theoretical knowledge. We doubt that the cross-grade coordination required to achieve these aims can happen in a system strongly characterized by private, autonomous instruction.

Linking academic work to social development. By now the reader may wonder whether we have a narrow view of what children learn in school that is of lasting value. In fact, we have a broad view of the skills and capacities schools help generate that are of long-term benefit to children. There is considerable evidence that suggests that schools can foster children's physical, social, and emotional development, which provides a foundation for later success in the labor market.[53] Schooling helps children develop the capacity for sustained, persistent effort as they learn to be punctual, to complete their work on time, to respond to positive and negative feedback, and to work collaboratively with other children. These skills and dispositions are equally if not more important than cognitive skills later in life. For example, research suggests that cognitive skills as measured by standardized tests explain only about 25 percent of the contribution of schooling to labor market success.[54] Employers recognize this, which is why credentials such as degrees are so important in signaling to an employer that an applicant for a job will be a reliable employee.

We also have good reason to believe that effective early schooling helps young children gain self-regulation and social skills that enable them to function effectively later on in school and in the job market. Effective schooling presumably fosters these skills (sometimes called "soft skills" or "noncognitive skills") that are not captured by tests of academic achievement. However, we take the view that children develop these skills as they engage in academic instruction. The highly skilled teacher organizes ambitious instructional activities that require attention skills, emotional regulation, and peer collaboration. As a result, a powerful system of instruction, by hypothesis, supports the development of both the cognitive and "soft" skills needed for academic and social success.

Conclusion

Current research provides a strong basis to believe that increasing the amount and quality of schooling can not only improve academic learning on average, but also reduce economic and racial inequality. Increasing the amount of schooling by increasing access to preschool education, increasing instructional time, extending the regular school day, and expanding summer learning opportunities can, in principle, help the children who currently depend most heavily on formal schooling for academic learning. Increasing quality by improving teacher knowledge and skill, enacting more effective instruction based on objective evidence, reducing class size, purposefully sequencing instruction across grade levels, and capitalizing on advances in instructional research also hold enormous potential for improving outcomes, on average, while reducing inequality.

However, if schools are to exploit these opportunities, it seems they must be organized to embrace and sustain powerful systems of instruction. Such systems can, in principle, coordinate prekindergarten, kindergarten, and postkindergarten instruction, integrate after-school efforts with the regular instructional program, and ensure that summer instruction is driven by objectively verifiable student needs and evaluated in terms of objectively verifiable student gains. Similarly, the existence of a powerful schoolwide instructional system can potentially enable schools to improve quality by compensating for shortages of teacher knowledge, building teacher knowledge and expertise, exploiting reduced class sizes, and incorporating the lessons from recent research. The aim of the work we describe in subsequent chapters was to craft developmentally sound sequences of instruction across the grades and to coordinate instructional efforts across subject areas in ways that develop high levels of reading comprehension, writing, and mathematical problem-solving, while developing students' motivation, persistence, and pro-social behavior. Those who designed UCCS concluded that the potential contribution of schooling to reduce educational inequality could not be realized within a system of teaching that emphasizes private, autonomous practice. They reasoned instead that ways of fulfilling this potential come into view within the framework of a schoolwide instructional system we describe and evaluate in this book.

In the next chapter, we describe an attempt by a group of dedicated researchers and practitioners from the Center for School Improvement at the University of Chicago to develop and implement such a system in conventionally organized schools. Their inability to fully realize this goal led to the establishment of the first campus of the University of Chicago Charter School.

CHAPTER 3 ORIGINS OF THE MODEL
LESSONS FROM PRACTICE (1989–1998)

In 1989, Anthony S. Bryk, Sharon Greenberg, and Sara Spurlark founded the Center for School Improvement (CSI) at the University of Chicago with the goal of improving teaching and learning in the Chicago Public Schools (CPS), starting in a small network of schools on Chicago's South Side.[1] A core aim of this work was to promote ambitious academic learning for every child. Its founders believed from the outset that they would need to create a new model of schooling involving radical changes in conventional school practice in order to achieve this. However, specifying the concrete programs, procedures, roles, and routines that this model comprises would require sustained, collaborative effort over the course of more than two decades. In this chapter, we recount how Bryk, Greenberg, Spurlark, and their colleagues began to develop the model we evaluate in this book and the obstacles they encountered along the way.[2] They discovered that it was exceedingly difficult, if not impossible, for teachers to enact the ambitious, responsive instruction they were promoting within the constraints of schools as conventionally organized. They ultimately decided to establish a new school, where these constraints no longer held. We describe the design for this new school in chapter 4.

An Attempt to Improve Teaching in South Side Schools

CSI began its work in a small network of low-performing CPS schools serving very disadvantaged[3] students. In 1993, CSI launched a comprehensive program for urban school development that began with a focus on providing ambitious literacy instruction that would challenge students intellectually and develop their capacities to reason, understand, and communicate significant ideas and concepts. By focusing on instruction—specifically, on enhancing teachers' pedagogical knowledge and skills and training principals to be instructional leaders—CSI's work differed markedly from both local[4] and national[5] school reform efforts at that time. Those reform efforts had focused primarily on issues of school governance, especially reducing bureaucracy and, in Chicago, increasing local, democratic control of schools. CSI's work, by contrast, focused on improving classroom instruction by enhancing the professional knowledge and skills of teachers and principals.

At the heart of the program was a literacy initiative developed in partnership with reading experts at the Ohio State University.[6] The literacy program provided teachers with a repertoire of instructional strategies, embodied in a framework for "balanced" or "comprehensive" literacy that included a combination of explicit instruction in word decoding, comprehension, writing, and oral language development. Starting in the earliest grades, it offered students varied contexts (both as a whole class and in small groups) in which to develop these skills, and emphasized creating enriched literacy environments in classrooms that increased students' access to books and the written word more generally and enhanced their opportunities to participate in conversations about the ideas books contain. The literacy initiative encouraged teachers to build classroom libraries with books that featured culturally familiar characters and celebrated the children's ethnic heritage and identities. The literacy framework also provided teachers with numerous opportunities to use what children know as a basis for building new knowledge. It emphasized honoring children's ideas and helping them elaborate and communicate their thinking via new literacy skills—especially reading and writing in academic English—without denigrating the vernacular children might speak in their homes or neighborhoods.

This involved major changes to the status quo of literacy instruction in network schools. For example, it involved more ambitious goals for student learning that included critical thinking and the capacity for complex oral and written expression. It also required that teachers move away from the common practice of teaching reading using a single textbook for all children in a class, with children typically organized into relatively static ability groups. Instead, the initiative asked teachers to tailor instruction to each student's distinctive skill profile; build classroom libraries geared at a wider range of reading levels and covering a wider variety of topics of potential interest to students; and offer students more choice in the selection of reading material from sets of books appropriate to their reading levels. Students would still be grouped for reading instruction, but the initiative asked teachers to continually assess students' skills and dynamically regroup children to receive instruction targeted at their changing skills as they emerged, to provide more differentiated instruction tailored to students' diverse needs and to use a wider variety of instructional materials responsive to those needs. The initiative also asked teachers to rely less on closed-ended instructional materials (such as worksheets) that focus on practicing skills in isolation from the contexts in which they might be used. Instead, teachers were to provide more authentic, open-ended tasks for students (such as writing a letter to a friend), creating more opportunity for extended self-expression and communication of ideas.

Teaching in this new way demanded more of teachers, including learning to assess students' literacy skills more precisely; thoughtfully designing lessons aimed at higher expectations for students' literacy development; and making strategic decisions on an ongoing basis about everything from how to regroup students for instruction so children could learn what they needed to next, to selecting books for these differentiated activities. Given the steep learning curve this involved for teachers, CSI asked participating schools to establish a role for a school-based literacy coordinator responsible for supporting teachers to learn a more complex instructional practice.[7]

CSI soon discovered that schools needed more detailed information on students' development as readers—not only to inform instructional decisions at the classroom level, but also to facilitate identifying students for supplemental services, to help make decisions about targeting professional development for teachers, and ultimately to increase teacher accountability for student learning outcomes. In response, Bryk worked with colleagues David Kerbow and Virginia Watson to develop the Strategic Teaching and Evaluation of Progress (STEP) literacy assessment (see chapter 5) and pilot it with the help of teachers and literacy coordinators in network schools.[8] CSI supported teachers and school leaders to gather and interpret evidence about student learning on a regular basis and to use this to determine next steps for instruction. Bryk and colleagues also urged principals to tie teacher evaluations to the results of the STEP assessment and to use these data to allocate professional development resources to help teachers improve. A key responsibility of the literacy coordinator was to monitor the effectiveness of teacher practice using information from the STEP assessment and plan targeted professional development for teachers based on these data.

Simultaneous with the effort to improve classroom instruction, CSI also helped schools construct a system of academic and social supports to ensure that each child could take maximum advantage of this improved instruction. The basic principle driving this effort was, according to Bryk, that educators should take "active accountability for the learning of every student" and provide whatever supplemental academic and social supports each student needed to get and stay on track to be proficient readers, writers, and mathematical problem–solvers by grade 3. Some children in network schools were so far behind their peers that they would require intensive tutoring to catch up. Others' difficult life circumstances impeded their ability to pay attention in class. The latter children needed counseling or other services to address social and emotional needs that were interfering with their learning. Bryk and colleagues believed that it was the responsibility of the school to ensure that the children who needed them received these supplemental supports; to accelerate the progress of struggling students; and, if students were not progressing, to try to understand why.

CSI built several mechanisms into the literacy initiative to systematically foster such accountability, identify students who were struggling, and ensure that every child was receiving the support he or she needed to make continued progress. The initiative required every teacher to meet at regular intervals with the literacy coordinator to undertake a "universal progress review" for each child in his or her classroom. This involved comprehensively evaluating every child along a host of academic and social dimensions. In the domain of literacy, CSI had established developmental norms within the STEP assessment to direct attention to children who were performing significantly below developmental level and might benefit from supplemental services. Using these tools, the literacy coordinator and teacher might decide that certain children should receive tutoring, while others who were having more significant difficulties should work more intensively with a literacy specialist. To facilitate collective problem-solving about the progress of such struggling students, CSI had also created a notation system within STEP to keep track of every supplemental service a child might be receiving. This made it easier for teachers and school leaders to take stock of which interventions they had already tried with a particular child and whether these were having the desired effect. The aim was to direct attention in a systematic way to the needs of struggling students and prevent such children from being overlooked or falling through the cracks. For example, if an individual teacher did not voluntarily refer a child for supplemental academic support, the need would still be identified via the mandatory universal progress review.

For students whom the teacher and literacy coordinator identified as particularly struggling or stuck and not progressing, Bryk and colleagues designed the universal progress review to trigger a more comprehensive process known as AS3, which stands for Academic and Social Support System. Students whom teachers referred to AS3 became the focus of a more intensive inquiry that brought together a range of adults (including the child's teacher, his or her parent or primary guardian, the school social worker, the literacy coordinator, and/or anyone else with relevant knowledge) at a series of meetings to talk about the individual student's difficulties and create plans for addressing them. Such plans might include modifications to his or her instruction inside the classroom, activities for parents to undertake with their child at home, or referrals for the student to receive supplemental academic and/or social services. Key to this process was the requirement that school staff undertake follow-up meetings to reflect on the effectiveness of any interventions a child had received and determine next steps for ensuring that child's continued progress.[9]

CSI also sought to increase instructional time for students and professional development time for teachers. For example, CSI staff helped network schools implement a variety of initiatives to extend or augment the school day, week, and year, including new prekindergarten programs, "extended-day" prekindergarten programming, full-day kindergarten, Saturday schools, and summer programs for students who were significantly behind their peers. They argued that without such extended time, children who were far behind academically stood little chance of ever catching up. CSI staff helped school leaders create extended instructional time for literacy and mathematics during the regular school day. Moreover, they tried to persuade schools to lengthen the school day to provide more instructional time for students and make possible professional learning time for teachers.

Finally, building an infrastructure to support family and community engagement was also a significant focus of this work. School leaders aimed to strengthen schools' relationships with parents and the community, particularly parents' capacity to support at home their children's learning at school. Following the lead of successful programs such as Head Start that mandate parent involvement, CSI encouraged schools to hire a parent coordinator whose work would complement that of the literacy coordinator. The parent coordinator would focus on bringing parents and teachers together to enhance children's literacy learning by supporting families' involvement with their children's learning, enriching the literacy environment of the home, and supporting teachers to become more familiar with and build on family literacy practices.

Obstacles to Improvement in Network Schools

The leaders of this work saw substantial improvement in individual class-rooms and even whole grades in some network schools. However, they found that no school in the network was able to embrace and maintain the type of instruction they advocated schoolwide, or to engage all the other organizational changes that this required. Three problematic conditions—and the lack of institutional authority to alter them—ultimately frustrated CSI's efforts to improve student achievement in network schools: (1) institutionalized barriers to extending time for student and teacher learning; (2) traditional occupational norms that inhibited sharing expertise among teachers; and (3) the professional isolation and demoralization of network school faculties. We elaborate each of these obstacles below.

Barriers to Extending Instructional Time

The literacy initiative asked schools not only to increase students' instructional time, but also to allocate significant time for teachers to learn to engage a more ambitious teaching practice. However, CSI was never able to secure this time for either student or teacher learning. All the schools in the network had adopted what was known in CPS as a "closed-campus" policy. This shortened the school day by forty-five minutes, to end at 2:30 p.m. To do this, schools eliminated recess and some preparation time and allowed teachers only twenty minutes for lunch, during which they were required to supervise their students.[10] In elementary schools, this meant there was no time in the school day for teachers to plan or meet together; thus professional development activities always required staying after school, which consistently met with great resistance from teachers and their union representatives, due to concerns about both safety and compensation. Many teachers in schools serving the most-disadvantaged students in CPS lived far from where they taught, adding to their reluctance to stay after school for professional development. Schools could get a waiver from the policy if 67 percent of the faculty voted to waive it, but teachers in network schools consistently and overwhelmingly supported the policy year after year. Indeed, closed-campus policies were an entrenched part of the culture of CPS. As Spurlark, cofounder of this work, explained:

With every school we've worked with, they all agree with us intellectually that closed campus is a terrible thing, and yet they all vote for it. . . . And all that's happened over thirty years [since closed campus policies originated in the 1970s] is that little by little, the number of schools on it have grown. And you have two generations of teachers and principals who don't know what a non-closed campus is like. Principals are worried about how they're going to supervise the kids [during recess and lunch] and that kids will come in after recess and [fight]. These are the kinds of philosophical and practical questions that we've tried to address. Although I think we've had great success with some ideas, there are some ideas that we have not been able to transfer from the intellectual to the practical.

Given the significant academic needs of students and the intense demands the literacy initiative made on teachers to learn new practices, it was impossible to achieve the goals of the literacy initiative without creating more time for both student and teacher learning. Consequently, the unwillingness of school faculties to waive their closed-campus policies posed a fundamental obstacle. Ultimately, the desire to create a school in which it was possible to lengthen the school day to increase the learning of both groups became a key part of the rationale for establishing a charter school. As we shall see, a fundamental element of the school's design was a longer day with extended time for student learning, a duty-free lunch period for teachers, and built-in time for teacher professional development and collaboration at the end of the school day.[11]

Barriers to Sharing Expertise among Teachers

The literacy initiative advanced an emergent conception of teaching as a shared, evidence-based professional practice.[12] The idea was that teachers should possess a common theory of how students develop as readers and writers, employ shared instructional strategies for supporting this development, and continually analyze evidence of student learning to plan their instruction. However, CSI confronted strong normative challenges to the new conception of teaching it promoted. These challenges stemmed from the traditional conception of teaching as a craft, rather than a profession. According to this view, teaching effectiveness is primarily a function of experience, intuition, or natural ability—personal qualities that are individually held and highly idiosyncratic. This conception of teachers' work has historically made it difficult to develop shared standards of best practice and to clearly define the meaning of teacher expertise.

Indeed, the craft conception of teaching has given rise to a constellation of interrelated professional norms that constrains the development, acknowledgment, and sharing of expertise among teachers.[13] By no means a uniquely urban phenomenon, these norms are an aspect of the private, autonomous approach to schooling that structures teachers' work in US schools more generally. However, they are particularly debilitating in low-performing urban schools because they deprive teachers of critical resources for instructional improvement and exacerbate the professional isolation and demoralization of urban teachers (a problem we discuss in the next section). Because inner-city schools, on average, have less-experienced and less-knowledgeable teachers to begin with (see chapter 2), a system that relies heavily on the individual skills of the teacher with little collegial support and no instructional guidance will tend to work especially badly in those schools.

The first of these norms—the privatization of practice—is most vividly expressed in the traditional "egg crate" structure of schools, the cellular organization of classrooms that keeps individual teachers isolated from one another for much of the day.[14] This norm involves the expectation that the work of teaching takes place behind closed doors: that each teacher's classroom is essentially his or her private, discretionary domain, off-limits to outside observers (including one's own colleagues) unless they are explicitly invited in. It socializes teachers to understand their work as a private endeavor of individual craftsmanship and to regard their instruction as an intensely personal activity. This leads to a conflation of professional critique with personal criticism and a strong tendency to avoid public acknowledgment or comparison of differences in the effectiveness of individual teachers in deference to teachers' feelings of personal vulnerability. This makes sense within a private, autonomously organized school where the lack of a shared instructional system limits the degree to which teachers can learn from one another because each teacher is likely doing something different in his or her individual classroom. Within this system, working hard and independently are the primary indicators of professionalism. In this context, teachers have little motivation to engage in public discussions of differences in teacher effectiveness and understandably interpret calling attention to such differences as cruel and unsympathetic.

A second, related norm is that of egalitarianism among teachers:

the idea that all teachers are equal, which deems it illegitimate for one teacher to be publicly acknowledged as more able or expert than her colleagues. The craft conception of teaching discourages the recognition of differential expertise among teachers because of its view of teaching as a highly individual, idiosyncratic practice, reinforced by the lack of common professional standards to distinguish more- or less-expert teachers. Reflecting this egalitarian norm, within the private, autonomous system, decisions about teacher promotion and distribution of professional rewards are generally driven primarily by questions of seniority—defined as longevity in the profession—rather than of effectiveness or expertise.[15]

The third norm is autonomy or individualism: the idea that each teacher should be able to do his or her own thing in his or her particular classroom. As a consequence of this norm, while individual teachers (or groups of teachers) might choose to exchange lessons or teaching strategies, adopt a new instructional approach, or aspire to particular professional standards, these activities are typically voluntary and inconsistently pursued; engaging in them is generally not an across-the-board expectation within a school or the profession at large. This "let a thousand flowers bloom" approach within schools further inhibits the development of common understandings of good practice and the acknowledgment of differential expertise among teachers. It also makes it much more difficult to coordinate instruction either within or between grades.[16]

Abiding by these three key norms (privatization of practice, egalitarianism, and autonomy) is arguably a precondition for fitting in and surviving socially within schools as traditionally organized; violating them brings no rewards to teachers and simply places one at risk of being perceived as critical, arrogant, or insensitive to other teachers' feelings and consequently being socially sanctioned by one's colleagues. Thus, teachers can hardly be blamed for adhering to these social norms and often come to do so reflexively or unconsciously. (Of course, some teachers may consciously disagree with them but still abide by them to avoid social sanctions). Nonetheless, this constellation of social rules and expectations severely limited the capacity of CSI's network schools to enact the literacy initiative, particularly because of how they constrained the work of school-based literacy coordinators.

For example, lacking formal role authority and given the norm of teacher autonomy, many literacy coordinators were forced to restrict their activity to working only with teachers who voluntarily sought or agreed to accept their assistance. Moreover, due to the norm of privatization, literacy coordinators also encountered various forms of resistance from teachers, some of whom were reluctant to permit them in their classrooms to observe instruction and to accept coaching based on these observations—central components of the professional development strategy within the literacy initiative. Even if a teacher agreed to work with them, the literacy coordinators still had to tread lightly on these traditional norms or risk teachers' withdrawing participation. For example, in deference to the norm of egalitarianism, literacy coordinators had to moderate the manner and extent to which they offered teachers critical feedback that might have improved teachers' practice. In some cases, literacy coordinators actually downplayed their own expertise in order to avoid being perceived by their colleagues as "uppity" or "holier than thou." In some schools, literacy coordinators acted as glorified teachers' assistants—for example, making copies and doing other favors—in an effort to ingratiate themselves to their colleagues so that they might eventually gain access to teachers' classrooms and engage the coaching and mentoring activities the literacy initiative intended.[17] Finally, these norms also limited the capacity of teachers to support one another in learning to enact new instructional practices because they discouraged observing each other's teaching, sharing information about the impact of instruction on student learning, or acknowledging differences in teachers' effectiveness or expertise.

Authoritarian leadership practices—unfortunately typical in urban schools—compounded the above challenges.[18] As a result of the norm of privatization discussed above, teachers in network schools generally were not accustomed to being observed by anyone other than the principal, and then often in a punitive fashion and for exclusively evaluative purposes. Consequently, they tended to perceive having their instruction observed and critiqued in a negative light, rather than regard this as an opportunity to learn and improve their practice. This was not only due to traditional professional norms, but it was also because principals at that time had not been trained or expected to actually provide instructional leadership to their faculties, and network school principals consequently lacked the expertise required for this.[19] More problematic still, literacy coordinators in some cases encountered political difficulties with authoritarian principals who felt threatened by their increasing expertise and actually tried to sabotage their efforts. In schools run by such leaders, literacy coordinators also faced resistance from colleagues who resented their promotion, perceiving this as a "cushy" job because it did not involve direct responsibility for students and suspecting that the literacy coordinator had been promoted based on favoritism or patronage rather than more legitimate professional criteria.[20]

Faculty Isolation and Demoralization

An additional set of obstacles arose from the difficult working conditions of teachers in network schools, which were some of the most challenging teaching environments in the city. Given the sink-or-swim situation that the private, autonomous model of schooling creates for teachers and students alike, a persistent, dysfunctional culture of low expectations had developed in some of these schools to compensate for teachers' lack of ability to be more effective with their students.[21] The private, autonomous model of teaching and school organization is virtually a recipe for demoralization in the most-disadvantaged urban schools, where one is most likely to find teachers working in isolation in settings with comparatively few resources, but where students have the highest needs and thus the tasks of instruction are most challenging. Consequently, large numbers of adults in network schools had seemingly resigned themselves to the likelihood of failure for the large majority of their students. As Spurlark recalled:

> When we started, a lot of urban schools did not even believe that the goal should be that every child should [learn to] read by third grade and that after that they should read to gain knowledge. There were tremendous numbers of parents and teachers who did not think it was criminal [that the majority of students in the school were not achieving this].

Teachers' diminished expectations for students translated into practices that denied students opportunity to engage in more ambitious intellectual work and thus demonstrate their capacity to do so, creating a self-fulfilling prophecy. Consequently, as Ann Grussing, a CSI literacy specialist leading this work, explained, "the move to work that was high level and high expectations" started with the most basic of changes: persuading school personnel to give students greater access to books. "Kids could not do high-level work if they didn't have real books. Or if the books were locked in the closet. . . . When you've had a scarcity of a commodity the tendency is to hoard and keep [it] locked up." She explained that another challenge was increasing students' opportunities to engage and express ideas in class:

> One of the hard parts for me was accepting how little respect some classroom teachers had for children and for the role of language in developing the life of the mind. Truly they didn't understand that words are tools for thinking and how critical they are to learning. . . . I saw a

little too much of "shut up and sit down" in the classroom, and conversation and storytelling [were] not a big part of too many classrooms. Developing oral language and written language and storytelling work together, and that was one of the things that we had to work toward: the idea that a silent classroom isn't always the best classroom and that children talking with each other around a story or activity was necessary to help them express ideas.

Network schools, like many low-performing urban schools, were also environments where the professional isolation that characterizes teaching was particularly marked. Most teachers in network schools had never seen a school or classroom in which disadvantaged students were achieving at high levels and had never actually seen the kind of instruction CSI was asking them to enact (and certainly not with disadvantaged students). There were also limited examples elsewhere in CPS. Isolation from other adults is a challenge for all teachers, but was all the more problematic in network schools because it denied teachers access to critical resources for improvement: knowledge that might help them be more effective with their students; evidence that disadvantaged students could achieve at higher levels; and a sense of hope and possibility that conditions in their school could be better. The core problem lay with the difference between understanding something in theory and observing it in action. Thus, even those teachers who might have been willing to believe in the principles of the literacy initiative were limited by the lack of opportunity to actually see instruction based on these principles.

The Decision to Start a New School

Bryk, Greenberg, Spurlark, and colleagues ultimately determined that their lack of authority to alter the above conditions constituted a fundamental obstacle to improvement in network schools. While the initiative had made some headway at every school in which they worked (for example, improving instruction in one or several classrooms), in no school were they able to implement and sustain all aspects of the initiative schoolwide. Moreover, CSI staff had never been able to get all of the teachers in a school to believe that students were actually capable of engaging in the ambitious intellectual activities CSI insisted were possible for them. Bryk, Greenberg, Spurlark, and their dedicated staff had limited power to reshape school schedules to create more time for student or teacher learning, influence workplace norms among teachers, or combat the sense of demoralization that prevailed in many network schools. They could not compel teachers to engage the new norms and practices that CSI staff members were promoting or oblige principals to support them. Their work occurred at the pleasure of the principal, and schools were free to withdraw from the program at any time. This meant that a principal's change of heart or a turnover in school leadership—a frequent occurrence in urban schools—could jeopardize several years of work. Moreover, administrators sometimes violated agreements that were critical to the success of the initiative. For example, network school principals agreed to create a full-time position for the literacy coordinator and to free this person from other administrative responsibilities so she could devote all her time to enhancing teachers' capacity to deliver more effective literacy instruction. In practice, however, it was not uncommon for principals to add additional administrative responsibilities to literacy coordinators' work portfolios, contracting the time they had to work with teachers.

The story of these early, frustrated efforts throws into sharp relief the limitations of the private, autonomous approach to teaching and school organization. It was not enough for CSI to bring more-ambitious, responsive instruction to conventionally organized schools, because this conventional structure made it exceedingly difficult for teachers to develop and share the expertise this instruction requires and for schools to provide students with sufficient time and resources to meet their instructional needs and address barriers to their learning. As we have seen, this conventional structure constrained collegial relations among teachers, inhibited the coordination of efforts to meet students' needs, and offered neither incentives for teachers to help one another improve nor mechanisms to support such improvement. The originators of the model we investigate in this book concluded that actually providing ambitious, responsive instruction for every child would require a complete reorganization of the schoolhouse in the core domains of instruction, the organization of teachers' work, the mobilization of broader supports for student learning, and the use of time.

This story also illustrates how the private, autonomous model of schooling constrains the capacity of universities to apply knowledge from research to improve school practice. Bryk and colleagues formed an extraordinarily committed and knowledgeable team of scholars and practitioners seeking to bring the best ideas from research to bear on key problems of school practice. Yet, the network schools where they worked were not organized well to either gain from or contribute to this knowledge. As discussed in chapter 1, when each teacher invents his or her own instruction and implements it autonomously, there is no systematic way for knowledge from research to influence practice. At the same time, the traditional occupational norms and prevailing craft conception of teaching associated with the conventional model of schooling left many practitioners uncertain about what it meant to be an expert teacher, how to develop such expertise, and the role that knowledge from research might play in this. The shared, systematic model of schooling that Bryk and colleagues ultimately developed, which we describe in the next chapter, implies a much stronger role for research in the improvement of practice. In chapter 9, we reason that a shared system of instruction such as the one we examine in this book provides a means for knowledge from developmental science to influence practice in the form of tools and materials that reflect the latest research on what children need to know, when they need to know it, and how learning accumulates. Such a system makes assumptions about learning more explicit and thus available for examination and possible revision. It can also incorporate new knowledge into successive iterations, regardless of whether such knowledge arises from research or from practice.

Bryk, Spurlark, and Greenberg initially believed that the main requirements for improving instruction in urban schools were (1) providing technical knowledge and training in best practices for effective instruction, school leadership, academic and social supports for students, and parent engagement; and (2) introducing more effective tools (such as STEP), roles (such as the literacy and parent coordinators), and processes (such as AS3) that would coordinate the efforts of adults and increase accountability, efficiency, and access to objective information about student learning. However, their experience trying to implement these changes in network schools quickly surfaced issues of human capital, problems of mistrust between and among teachers and parents, normative challenges, and other impediments that could not be solved by purely technical or structural solutions. Reflecting on this fact, Bryk explained that he and his colleagues "gradually came to see the deep cultural dimensions of change." Another major lesson of their work in network schools, therefore, is that school cultures are very powerful, are highly resistant to change, and can act as serious impediments to school improvement—a conclusion borne out by decades of qualitative research on efforts to implement reform in urban schools.[22] Indeed, Bryk concluded that changing an existing school culture is much harder than creating a new one.

As we discuss in the next chapter, Bryk and colleagues ultimately decided to establish a new charter school that would give them the opportunity, they hoped, to pursue their ambitious goals for student learning with a greater chance of success. Yet the conclusion that they could not accomplish their goals in conventionally organized CPS schools raised a number of crucial questions, which we address in the second and third parts of the book. The first, which we probe in chapters 4 through 7, is: If they started a new school from the ground up, what would it take to make the more ambitious, responsive instruction they envisioned for urban students actually happen there? The next question, which we consider in chapter 8, is: If they succeeded in making such instruction happen, would students in fact learn more and achieve at higher levels? The final questions, which we ponder in chapter 9, are Could the success achieved in such a novel, less constrained setting contribute to or be relevant to improving existing urban schools? Or would the only conclusion to be drawn from their success be that it is necessary to start a new charter school to achieve ambitious learning goals for urban students? We begin our examination of these questions in the next chapter, which summarizes the new elementary school model that Bryk and colleagues created, and that successive school and university leaders further developed and refined.

PART II

A MODEL OF INSTRUCTIONAL PRACTICE AND SCHOOL ORGANIZATION

CHAPTER 4 ORGANIZING PRINCIPLES OF THE UNIVERSITY OF CHICAGO CHARTER SCHOOL (2008–2012)

The passing of Illinois's first charter school law in 1996, granting fifteen charters to the Chicago Board of Education, offered a singular opportunity to circumvent the obstacles Anthony Bryk and colleagues had faced in conventionally organized CPS schools. Seizing this chance to fundamentally rethink many aspects of urban school practice, Bryk, Sharon Greenberg, Sara Spurlark, and Marvin Hoffman established the first University of Chicago Charter School (UCCS) campus in 1998, the North Kenwood/Oakland (NKO) campus. Hoffman—a leader of the literacy initiative in network schools for the Center for School Improvement (CSI)—was NKO's founding director. Barbara Williams, a leader of CSI's parent and community engagement and social support initiatives in network schools, later became its codirector.

With the opening of NKO, Bryk and colleagues sought to create a proof of concept that disadvantaged students could achieve at high levels. They also wanted to create a place where teachers from other schools could see and learn how to produce such results for themselves. To that end, they designed NKO as a professional development site, with the intention that the school would host professional learning activities for other CPS teachers who would visit the school to observe and learn.[1]

Following the success of NKO, the University of Chicago agreed to open a second campus, Donoghue, in 2005. The design team for Donoghue built upon and elaborated NKO's initial design, further specifying the model this book investigates. This team included Timothy Knowles, Linda Wing, Hoffman, Sybil Madison-Boyd, and Tamara Gathright Fritz. Nicole Woodard-Iliev and Todd Barnett joined the team after they had been hired as campus director and director of family and community engagement, respectively. Knowles had come to the university in 2003 and succeeded Bryk in leading what became the Urban Education Institute (UEI), established in 2008.[2] Knowles worked closely with Woodard-Iliev to develop a set of common norms and practices across the two campuses. Successive campus leaders have struggled to further develop and refine these practices.[3] Together, these two campuses provide all elementary schooling for UCCS.

During the main period of our research, from 2008 to 2012, we noted a fairly high degree of consistency in both espoused belief and observed practice across the two campuses.[4] However, not all the elements we describe in this and subsequent chapters were in place at both campuses from their inception, due to the unique conditions and somewhat different circumstances and time periods under which each was established. Rather, some of the elements we describe as common to the two campuses originated at one campus and were subsequently adopted or "replicated" at the other.[5] Consequently, what we portray as a fully formed model necessarily glosses over the years of experimentation, refinement, and iteration that comprised its development. In so doing, our analysis also conflates some of the differences between the two campuses in favor of a focus on their commonalities, which was our central concern in articulating the model. Unfortunately, space does not permit us to describe in detail these differences or the process by which the two campuses became more similar over time. However, we observed increasing convergence between the two campuses over the years as it became clearer to UEI and school leaders what would be necessary to put their vision of effective urban elementary schooling into practice. By the same token, when we refer in this chapter and throughout the book to "the designers of the UCCS model," we are referring not only to the original designers of the first campus, NKO, but also to a succession of other leaders who built on and further refined their work.

A Snapshot of the Two Campuses

The two elementary campuses of UCCS were similar in many ways to other urban public schools. Both NKO and Donoghue were located in neighborhoods on the predominately African American South Side of Chicago, where many public schools have proven ineffective. Admission was by lottery, and there were no criteria for acceptance, except that neighborhood children received priority in the lottery over children who resided outside the school's CPS-designated attendance zone.[6] As was the case with many other public schools in a city still marked by high degrees of residential segregation, all but a few students who attended the two campuses were African American. Similarly, many students came from families who struggled to make ends meet. In 2009, 78 percent of students who attended NKO and 82 percent of students who attended Donoghue qualified for free or reduced-price lunch. As in many other elementary schools, children at NKO and Donoghue were grouped into two classes per grade level, from preschool through fifth grade.

However, in many significant ways, NKO and Donoghue also looked quite different from typical public schools. For one thing, they were smaller than average. For example, in the academic year 2010/11 (the midpoint of our study), NKO had 344 and Donoghue had 425 students in grades pre-K through 5, whereas the average enrollment of Chicago public elementary schools was approximately 500.[7] Most important, NKO and Donoghue operated with greater autonomy and were consequently organized fundamentally differently than regular CPS schools.[8] The district granted substantial freedom to charter schools and gave their operators authority over all aspects of the school's design, ranging from the selection of school directors to the hiring and termination of teachers, and from the choice of curricula and assessments to the length of the school day and year. For example, NKO and Donoghue did not have to use district-approved or mandated curricular materials, promise teachers tenure, or engage every new reform initiative emanating from the central office. By the same token, engagement with the new ideas, practices, and norms that comprised the model we investigate in this book became mandatory in the new charter school, unlike in the network schools described in the previous chapter, where school leaders and teachers could implement parts of the model piecemeal or opt out entirely. At the same time, university and school leaders also had the authority to recruit teachers who wanted to work in these novel ways.[9] NKO and Donoghue leaders used these freedoms to align their budgets, staffing, and school calendar and to flexibly allocate key resources—especially time, people, and money—to meet the changing needs of students.

The authority and flexibility that the charter afforded provided the conditions for the founders of this work to develop, test, and refine the model now in place at the two campuses. What emerged from their efforts was a shared, systematic model of urban elementary schooling that stood in stark contrast to the prevailing private, autonomous model. In the previous chapter, we examined the numerous barriers that impeded the success of Bryk and colleagues' work in network schools. These obstacles were not unique to the Chicago Public Schools, but had great resonance in urban districts across the country. In this chapter, we summarize the model of schooling that the designers of UCCS created to surmount these obstacles as we observed it from 2008 to 2012. Our discussion contrasts the conditions they encountered in conventionally organized public schools with what they wanted to create, focusing on their three major imperatives of (1) ambitious instruction, (2) organizing teachers' work to ensure such instruction occurred for every child, and (3) mobilizing broader supports for student learning.

Instruction

At the heart of the elementary school model were ambitious learning goals for students. The designers of this model believed that school subject matter should be engaging, intellectually challenging, and relevant to students' lives. They argued that instruction should take as its central aim children's cognitive development—especially the development of conceptual understanding of subject matter and the ability to apply such knowledge to solve intellectually challenging problems. They advocated a diagnostic approach to instruction that involved carefully assessing and responding to each child's learning needs so as to advance his or her development along an explicit trajectory of learning that would result in high levels of reading comprehension, mathematical understanding, and computational fluency by grade 3. Finally, they conjectured that ensuring each student's adequate progress along these learning trajectories would require not only significantly more time for both student and teacher learning than was available in traditionally organized schools, but also the ability to more flexibly allocate such time in response to students' needs. Below, we discuss how the school's designers conceptualized the imperative of ambitious instruction and compare the shared, systematic model they developed with the private, autonomous model, focusing on two dimensions in particular: (1) their vision of curriculum, assessment, and pedagogy; and (2) their stance toward the use of time.

Curriculum, Assessment, and Pedagogy. The school's designers argued for what Bryk called "ambitious intellectual work for every child." They aimed to engage students in meaningful tasks that involved sustained inquiry into challenging topics or problems, while also ensuring that students acquired basic skills such as the ability to decode text fluently and apply appropriate mathematical procedures to solve problems accurately and efficiently. They especially aimed for students to develop "higher-order" abilities such as the capacity to synthesize and explain complex ideas, interpret and construct arguments, test hypotheses, discover patterns, evaluate claims, and support conclusions with evidence.[10]

The school's designers questioned the assumption—which they had found to be common among network school teachers and leaders—that urban students were best served by didactic approaches to teaching that emphasized the absorption of facts and procedures and seldom engaged students in the disciplined exploration of ideas. Instead, they argued that instruction should maximize opportunities for students to discuss and explore ideas; test any developing understandings against evidence; explain the reasoning; and apply, interpret, and integrate new knowledge into prior understandings. They reasoned that teachers should function as facilitators of student learning by creating environments that actively stimulated processes of knowledge construction and sense-making in particular subject areas. The teacher's role was to create activities that nurtured deep understanding of the core ideas that constitute particular disciplines and the relationships among these ideas; and to hold children accountable for explaining concepts, elaborating their thinking, and justifying their reasoning using established principles of logic and evidence. The designers argued that such interactive instruction—which required students to elaborate their ideas—would provide teachers with more diagnostic information about students' intellectual development than the commonly used didactic methods, where the focus was more on imparting information than on eliciting student thinking.[11]

This model of instruction conceptualized teaching as a shared, systematic practice responsive to each child's individual learning needs. This conception involved not only a distinctive approach to instruction inside each classroom, but also a different way of organizing instruction schoolwide, with large implications for curriculum, assessment, and pedagogy as well as for the use of instructional time. The designers of UCCS had found that in conventionally organized schools operating under what we call the private, autonomous model, teachers exercised enormous discretion but received minimal guidance concerning the instruction they delivered to students, with the result that teacher practice was highly variable and idiosyncratic. The shared, systematic approach they developed for the charter school, by contrast, required that teachers give up some of this autonomy to enact a common practice that offered intensive guidance and support for teachers.

Shared instructional systems for reading and mathematics provided a careful sequence of coordinated, developmentally driven instructional tasks for students in both subjects. Teachers devised new instructional strategies dynamically, based on changes in student skill revealed by the assessment system, using approaches that were shared schoolwide. The assessment system reflected a developmental theory of how requisite skills and knowledge at one level become the foundation for skills and knowledge at the next highest level. UCCS's designers intended these shared systems of instruction (which we describe in chapters 5 and 6) to enable close coordination and common language among teachers, other staff, and parents, with the aim of maximizing the coherence of instruction as students proceeded through the grades.

The school's designers believed that teachers in conventionally organized schools often relied too heavily on standardized instructional materials and used them in a generic, one-size-fits-all way rather than tailoring instruction to highly varying student needs. They consequently built tools for systematic diagnostic assessment (such as the STEP assessment discussed briefly in chapter 3 and in greater detail in chapter 5) into the design for the school. The assessment data would enable teachers to tailor instruction to the academic strengths and weaknesses of particular students. The main idea was for teachers to collaboratively develop and administer instructional plans for each child—working closely with school leaders, social workers, tutors, and extended-day staff—over the whole of each child's school career.

Use of time. The school's designers discovered through their work in conventionally organized CPS schools that numerous factors limited students' instructional time, including collective bargaining agreements; budgetary constraints; and traditional notions of what the school day, week, and year should look like. By contrast, in the UCCS model, consideration of the needs of students and their families drove the school schedule and calendar to a much greater extent. The regular school day began at 8:30 a.m. and ended at 3 p.m., in contrast to the closed-campus schedule described in the previous chapter. This afforded longer blocks of time for literacy and mathematics instruction, with extended programming available before and after school, as we discuss below. UCCS teachers also had a longer work day, ending at 4:30 p.m., with ninety minutes of time built into the schedule for professional learning, meeting, and planning together at the end of the regular instructional day. As we discuss in chapter 7, UCCS teachers also were expected to use this time, on a regular basis, to collectively analyze evidence of student learning and plan subsequent instruction.

Another driving principle was extended instructional time for students who needed it. The model held that school leaders should flexibly allocate such time via a school day with extended hours and that students should receive social and academic supports aligned with their particular needs before, during, and after school. The NKO and Donoghue campuses offered extended-day, extended-week, and extended-year programming in five categories: before school, during school, after school, weekends, and summer. School leaders and teachers worked together to develop a particular portfolio of programs for each student, based on their diagnosed instructional needs. Before-school programming began at 7 a.m. and ran until 8:10 a.m. Participants engaged in group games, art projects, library time, and literacy learning. Extended-day programming began after school at 3 p.m. and ended at 6 p.m. Participants received homework help, tutoring, and academic enrichment activities, as well as music, dance, peer mentorship activities, and character education. Weekend programming ran from 10 a.m. to 2 p.m. on Saturdays. There were three different Saturday programs, including tutoring, boys' mentorship programs and girls' mentorship programs. Two different summer school programs ran for four weeks: one in the morning, from 8 a.m. until 12 p.m., and an extended summer school in the afternoon, beginning at 12 p.m. and ending at 5 p.m. The intensity of instruction varied across activities. For example, a reading specialist provided one-on-one tutoring for students who were more than two grades below grade level. But students who were one year behind in their reading level participated in small group tutoring lessons during school, with a teacher student ratio of 1:4, providing a slightly lower degree of individualization.[12]

The designers of the school had observed that while some public schools in CPS offered before- or after-school programming or summer school for those who qualified, the after-school instruction tended to occur independently from instruction during the regular instructional day. In contrast, the design for such extended programming at UCCS aimed to accelerate, reinforce, and augment academic instruction for each child, via a deliberate alignment of regular and extended-day programming. They designed this alignment to occur in three ways.

First, extended-day staff members overlapped their work shifts between the regular school day and the extended day, allowing extended-day staff members and regular classroom teachers the opportunity to share information about each student's daily problems, progress, and needs. Regular teaching staff also supported extended-day programming in various ways. For example, at Donoghue, classroom teachers provided homework support and the technology coordinator ran the technology club during extended-day programming. Teachers and social workers were often expected to provide timely information about specific students and their academic, social, and emotional needs to extended-day staff and parent volunteers. Second, classroom teachers, social workers, and coaches trained all extended-day staff and tutors in the same academic and behavioral expectations and practices that were in place during the regular school day. Third, school directors ensured that all extended-day partners aligned their programming to support the social and academic goals of each school. Both campuses required all external staff to coordinate closely with school leaders and classroom teachers and receive training in the school's instructional systems. In some cases, after-school programming was literally an extension of the schools' regular instructional programs. For example, both campuses used an after-school mathematics curriculum developed by the creators of *Everyday Mathematics*, which also provided the curriculum for mathematics instruction during the regular school day (see chapter 6).

Table 4.1 compares the model of instruction in conventionally organized schools (what we are calling the private, autonomous model) with the shared, systematic model the school's designers created for UCCS, contrasting how each approached issues of curriculum, assessment, and pedagogy, and the use of time.

Organizing Teachers' Work

Enacting the instruction described above required systematic support from school leaders and the organization as a whole. The model demanded close coordination among teachers, parents, and other school professionals; a shared, public teaching practice; common language; and shared expectations of students. It also involved increased public accountability for student learning, increased scrutiny of teacher practice, and increased expectations on—as well as support for—teachers to develop and share expertise. This shared, systematic approach to the organization of teachers' work contrasted sharply with the "loosely coupled" way that schools have traditionally been organized, in which teachers' work is minimally coordinated and norms of privacy, egalitarianism, and autonomy prevail.[13] Below, we discuss how the school's designers conceptualized the organization of teachers' work and the contrast they drew between conventional practice and what they wanted to create, with reference to three key dimensions: (1) collective and individual accountability, (2) professional relations among teachers, and (3) leadership and professional development.

Collective and individual accountability. The school's designers knew that conventional CPS schools typically provided minimal oversight of teach-

TABLE 4.1. Contrasting ways of organizing instruction

Dimension of school practice	Private, autonomous model	Shared, systematic model
Vision of curriculum, assessment, and pedagogy	Great variability in teachers' goals and practices; some common materials, used in variable ways	A schoolwide commitment to ambitious learning goals and diagnostic, responsive instruction; a common view of student learning; shared materials, assessments, and practices used in common ways
	Emphasis on teacher autonomy; efforts at instructional alignment largely voluntary	Systematic effort by school leaders to align and coordinate instruction schoolwide
	Enormous teacher discretion, but limited instructional guidance	Limited discretion for teachers, but more systematic instructional guidance and support
	Teachers decide whether and how to modify instruction in response to evidence of student learning	Collective analysis of school- and classroom-level evidence to inform changes to curriculum and instruction as well as teacher professional development
Use of time	Student and school schedules were standardized by grade level and generally do not change throughout the year	Student and school schedules flexibly allocated and continually adjusted based on ongoing analysis of student needs
	Extended-day and summer programming, if they exist, were independent of programming in the regular school day	Strategic alignment between regular, extended-day, and summer programming

ers' work and little incentive for teachers to cooperate, and that traditional occupational norms actively discouraged such mutual assistance. Consequently, they put organizational structures in place at UCCS to promote accountability for the learning of every child, provide close monitoring of student learning and teacher effectiveness, and motivate collaboration and continuous improvement. School leaders expected information from diagnostic assessments to become the shared knowledge of all teachers within the school, creating a strong social press for each teacher to meet public benchmarks for student achievement and encouraging a heightened sense of internal accountability for student learning. In both one-on-one coaching sessions and gatherings of the faculty, teachers reflected on their practice and the evidence of its effectiveness and collaborated to devise ways to better address the needs of students when necessary. As we discuss in chapter 7, school leaders also set an expectation that more-effective teachers should share their knowledge with colleagues who may be struggling and that the latter should accept such collegial assistance.

In addition to these internal accountability structures (those that operated primarily within the school) were a variety of mechanisms designed to foster a sense of external accountability.[14] NKO and Donoghue were part of a network of four UCCS campuses that also included Woodlawn and Carter G. Woodson, a high school and a middle school campus established in 2006 and 2008, respectively. Campus directors were directly accountable for student learning to a variety of external actors. The first of these was UEI, which operated the four campuses. Campus directors reported to and received guidance from both the director of UCCS at UEI, who oversaw all four campuses, and the director of UEI itself. A three-member board of directors and a twelve-member governing board composed of parents, community leaders, and university faculty and administrators also oversaw the four campuses. Finally, the university itself was accountable to various criteria set forth in its charter agreement with the district as well as to applicable federal, state, and local laws. This dual (internal and external) accountability system aimed to align the interests of teachers and campus directors, motivating cooperation toward continually improved results for students.

Professional relations among teachers. As discussed in chapter 3, the school's designers had found that in conventionally organized schools, elementary teachers did not typically collaborate to address shared problems of practice, coordinate their instruction, critique one another's work with students, or mentor one another in systematic ways. Rather, they tended to teach privately and autonomously, keeping their expertise to themselves and being careful to avoid any criticism of other teachers' practice. Indeed, UCCS's founders discovered that even in more collegial school environments where such collaboration could more readily occur, teachers tended to avoid sensitive or loaded questions about the relative effectiveness of different teachers' practices in favor of "safer" collaborative activities, such as jointly planning field trips or codeveloping thematic units for students.

Campus leaders, by contrast, expected teachers to adhere to new professional norms that directly challenged these tacit expectations. These included engaging a shared, public (rather than idiosyncratic and private) practice; acknowledging differential expertise and effectiveness among teachers; and participating in critical dialogue about evidence of student learning in service of improving practice (rather than the avoidance of such criticism in deference to teachers' feelings of personal vulnerability). As we elaborate in chapter 7, the model involved a constellation of specific organizational roles, routines, and practices designed to facilitate the sharing of expertise, the development of more collegial relations among teachers, and collaboration to improve instruction schoolwide. Teachers also participated in a larger professional community that included all four UCCS campuses. These campuses shared a common mission to prepare all students for success in college and aimed to constitute a pre-K–12 pathway to attaining this goal.

Leadership and professional development. The school's designers had also observed that in conventionally organized CPS schools, the work of school leaders rarely penetrated the day-to-day activities of classroom instruction. Teachers enjoyed considerable autonomy but few opportunities for collegial dialogue or professional growth. Since practice was private and egalitarianism the norm, teachers were unaware of differences in expertise among their colleagues. Compensation was based solely on seniority and credentials. To the extent that professional development was available, it often came from external service providers and tended to be standardized, rather than tailored to specific, local challenges. In contrast to this conventional scenario, UCCS leaders sought to create a school in which the work of leaders was much more tightly coordinated with that of teachers. In the UCCS model, school leaders were required to work closely with teachers to analyze evidence of student learning in an effort to ensure instruction tailored to student needs.

Campus directors were also expected to identify, train, and promote instructional subject-area leaders from within the ranks of teachers and require all school staff members to cooperate with their efforts to improve teaching and learning in the building. These coaches earned their positions based on their demonstrated effectiveness at using the school's instructional systems in their particular subject areas. Their extra responsibilities as leaders also earned them increased compensation. As we illustrate in chapters 5 through 7, subject-area coaches provided one-on-one coaching and mentoring to improve each teacher's practice and also led professional development and data analysis sessions for groups of teachers. Coaches shaped teacher interactions and expectations by facilitating professional dialogue focused on evidence of student learning; coordinating instruction across classrooms; and enforcing new professional norms of collegiality, public practice, and acknowledgment of differences in

TABLE 4.2. Contrasting ways of organizing teachers' work

Dimension of school practice	Private, autonomous model	Shared, systematic model
Collective and individual accountability	Teachers permitted to practice autonomously with sporadic monitoring by school leaders	Ongoing close analysis of teacher practice and evidence of student learning
	Accountability mechanisms primarily external to the school; sharing of expertise among teachers strictly voluntary	Aligned internal and external accountability mechanisms to motivate continuous learning and incentivize the sharing of expertise
Professional relations among teachers	Teachers work independently; collaboration generally voluntary and uneven	Common system of instruction and mutual support and accountability to enact it
	Traditional norms of privacy, autonomy, egalitarianism, and avoidance of critical dialogue about teacher practice	New norms of shared, public practice; recognition of differential expertise; and critical dialogue about the effects of instruction on student learning
Leadership and professional development	School leaders as managers focused primarily on operational issues rather than instruction	School leaders guide a common instructional program
	Flat career trajectory for teachers; promotion and compensation based on seniority, credentials	Leadership roles for teachers with promotion and compensation based on expertise in shared instructional systems
	Sporadic, standardized professional development, usually externally provided	Ongoing pedagogical guidance tailored to local problems of practice, generally provided by leaders internal to the school

expertise. Table 4.2 illustrates the contrast the school's designers drew between conventional practice and the model they were trying to create with respect to the organization of teachers' work.

Mobilizing Broader Supports for Student Learning

The model we examine in this book also involved a distinctive approach to providing academic and social supports for students as well as to engaging parents. This approach, which we discuss below, was consistent with the principles of shared, systematic practice the school's designers applied to both instruction and school leadership.

Academic and social supports for students. The designers of UCCS noticed that in conventionally organized CPS elementary schools, classroom teachers often struggled on their own to manage children's social, emotional, and behavioral challenges. Parents also struggled with these same challenges in isolation at home. And while all public schools provide some academic and social support for their students, the designers noted that the social workers and other specialists who provided these supports most often worked in a different organizational environment from that of classroom teachers. They were frequently part-time staff and were often employed by and thus accountable to the district central office rather than to the school principal. Moreover, social workers often worked across several schools at once and focused on applying interventions mandated by legal agreements or professional standards. These structures and responsibilities made it very difficult for them to align their interventions with everyday classroom instruction. Moreover, only a small subset of children typically received these specialized interventions. Indeed, the only students who typically came to the attention of school social workers were those whose struggles had escalated to an unmanageable level, where the classroom teacher could no longer handle them alone. Social workers and clinicians then sorted students by the severity of their needs and assigned those students whose challenges were most severe to a separate system of special education. Similarly, in most schools, resources for struggling students were generally distributed ad hoc, as teachers or parents requested them or disruptions in the classroom or school demanded them. In many schools, only students with the most severe needs received these services. Teachers developed their own methods for determining their students' needs and then competed with one another for resources to address them. Principals then had to adjudicate between different assessments of students that were based on different kinds of evidence to determine how to distribute scarce school resources.

In contrast to this conventional scenario, in which overburdened teachers and overwhelmed parents referred "problem" students to a separate clinical service system, the school's designers developed a model that called for close monitoring of all children and focused on prevention rather than primarily on treatment. The key idea was to keep small academic, social, and/or emotional challenges from escalating into big ones, so that the number of children who required intensive remediation or intervention remained small. As we discuss in chapter 7, NKO and Donoghue each had a full-time lead social worker, who closely coordinated their efforts with other school staff and were themselves supported by the school's shared instructional system. The lead social worker belonged to the school's senior leadership team and was assigned to work with the team to assess and support the academic, social, and emotional development of every student and foster a campus environment conducive to this. The prominence of the social worker on the school's leadership team was not accidental. Rather, it reflected a conviction on the part of the school's designers—especially Tamara Gathright Fritz, who co-led the development of UEI's Academic and Social Support Initiative—that urban schools serving disadvantaged populations of students must (1) give serious, sustained attention to providing academic and social support for children and families to ensure that children could take advantage of strong classroom instruction; and (2) integrate this support into the daily life of the school. Both campuses were designated Chicago Public Schools "Community Schools," which allowed them to offer academic and social programming for students, families, and community members beyond the traditional school day. This designation gave school leaders additional resources and flexibility to address students' academic and social needs, as well as engage more deeply with parents.[15]

Finally, using a schoolwide assessment system, school leaders and teachers were to routinely obtain evidence of the needs of each child and to allocate supports to address them before, during, and after school as well as during the summer. The purpose of this ongoing activity was to keep smaller academic and social challenges from escalating into bigger problems and to intervene as early as possible so that each child received the supports he or she might need to get and remain on track to achieve at high levels, ultimately leading to college graduation.

Relations with parents. In many urban public schools, UCCS's designers observed administrators and teachers engage parents on an ad hoc, case-by-case basis—most often when children experienced serious problems. In contrast, as we discuss in chapter 7, the school's designers created the role on each campus of director of family and community engagement (FCE director), who was responsible for systematically engaging parents while also managing extended-day programming and performing everyday disciplinary duties with students. This role combined the traditional responsibilities of a vice principal with a novel emphasis on community and parent engagement and outreach.[16]

TABLE 4.3. Contrasting ways of mobilizing broader support

Dimension of school practice	Private, autonomous model	Shared, systematic model
Supplemental supports for students	Offered via a separate system of services for those deemed most in need of extra help	Academic and social supports integrated with regular system of instruction; social worker embedded in school leadership team
	Targeted toward small numbers of students facing the greatest difficulties and needing remedial and special education	Focused on prevention of problems via continuously monitoring social/emotional needs of all students, creating pro-social school climate
Relations with parents	Teachers engage parents as needed, on a case-by-case basis, varying greatly in the extent to and manner in which this occurs	Systematic approach to parent engagement, focused on providing knowledge of the instructional system and how parents can support their child's learning within it

In addition, all school staff members were to provide parents (1) ongoing, specific, timely information about their child's individual learning trajectories; (2) training in the school's assessment tools and assistance interpreting assessment results to better understand their child's academic strengths and needs; and (3) guidance on how to support their child's academic and social learning needs at home. School staff members also reached out to parents as needed every six to eight weeks when teachers and leaders met for their "classroom monitoring meetings" to review the progress of every child in each class (see chapter 7), to talk with parents about issues they were facing with their children at home, offer support, and craft a plan of shared responsibility for addressing individual student's learning challenges.

Finally, as we discuss in chapter 7, the Donoghue campus had a parent resource center staffed by a full-time parent coordinator.[17] This center offered educational enrichment programs for parents before, during, and after school, such as book clubs, standardized test prep advice, training in the school's shared assessment systems, salsa dance classes, and workshops on financial literacy. As a by-product of such programming, the center also built parent networks that facilitated the flow of information and support between the school and the home. Table 4.3 contrasts the shared, systematic approach that UEI and school leaders developed for marshaling broader support for the work of schooling with the private, autonomous approach they had encountered in conventionally organized CPS schools.

Conclusion

Thus far, we have described the UCCS model in somewhat abstract terms, focusing on three imperatives of (1) ambitious instruction; (2) organizing teachers' work to ensure such instruction occurs for every child; and (3) mobilizing broader supports for student learning. In the next part of the book, we elaborate more concretely how school and UEI leaders and staff actually pursued these imperatives in practice. Chapters 5 and 6, which discuss reading and mathematics instruction, respectively, concentrate on the first imperative. Chapter 7 focuses on the second and third imperatives of organizing teachers' work to support such instruction and mobilizing broader supports for student learning, showing in detail how school leaders organized the work in their buildings to enable the ambitious instruction for reading and mathematics described in chapters 5 and 6. As we shall see, the model of instruction in these two subject areas shared a number of common features or guiding principles: (1) *ambitious learning goals for students*, such as we have begun to describe in this chapter; (2) *ambitious curricula* that challenge and support students to achieve these far-reaching goals; (3) *shared, systematic collection and use of formative assessment data* to inform tailoring instruction to address students' individual learning needs; (4) *intensive pedagogical guidance* for teachers to enact this dynamic, responsive instruction; (5) *extended instructional time*; and (6) *engaging parents* as partners in advancing students' learning.

CHAPTER 5 DESIGNING READING INSTRUCTION TO OVERCOME EDUCATIONAL INEQUALITY

Any attempt to improve American schooling will immediately confront the problem of teaching reading. No other aspect of schooling has been more studied, and no line of educational research has produced more conclusive findings. Yet it remains true that many children, disproportionately from low-income and ethnic minority families, experience reading difficulties during elementary school.[1] Poor reading skills significantly diminish subject-matter learning and chances of high school graduation, college attendance, and college completion,[2] all of which are important for succeeding in the labor market, staying out of trouble, and living a long and healthy life.

Why does inequality in reading remain large despite the fact that we have learned a great deal about how to teach reading? Part of the answer seems to be that schools have not fully implemented best practice for reading instruction. But a deeper problem looms large. It has to do with the varied learning opportunities children have before they enter school and the challenge this poses elementary schools. Reading research has comparatively little to say about this deeper problem.

Most research on reading instruction focuses on early reading, when children learn how words and sentences are represented on the printed page. This stage of reading is called "decoding familiar text," and it is a crucial skill. To decode well is to recognize in printed text the ideas, vocabulary, and sentence structures that virtually every child knows from experience in conversations.

The problem is that learning how to decode simple texts, while essential, is not sufficient to enable children to comprehend the texts that they will encounter later when they study science, history, and literature. Those texts use a large vocabulary and arrange words and phrases in complex ways to clarify, compare, analyze, and synthesize new concepts. In reading such texts, children who have an extensive vocabulary and who are familiar with academic syntax will have an advantage over children who don't. To a large extent, these language skills develop before school entry. The problem is that children's learning environments before schooling vary dramatically. As a result, children enter school with widely varied oral language skills. Therefore, even if all children are taught to decode simple texts during kindergarten and grade 1, we can expect wide variation in children's reading comprehension in later grades—unless schools find some effective strategies for coping with the heterogeneity of early oral language skills that children bring to school.

Redesigning reading instruction was the first order of business when the North Kenwood/Oakland (NKO) Campus, the first campus of the University of Chicago Charter School (UCCS), was founded in 1998. The model for literacy instruction looked very different from conventional approaches. One aim was to capitalize on research about how to teach early reading with a focus on decoding familiar text. A more ambitious goal was to immerse all children in an enriched language environment. Here the challenge was to design a system that could cope with the great heterogeneity in language skills that children brought to school. The system required frequent assessment of children's skills and individually tailored instruction for each student.

Embracing such a system significantly increased the complexity of teachers' work. To some considerable extent, how to help children of varied backgrounds move toward ambitious learning goals was not known and had to be collectively learned. This required breaking down the barriers that separate teachers, opening practice to public scrutiny, and collectively trying out new ideas during instruction. An additional question was how to mobilize enough instructional time to ensure that children could achieve the school's ambitious goals.

When Timothy Knowles hired Nicole Woodard-Iliev to launch the Donoghue campus in 2005, Woodard-Iliev and her colleagues increased the intensity of support for children who were furthest behind, leading to more radical changes, including dramatically increasing instructional time in reading, extending the school day and school year, and concertedly engaging parents in new ways. In time, as each campus adopted the innovations generated in the other campus, a distinctive and coherent schoolwide approach emerged; and that approach, shared by the two campuses, is the focus of this chapter.

The key aims were invariant over time: to immerse children in rigorous intellectual work from the time they first entered school, and to assure that all children could read with high levels of comprehension by the later elementary grades. Accomplishing these aims required a schoolwide literacy framework, frequent assessment of student progress, instructional plans tailored to each student, intensive pedagogical guidance, flexible use of instructional time, and the active engagement of parents. Pulling this off required significant changes in school organization, which we describe in detail in chapter 7.

In this chapter, we first review research on how children learn to read and why inequality in reading is so dramatic. We'll see that the research provided some answers but raised many challenging questions about how schools can overcome inequality. Grappling with these questions led to the development of the novel and unusually ambitious approach to reading instruction that we describe in some detail later in the chapter.

Elementary School Reading Instruction and Inequality

There has been long-standing controversy regarding the best way to teach children how to read. One key question involves the emphasis on "word decoding" and, in particular, whether it is useful to focus instruction on the relationship between letters and sounds, often called "code-based" instruction. Some who advocated an emphasis on "whole language," or meaning-based, instruction[3] have criticized approaches that emphasize letter-sound relationships that are divorced from the meaning of the text. Others have advocated various combinations of phonetic and meaning-based approaches.

Advances in Research on Early Reading

By 2000, a scientific consensus had emerged about how children learn to read. Based on careful review of thousands of studies, the National Reading Panel confirmed four powerful approaches to instruction that influence early reading skills. These findings regarding early reading are remarkably convergent, though important questions about the later emergence of reading comprehension remained unanswered.[4]

First, explicit instruction in "phonemic awareness" is helpful. This entails learning how to identify and categorize particular sounds, how to blend these sounds to make words, how to segment words into their component sounds, and how to relate the sounds with which children are familiar to the particular letters and words they are learning. Teaching phonemic awareness in small groups and applying these techniques to particular reading tasks has been found to promote successful word decoding, allowing children to link written words to words familiar to their ear, and to promote spelling accuracy.

Second, findings confirmed that systematic, explicit instruction in word decoding is far more effective in promoting early reading than the use of approaches that emphasize the meaning of words without instruction in word decoding. In particular, early word-decoding instruction has been found to have powerful effects for children at risk of reading disorders. The vast majority of children respond positively to early instruction in phonemic awareness and word decoding; the small fraction of children who do not can then be assigned intensive clinical interventions (for example, instruction of groups of two children over eighty hours) that have proven quite effective. When children are not exposed to early instruction in word decoding and phonemic awareness, a large fraction will experience problems mastering early reading, making it difficult to target intensive and expensive clinical interventions.

Third, guided oral reading—typically conducted in small groups—significantly improves reading fluency (defined as reading accurately, reasonably quickly, and with expression), as well as word recognition and reading comprehension. In contrast, researchers have found little evidence that independent, private reading is helpful for beginning readers, although this question has not received sufficient attention in the research literature.

Fourth, the reviewers found some evidence that teaching children certain cognitive strategies can increase reading comprehension. These include helping children to ask and answer factual questions such as who in the text is involved, where, and when; teaching children to answer more conceptual questions about why things are happening and what will happen next; encouraging children to write and draw pictures about what is happening in the text; and asking children to summarize in their own words what is happening and why. Such strategies can be used in combination with word-decoding strategies based on letter-sound relationships to identify the meaning of new words.

These strategies enable nearly all children to succeed at what Jeanne

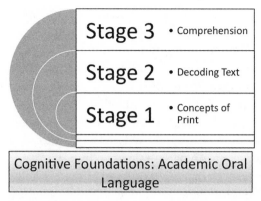

FIGURE 5.1. Stages of reading development

Chall has called "decoding familiar text,"[5] the essence of early reading. Familiar text includes ideas, vocabulary, and syntax that are familiar to nearly all children in their experience as listeners and speakers. Decoding enables children to connect what they already know from their experience in the world of oral language with the printed word.

However, there is also an emerging consensus that learning to decode familiar text is a necessary but not sufficient condition for learning to read unfamiliar text with a high level of comprehension. Also essential is the child's mastery of vocabulary and complex syntax. In essence, a child's oral language experience before school entry shapes the later emergence of reading comprehension, even if that child has become a skilled decoder of familiar text (see figure 5.1).[6]

Early Sources of Inequality in Oral Language and Print-Related Skills

Children first learn language and vocabulary skills in their home environments with their parents and other caregivers.[7] Some parents—particularly those with high levels of education—provide reasonably systematic instruction to their children at home in vocabulary, syntax (how words and phrases are arranged in sentences), narrative skills, and general knowledge required for academic discourse in school settings. For these children, language at home closely approximates "academic English"[8] and therefore is similar to the language applied to subject matter at school. However, many low-income and ethnic minority children use languages, linguistic codes, and dialects at home and in community settings that are different from the language most often used in school settings. To be sure, these children will become effective communicators in a variety of cultural settings. However, research suggests that exposure to academic English vocabulary, syntax, and narrative skills is particularly important for the later emergence of reading comprehension, given that written texts almost invariably use academic English.[9]

As children mature, parents tend to use increasingly complex sentences and narrative structures as well as more diverse vocabulary.[10] Such early interactions between parents and children constitute a form of oral language development that gives children of more–highly educated parents a significant advantage in academic settings over peers from cultures with different styles of communication that do not directly conform to the language of instruction taught in American schools. These differences in early literacy experiences may not seem important during early reading instruction, when children focus on decoding short sentences that use familiar words and syntax. However, the resulting differences in oral language skills emerge as crucial when children have mastered basic decoding and the focus shifts to comprehending texts that present new ideas and vocabulary.[11]

Young children also vary in their exposure to printed materials at home, leading to differences in what developmental theorists call "concepts about print."[12] These skills include understanding how books work (such as how to follow text from left to right and down the page, how and when to turn the page to follow the text), knowing the alphabet, and understanding that certain sounds associate with specific letters. Until a child can accurately point to individual words within a line of text, he or she will be unable to learn new words while reading or to attend effectively to letter-sound cues at the beginning of words.[13] Such early concepts about print create a context for building knowledge of letters and sounds related to a written word and ultimately for matching written words to spoken words as the child reads. Interactions that children have with their families at home around print can engender these prereading skills, conferring later advantages in school settings. Such exposure to printed text and the consequent development of such early skills are most likely to occur in the homes of highly educated parents.[14] The children in these homes learn at a young age not only how books work, but also how to enjoy and discuss books. From these early interactions with books, children learn that reading words and making sense from text go hand in hand. Thus, book reading with parents not only supports knowledge about text, but also supports language development.

The Challenge Facing Elementary Schools

In summary, the period between birth and age five represents a significant opportunity for oral language development in academic English and also early understandings of written text that confer benefits which last throughout the school years. Children who lack exposure to academic literacy input at home often start school behind their peers and then tend to fall further behind because their parents often do not have the social, cultural, and financial resources[15] to address at home the increasing challenges students face at school.[16] This variation in children's prior experiences with academic English and printed text at school entry poses formidable instructional challenges to teachers who wish to ensure that all children will read with high levels of comprehension by grade 3. These are the challenges taken up by the founders and subsequent leaders of the University of Chicago Charter School (UCCS).

A Schoolwide System of Reading Instruction

The major advances in research on reading, described above, have been successful primarily in helping children decode familiar text. Embracing this research has great potential to help overcome inequality in children's print-related skills and to ensure that the vast majority will learn to "crack the code." But the research consensus had comparatively little to say about how to overcome inequality in academic vocabulary and syntax—knowledge that is foundational for "reading to learn," beginning typically in second grade.[17] As a result, the leaders of UCCS reasoned that elementary school literacy instruction was not sufficiently ambitious to overcome inequality at school entry. To cope with this challenge, leaders at the school developed a system characterized by six guiding principles.

1. *Immerse all children in ambitious learning.* UCCS sought to enable all children to achieve high levels of reading comprehension so they could engage in ambitious subject-matter learning by grade 3.
2. *Adopt a schoolwide framework for reading.* UCCS faculty and staff emphasized the importance of a curriculum that promoted oral language development as well as proficiency in word decoding.
3. *Frequently assess student learning and tailor instruction to students' current skill.* Teachers frequently diagnosed their students' reading skill and devised child-specific instructional plans.
4. *Provide teachers with sustained pedagogical support.* Ongoing pedagogical

support was essential to sustain a complex practice that used frequent assessments to guide reading instruction tailored to individual students.

5. *Expand instructional time.* To ensure that every child was on track for success required extending instructional time during the school day, after school, and, if necessary, during the summer.

6. *Continuously engage parents.* Rather than contacting parents during crisis situations or infrequently scheduled conferences, teachers and school leaders continuously engaged parents in advancing their child's reading progress.

In the remainder of the chapter, we elaborate each of these principles.

1. Immerse All Children in Ambitious Learning

The goal was ambitious: to ensure that every student would be reading with high levels of comprehension and thus be prepared for ambitious subject-matter learning by grade 3. School leaders sought to mobilize staff and parents in a relentless campaign to achieve this goal.

An example from the Donoghue campus illustrates this clearly. Many students entering Donoghue in the opening year faced difficulties learning to read. At the beginning of the 2005/06 school year, campus director Woodard-Iliev and her teaching team discovered from the initial round of baseline literacy assessment that only 18 percent of kindergarteners could identify letter names and connect them to their sounds or talk about or retell specific parts of stories. Many were unable to recognize letters in their names. These were milestones that Woodard-Iliev had expected all students to achieve by kindergarten to be on track to read with high levels of comprehension by the end of grade 3. First, second, and third graders were also falling short of critical literacy benchmarks. Among first graders, only 16 percent could hear and write down the initial and ending sounds in words or add up clues from a text to make sense of and talk about stories. Only 4 percent of second graders were reading at expected levels; 96 percent of them were unable to ask questions about or discuss characters' actions, motives, and feelings in a story, or figure out irregularly spelled words. Only about one in five third graders could build and revise their understanding of a text as they read or write elaborate responses to thought-provoking questions. Woodard-Iliev and her team pursued multiple strategies to solve this problem, including dramatically expanding reading instructional time, reshuffling classroom teaching assignments, splitting larger classrooms into smaller classrooms, and launching an after-school tutoring program. In short, school leaders used every organizational device under their control to make sure that all students were on track for success.

2. Adopt a Schoolwide Framework for Reading

In close collaboration with Gay Su Pinnell of the Ohio State University, the founders of the charter school adopted as their framework for reading instruction "balanced literacy," an instructional approach that involves guiding children through the stages of learning to read.[18] The framework emphasized instruction in decoding in combination with guided oral reading in small groups and the use of comprehension strategies found effective in the research. It encouraged vocabulary growth and provided opportunities for children to discuss complex ideas and information that arose in books of varying difficulty. For example, teachers engaged in the following practices: (1) reading challenging texts to children and stimulating discussion about these books to stretch children's vocabulary and higher-order thinking skills; (2) guiding children in small groups to read books that were just beyond students' current reading ability to provide direct instruction in word decoding and comprehension strategies for new vocabulary; and (3) providing children simpler texts that they could read independently, or with minimal teacher assistance, to practice their decoding and comprehension skills.[19] The teachers used the assessment system we describe below to select texts to match each child's current level of reading skill.

Cultural responsiveness. Along with Ladson-Billings and others,[20] UEI and UCCS leaders reasoned that children bring to school ideas, interests, experiences, and cultural identities that teachers could use as a foundation for building new knowledge. The aim was to build a school environment that affirmed students' cultural identities[21] and offered a counternarrative to race, class, and gender stereotypes. Books and other instructional materials featured characters with whom students identified and situations with which they were familiar.

At the same time, UCCS leaders reasoned that schooling should also expand children's experiences beyond their families and communities, providing children opportunities to develop skills in speaking and acting in ways that are required for success in mainstream institutions. The aim was to expand children's repertoires so that they could operate effectively in the widest variety of cultural settings.

Dynamic grouping for instruction. The reading model used small-group reading instruction to help students practice academic language, habits of discussion, and rich vocabulary. Teachers were expected to challenge children to express their ideas about books in these small-group settings, back up their ideas with evidence from the text, and listen to and evaluate their peers' thinking.

Grouping children for reading instruction has been a pervasive practice in US elementary schools. Critics have claimed that separating children into groups based on skill can stigmatize the least skilled children and generate low teacher expectations for child learning. More recent research suggests that homogenous grouping works well if it is combined with adequate instructional time[22] and when it is designed to ensure that all children reach a high level of comprehension. At the UCCS campuses, teachers implemented frequent objective assessments (see below) designed to facilitate "dynamic grouping": based on the most recent assessment, teachers brought students together around particular skills to ensure that all were on track for success, and children were regrouped as they progressed, based on evidence of each child's emerging skills.

A recurrent criticism of grouping is that the high-skill groups gain experience in higher-order reasoning while low-skill groups drill in rote memorization. UCCS designers adopted a very different policy. Regardless of a child's current skill, there was an emphasis on using discussions to make sense of text. Of particular importance was the balance between word decoding instruction and comprehension, generating in all groups strong habits of discussion and the ability to articulately express ideas orally and in writing.[23]

3. Frequently Assess Student Learning and Tailor Instruction to Students' Skills

Given the multiplicity of tasks facing the primary school teacher and the wide variability in children's language backgrounds and early decoding skills, UCCS leaders recognized that a range of instructional errors—which might be regarded as errors of emphasis and sequencing—prevented many children from successfully making the transition from word decoding (stage 2) to reading comprehension (stage 3; see figure 5.1). Consider a child who starts out at kindergarten behind in academic English skills as well as decoding skills. One common error would be to set aside the need for language development entirely and instead teach only word decoding. With this approach, we would predict success on early tests of decoding in kindergarten and grade 1 with disappointing results in reading comprehension in grades 2 and 3. This error of sequencing appears common in US schools.[24] Another possible error would involve a premature move away from an emphasis on decoding. This instructional error would rob children of the opportunity to master decoding, a foundation for later reading comprehension and accurate spelling.

A third kind of error affects those children who learn to decode very rapidly. For these children, there is a risk that teachers will persist in emphasizing the most basic decoding skills, delaying the transition for those who are ready to "read to learn." UCCS leaders suspected that this error was quite common in schools serving low-income children, particularly when children who had rapidly gained decoding skills were in classes where most other children had not yet gained those skills. This error would more commonly occur when the teacher instructed the whole class or when the school followed a "scripted curriculum" that prevented teachers from grouping to accommodate the varied skill levels of individual students.

It is a tall order to correct these errors and make certain that each child receives instruction optimally tailored to his or her particular mix of oral language and reading skills. UCCS designers reasoned that avoiding these errors required detailed, objective information about the skill level of each child. It also required knowledge of the optimal instruction that matched the identified profile of skills. Such a system makes reading instruction complex because (1) teachers must simultaneously attend to multiple skill domains (language development, word decoding, and reading comprehension); (2) children's skills in each of these domains vary widely; and (3) the teacher must continuously manage the instructional activities of a large number of children.

The STEP assessment system. To manage these challenges, the school's founders adopted a schoolwide literacy assessment system, discussed in chapters 3 and 4. It tracked children's developing skills in oral language, word decoding, and comprehension between kindergarten entry and grade 3. The system would no doubt reveal substantial inequality in skill at school entry and thereafter. The key was to tailor instruction to the current level of student skill to ensure that every child made rapid progress. This entailed a dynamic system of grouping children for instruction, assessing them, and regrouping as needed. Teachers emphasized oral language and comprehension skills in every group, along with the level of phonetic instruction needed.

As discussed in chapter 3, Anthony Bryk and David Kerbow worked with Virginia Watson to develop the formative literacy assessment, organized around a developmental trajectory of progress from prereading to high levels of reading comprehension, called Strategic Teaching and Evaluation of Progress (STEP).[25] The STEP assessment consisted of twelve distinct "steps" from prereading to step 12. The assessment provided a comprehensive map of students' reading skill acquisition, reflecting expectations for students' skill development from kindergarten to the end of grade 3 (figure 5.2[26]).

Note that a child at step 12 was reading with high levels of comprehension. Such a child could "acquire new vocabulary and concepts through independent reading, comprehend texts that are removed from personal experience, and entertain and evaluate different interpretations" of text. The key aim was to get every child to this level by the end of grade 3. Achieving this level required a combination of decoding and comprehension skills developed in earlier steps.

Steps 1 through 6 included print-related skills that enabled a child to be a fluent decoder of familiar text, beginning with knowing the letters of the alphabet and recognizing that print corresponded to words being read; breaking down long words into syllables; and figuring out how to spell irregular words. At the same time, starting at step 1, each step also included assessment of oral language and comprehension skills. Linked to each step in the assessment was a set of books at incrementally increasing levels of reading difficulty corresponding to the trajectory of reading skill development that STEP measures.

Primary-grade teachers explained to us that they administered the STEP assessment to every child every ten to twelve weeks over a period of several days, during individual conferences of ten to fifteen minutes, recording information about each student's reading accuracy and fluency. Teachers also reported that they provided interim STEP assessments for students who were either rapidly progressing or seriously struggling in their small reading groups. Teachers compared data from one time point to the next, enabling them to assess child progress and evaluate the efficacy of earlier instructional efforts.

With step 12 as the goal for the end of third grade, the assessment maps backward in time to determine appropriate end-of-year benchmarks for kindergarten through third grade as well. Thus, children were expected to be at step 9 by the end of second grade and at step 6, which signified the end of the "early reading" stage, at the end of first grade. At this time, children were learning to combine "code breaking" and "meaning making." Finally, the benchmark for the end of kindergarten was step 3, marking the end of the "emergent" stage of reading in which the stu-

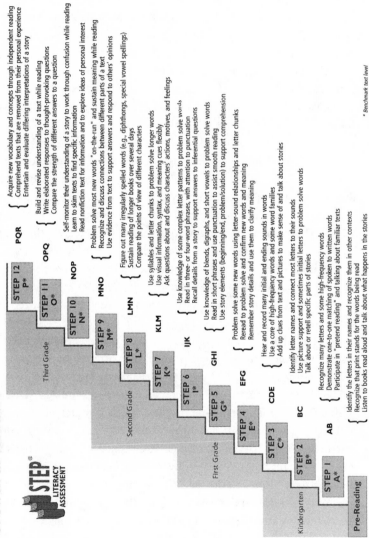

Developmental Map of Students' Growth as Readers

STEP LITERACY ASSESSMENT

Instructional Book Levels

At this STEP, students can

* Benchmark text level

STEP 12 P* — PQR
- Acquire new vocabulary and concepts through independent reading
- Comprehend texts that are removed from their personal experience
- Entertain and evaluate differing interpretations of a story

STEP 11 O* — OPQ
- Build and revise understanding of a text while reading
- Write elaborated responses to thought-provoking questions
- Compare the strength of different answers to a question

STEP 10 N* — NOP
- Self-monitor their understanding of a story to work through confusion while reading
- Learn to skim texts to find specific information
- Read nonfiction text for information and to explore ideas of personal interest

STEP 9 M* — MNO
- Problem solve most new words "on-the-run" and sustain meaning while reading
- Recognize and discuss connections between different parts of a text
- Use evidence from text to support answers and respond to others' opinions

STEP 8 L* — LMN
- Figure out many irregularly spelled words (e.g., diphthongs, special vowel spellings)
- Sustain reading of longer books over several days
- Compare the points of view of different characters

STEP 7 K* — KLM
- Use syllables and letter chunks to problem solve longer words
- Use visual information, syntax, and meaning cues flexibly
- Ask questions about and discuss characters' actions, motives, and feelings

STEP 6 I* — IJK
- Use knowledge of some complex letter patterns to problem solve words
- Read in three- or four-word phrases, with attention to punctuation
- Recall details from a story to support answers to inferential questions

STEP 5 G* — GHI
- Use knowledge of blends, digraphs, and short vowels to problem solve words
- Read in short phrases and use punctuation to assist smooth reading
- Use story elements (beginning/end, problem/solution) to support comprehension

STEP 4 E* — EFG
- Problem solve some new words using letter-sound relationships and letter chunks
- Reread to problem solve and confirm new words and meaning
- Remember story details and use them to clarify meaning

STEP 3 C* — CDE
- Hear and record many initial and ending sounds in words
- Use a core of high-frequency words and some word families
- Add up clues from text and pictures to make sense of and talk about stories

STEP 2 B* — BC
- Identify letter names and connect most letters to their sounds
- Use picture support and sometimes initial letters to problem solve words
- Talk about or retell specific parts of stories

STEP 1 A* — AB
- Recognize many letters and some high-frequency words
- Demonstrate one-to-one matching of spoken to written words
- Participate in "pretend reading" and talking about familiar texts

Pre-Reading
- Identify the letters in their names and recognize them in other contexts
- Recognize that print stands for the words being read
- Listen to books read aloud and talk about what happens in the stories

Third Grade

Second Grade

First Grade

Kindergarten

FIGURE 5.2. STEP Development Reading Map

dents' greatest challenge was learning concepts about print, breaking the alphabetic code, and applying phonological awareness to book reading while also developing oral language skills.

Tailoring instruction to student differences in skill. Teachers examined assessment data together, with guidance from the literacy coach, to determine next steps for small-group instruction in word decoding. After teachers administered the STEP assessments and reviewed the results on their own, literacy coaches met with teams of teachers to help them develop a six- to eight-week instructional plan for meeting the students' needs based on their STEP results.

The following account of one such meeting illustrates how teachers used information from the STEP assessment to plan small-group word-decoding instruction that would help children advance to the next STEP level. At this particular meeting, the discussion aimed to understand why a significant number of kindergarten readers who achieved step 1 had not been able to achieve step 2. Teyona James, the literacy coach at Donoghue, explained:

> We looked specifically at the various components of learning to read at [step 2] and how performance on the various tasks might help us understand what was needed instructionally. A trend arose that most of the students were able to name all of the letters and all letter sounds as well. They also met the targets for segmenting words. . . . They knew how to match their finger to the print. However, . . . in their reading of a short patterned book . . . with one sentence per page and large pictures that supported comprehension, the students were not able to correctly read the words that changed within the patterned text, even though there was picture support. . . . In the second patterned text they read at step 2, the pattern changed in the book on the last page. We noticed a trend that the students just continued the pattern, even though the pattern of the sentence had eight words, and the last page of the text only had three words. . . . [We concluded that] these students' struggle is attending to print and attempting words based on first letter sounds and pictures, versus guessing at words based on pictures alone. Specific instructional approaches to teach children that are moving from step 1 to step 2 to read more successfully [are] teaching them to cross-check between the picture and the first letter of the word on the page and to attend to the print on the page and use a finger to point to each word in the text. Because we know they know how to match one-to-one, and

know the letter sounds, [we determined that] instruction in these reading strategies and practice in small-group instruction with appropriate
texts will facilitate their reading development and allow them to become independent in reading at this STEP level and ready for instruction at the next STEP level.

This example shows how information from the STEP assessment supported teachers' efforts to provide small-group word-decoding instruction targeted to the needs of particular groups of students. Without such
a shared system of instruction and assessment, teachers would be left
largely on their own to diagnose students' word-decoding difficulties and
devise strategies for addressing them.

4. Provide Teachers Sustained Pedagogical Support

To enact the instructional system required substantial expertise. Balancing language development and word decoding, frequently and accurately assessing these skills, designing small groups for instruction, and
integrating regular classroom work with after-school and summer work
made the teacher's task complex and intellectually demanding. Standard
teacher-training programs did not prepare teachers for such ambitious
work. Occasional outside professional development seminars could not be
adequate to the task of in-service training. What was required was an intensive system of pedagogical support built into the routines of everyday
school life.

UCCS leaders reasoned that teachers in conventionally organized
schools typically do not have the time required to collect and analyze data
and plan instruction in response to evidence about the learning needs of
each child in their classroom. Such time constraints imply the need for
more time during the school day and after school to improve teachers'
expertise in teaching reading. This likely also requires increased collaboration and sharing of knowledge among teachers, an issue we address
in detail in chapter 7. However, as we saw in chapter 3, when the norm of
teacher autonomy held sway, it became difficult to mobilize advice and
support networks among teachers that encouraged mutual observation
and feedback, shared evidence of student progress, and joint planning of
next instructional steps.

Collaboration and mentoring. The system of pedagogical support at UCCS
included not only training by the literacy coach in using the school's in-

structional system, but also—as we have seen—participation in meetings in which groups of teachers collectively analyzed information from the STEP assessment alongside other data to develop instructional action plans for students. Teachers working in isolation and without support from a literacy coach would vary widely in their motivation and capacity to engage in this kind of analysis as well as their knowledge of instructional strategies to move children from one STEP level to the next. Meetings where teachers put their heads together to solve difficult problems with expert guidance from a coach helped teachers deepen their expertise at using the instructional system to advance student learning and also at reflecting on their practice and its results.

For example, during "analysis meetings" at NKO (where teachers from a range of grade levels met together and shared and analyzed STEP data), teachers described the strategies they used to move a particular student or group of students to the next STEP level and offered collegial advice on how they solved particular instructional problems. Shannon Justice, a third-grade teacher, explained how this worked at NKO:

> The professional development we have in the building is focused on bringing us teachers together because we can provide specific information about our students that will provide next steps for another teacher. There's always a shared conversation about a student in my class [third grade] or a particular student in Karishma [Desai's] class [a fourth/fifth-grade teacher]. Everyone knows where that student was when he was with me and where he is now. In those meetings, I'm working to support Karishma in helping a particular student progress to their next level, and in doing so I am contributing to the whole-school investment that we have in each kid. It's particularly great to see kids really build on the progress that I was able to achieve with them.

While the outside world might view such meetings as a means of monitoring teachers for accountability purposes, Justice described these analysis meetings as a form of professional development. Her reference to "the whole-school investment that we have in each kid" also points to the role of such meetings in cultivating a sense of internal accountability for the progress of every child in the building, a topic we address in detail in chapter 7.

The literacy coach's role in leading these discussions was not only to support teachers' analysis of assessment data, but also to prompt partic-

TABLE 5.1. Literacy coach schedule

Time	Activity	Role
7:30 a.m.	First-grade team meeting	Coach
8 a.m.	Kindergarten team meeting	Teacher and coach
9 a.m.	Coaching observation of first-grade teacher	Coach
10 a.m.	Coaching debrief with first-grade teacher	Coach
11 a.m.	Lunch	Teacher
12 p.m.	Teaching literacy block in own class	Teacher
1 p.m.	Teaching literacy block in own class	Teacher
2 p.m.	Teaching literacy block in own class	Teacher
3 p.m.	Leadership team meeting	Teacher and coach
4:30 p.m.	Prep time for data analysis of own students	Teacher

ular kinds of interactions—especially sharing expertise—among teachers. As Desai explained,

> Our literacy coach turns to one teacher and says, "Well, you were struggling with that group [or with a similar challenge]—how did you get them over the hump?" Or she can help us have a broader discussion about the present problems by helping us to talk about what's worked in the past.

Such conversations might occur among teachers more informally. However, given the traditional professional norms of egalitarianism and privatized practice discussed in chapter 3, this rarely occurred in traditionally organized schools. Rather, creating a school environment in which such conversations could occur involved an ongoing process of culture building that was a conscious focus of leadership activity.

A day in the life of a literacy coach. Subject-specific coaches at each campus were tasked with helping advance teacher expertise. To explain how coaches did their work, we provide an example of the schedule of activities on March 24, 2010, of Teyona James, who was both a kindergarten teacher and the primary literacy coach at Donoghue (see table 5.1).

James started her day at 7:30 a.m. by attending the weekly team meeting of the first-grade teachers. During part of the team meeting, she coached first-grade teachers on how to use the running-record technique, which allows a teacher to systematically record the errors students make as they read a written passage. James next attended the kindergarten team meeting, where she was both a leader and a participant. In addition to discussing specific concerns about the kindergarten children, during this particular grade-level meeting, James also trained her fellow kindergarten teacher how to keep running records: one of the kindergarten teachers was a first-year teacher, so James also provided additional training for the new teacher in how to analyze the running record and use information from the analysis to alter reading instruction during the reading teaching time.

At 9 a.m., James conducted a classroom observation of one of the first-grade teachers. The first-grade teacher had requested that James visit her classroom to observe her guided oral reading techniques with a particular reading group of struggling students.[27] James recorded her observations of the teacher's interactions with struggling students and then followed up immediately with a one-on-one coaching session during which she discussed her comments and planned for her second visit to observe changes. After her coaching session, James ate lunch and prepared to teach the literacy block in her own kindergarten classroom, where she worked in partnership with her coteacher to conduct running records with her own students.

At 3 p.m., James attended an instructional leadership team meeting, where all school leaders met to discuss different issues, such as individual student progress, classroom dynamics, and school-level curricular issues. James explained,

> At that meeting, the leadership team realized that our students were good at [comprehending and writing] fiction but their gaps were in non-fiction. We used assessment from kindergarten through fifth grade to figure this out. We discussed that we were relying heavily on fiction texts in the early grades, but the upper-grade literacy coaches were seeing kids struggle to write nonfiction reports and other forms besides fictional stories. The science and social studies teachers also weighed in so we knew we had to find some way to identify and address those gaps. So we sought out different ways to incorporate nonfiction into our reading teaching.

Finally, at 4:30 p.m., James devoted some time to analyzing her own students' literacy data in preparation for an upcoming literacy analysis meeting.[28] Analysis meetings usually lasted up to two hours per grade level and teachers left them with detailed instructional plans to move each student from their current STEP level to the next.

Every aspect of the literacy instruction program at UCCS had implications for how the school functioned as an organization. When teachers frequently assessed their children's skills one-on-one, arrangements had to be made to ensure that the classroom was being taught well—typically by a literacy coach, the campus director, or other administrator—during assessment times. Planning instruction tailored to the assessments required meetings between a teacher, a literacy coach, and possibly others. Integrating the extended-day program with regular instruction required planning and training. Learning to advance students' reading skills required pedagogical support that could occur only if the requisite professional development was in place. We consider how UCCS designers organized school leadership to achieve these tasks in chapter 7.

5. Expand Instructional Time

Extending instructional time and using that time effectively seemed to be another crucial ingredient for implementing ambitious instruction for each child.[29] Extending the school day and the school year, as reviewed in chapter 2, appear especially essential for those children displaying the least favorable school-entry skills. There is also good evidence that summer instruction can pay off, enabling children who are behind to catch up.[30] As discussed in chapter 2, conventional schools rarely devote sufficient instructional time to enable children who start farthest behind to become strong readers by grade 3.[31]

UCCS leaders were convinced that broadening the reading instruction agenda to include the development of oral language, explicit decoding, and reading comprehension would require more time than was typically devoted to literacy instruction. They relied on three main research findings that support extending instructional time. First, students need time, not only to learn to decode unknown words but also to build comprehension, vocabulary, and fluency to comprehend higher levels of written texts.[32] Second, instruction in writing also contributes substantially to children's understanding of words, as they simultaneously learn to look at letters and words and hear the sounds in words (to develop "phonemic awareness").[33] Finally, developing oral language skills requires substantial time as well. When the amount of instructional time is constrained, it forces a competition among these basic aspects of instruction. To some large extent, the "reading wars" from earlier decades were territorial fights over limited instructional time.[34] Given limited time, "whole language" advocates emphasized comprehension skills and language development, while advocates of "word decoding" were committed to mastery in explicit decoding. Removing the constraints on instructional time for reading allowed UCCS practitioners a comprehensive approach for this foundational subject, while, in principle, laying to rest this unproductive controversy.

The reorganization of extended time during the school day. There is increasing evidence that disadvantaged students improve their literacy skills in schools that organize longer periods of literacy instruction during the school day (60 to 120 minutes), using a mix of heterogeneous and homogeneous literacy skill–based groups.[35] Leaders at UCCS sought to maximize each student's exposure to relevant instruction in literacy by dramatically increasing instructional time during the school day. We mentioned earlier that when Donoghue director Woodard-Iliev launched the campus's first year, she and her teaching team discovered that many children were behind in oral language and print-related skills. In response to this evidence, Woodard-Iliev and her team drastically increased instructional time in reading.

Extended reading instruction after school. Because many disadvantaged students start schooling behind their more advantaged peers in oral language and print-related skills, extending the school day and the school year is of potential benefit to students who need to accelerate their learning to catch up with their peers. However, extended-day and extended-year programs are frequently offered by outside service providers and may not be aligned with instruction provided during the regular school day.[36]

The UCCS campuses aligned reading instruction before and after school by training extended-day staff to target reading goals for individual students during their tutoring sessions in the extended-day setting. In the traditional after-school setting, there is no staff overlap in work shifts between teachers and after-school staff. After-school staff begin their work once regular staff leave at the end of the school day. The UCCS elementary campuses developed an extended-day model to solve this problem. They scheduled overlapping work shifts so that school leaders and classroom teachers could provide training to extended-day staff. That way, the efforts of the extended-day staff would support the instructional plan teachers were pursuing during the regular school day.[37] After-school staff arrived at 1 p.m. and worked in classrooms with teachers in the afternoon. The director of the extended day also started the day at 10 a.m. and worked through 6 p.m.

For example, at the beginning of the school year, each campus hired tutors from City Year, a federal government program, to work with students after school. Classroom teachers and coaches trained the tutors in balanced literacy and the STEP assessment and collaborated with the tutors in pursuing each student's instructional goals. At both schools, the City Year tutors, along with the extended-day staff directors and their other staff members, began their work in regular classrooms at 1 p.m., before the end of the regular school day, to build continuity between regular school instruction and after-school instruction. The City Year tutors followed the instructional plans with students one-on-one during the regular school day and also ran similar small-group tutoring events for extended-day students. Teachers were expected to schedule regular weekly meetings with City Year tutors to discuss each child's progress.

This redundancy in scheduling made close collaboration—based on emergent evidence of student learning—logistically possible. School directors also told us that they worked closely with extended-day directors to continually evaluate the City Year programming to make sure that their programs aligned with the academic and social goals of the school. Todd Barnett, the family and community engagement director at Donoghue, explained that if external-program providers refused to align their services, their contracts were discontinued. This illustrates the kind of organizational adjustments that UCCS leaders made to align reading instruction around each child's assessed skill profile and to coordinate the work of adults to both extend instructional time and maximize its potential learning benefits.

6. Continuously Engage Parents

At both NKO and Donoghue, leaders and teachers made considerable effort to communicate with parents about how children were progressing in their reading skills and to encourage parents to work at home with their children on reading. James described how, in her role as a kindergarten teacher, she built common understandings with parents. She emphasized the importance of sharing the STEP assessment with parents.

> When my kids come to me [at the beginning of the year], I tell their parents, "I'm going to get your child to be the best that they can be." My work as a teacher starts there. Getting the parents to get on board with that from the beginning and also getting the kids to buy into that from the beginning is key. This motivates me; it helps me to stay focused and it helps me to stay sharp. Because when you get kids, they come in at all different levels. And so if I can stay sharp, then I have the tools that I need to help the highest kid in the class and the kid who is struggling

in the class. The STEP assessment is just basically a tool that kind of gives me a nudge to say, "Okay, they really didn't get this today." So I need to rethink how I taught that, or maybe they were just tired, you know? So those assessments kind of drive my work in the sense that it makes me reflect on my teaching. So it is data [about the student] that is concrete, and I can say, "Okay, is this kid really [at] this level, based on their comprehension? Even though the rest [of the assessment] looks fine, they really can't comprehend; even if they got other questions correct, the assessment suggests that they're not really comprehending, so maybe we ought to think about that." So the observations and the results drive that work. . . . And so with parents, it's very essential that they see achievement. The STEP assessment really is a way to show them achievement, whether it's little or big.

School leaders also provided ongoing discussion about literacy assessments and student progress during Parent, Teacher, and Community Organization (PTCO) meetings. In addition to learning about how to interpret their own child's progress, parents learned about how all students were progressing at the school. Campus leaders also encouraged more-informed parents to help less-informed parents understand literacy assessment at the school. Woodard-Iliev explained,

We were talking this year at the first PTCO meeting back after the holiday, and the parents were asking questions about the standardized tests [from the previous year]. And we were just going over the format and I drew the distinction for them again between a formative and a summative assessment. And I said, "You know, when you look at where our third graders were in March, less than 20 percent of them were at the STEP benchmark for third grade, [however] over 40 percent met or exceeded the state benchmark for third grade. So you have to ask, 'Okay, which one of these tools is more valuable?'" So I try, every time we have a conversation with parents, to really help parents understand how to get real information about what their child knows how to do. That's going to help them later, so we really focused on STEP. I can remember PTCO meetings at the beginning of the year after we went through the STEP test for the first time and parents would raise their hands and say, "I don't understand why my child is only a step 5." They told me, "My child didn't pass the developmental spelling!" or "My child didn't pass the comprehension!" Other parents would raise their hands and they would respond [to the parent's questions about the STEP assessment].

From the beginning, there was a group of parents who really understood the STEP assessment, but it's been our goal to grow that group of informed parents and grow their ability to share their understanding with other parents, because they're our best allies.

Teachers perceived parents as partners not just for their own child, but also as partners in the overarching goal of providing ambitious literacy instruction for all students at the school. Training parents how to interpret the STEP literacy assessment allowed for more ambitious partnerships between home and school.

Conclusion

UCCS organized reading instruction around six guiding principles that were designed to close gaps in reading achievement for all students. First, all teachers, school leaders, and parents shared the ambitious goal for all children to achieve high levels of reading comprehension so they could engage in more complex subject-matter learning by grade 3. Second, UCCS teachers and staff shared a schoolwide curriculum tailored to achieve ambitious reading comprehension goals. Third, frequent assessments of student skill guided all instruction for reading. Fourth, school leaders and literacy coaches provided ongoing support to help teachers figure out how to help their students learn to decode and to read at high levels of comprehension. Fifth, teachers and extended-day staff worked together to pursue reading goals for each child. Last, the staff initiated partnerships with parents to support their children's progress in reading. In the next chapter, we discuss how UCCS organized math instruction, and we consider the similarities and differences between the reading and math approaches.

CHAPTER 6 DESIGNING MATH INSTRUCTION TO OVERCOME EDUCATIONAL INEQUALITY

US math achievement results are deeply disappointing. Countries that spend much less on education—and that hire teachers with much less training—do far better than the United States in math.[1] Results from the 2009 Programme for International Student Assessment (PISA) vividly illustrate the relatively poor math achievement of US students (see figure 6.1[2]). Compared to thirty-three other developed nations, the United States ranks 25th in math, with seventeen nations scoring statistically significantly higher than the United States, and US students score significantly below the Organisation for Economic Co-operation and Development (OECD) average.[3]

The persistently low average math achievement of US students has generated heated debate. Some scholars and policy makers have viewed these results as evidence that math curriculum and instruction in the United States are decidedly inferior to curriculum and instruction in other countries—most notably Korea, Finland, Japan, Canada,[4] and, most recently, China.[5] Others have claimed that poor US math results reflect extreme social class and racial inequality in the economic outcomes, neighborhood conditions, and family circumstances of the most disadvantaged American youth rather than shortcomings in US schooling.

Cross-sectional test scores collected across nations cannot clarify causal mechanisms, so international comparative data cannot resolve these disputes. However, one aspect of these data offers a clue that deserves investigation. Specifically, inequality in test scores is particularly pronounced in the United States. For example, the top 10 percent of Korean students score about .25 standard deviations higher than do the top 10 percent of US students. This is a sizeable difference. It means that if we consider the

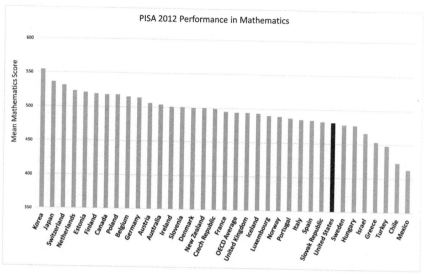

FIGURE 6.1. The United States' standing in mathematics performance, Programme for International Student Assessment (PISA), 2012

highest scorers in the United States (those in the top 10 percent of the US distribution) alongside the highest scorers in South Korea (those in the top 10 percent of the Korean distribution), the typical high-scoring Korean student would outscore 60 percent of the high-scoring US students.

However, this difference pales in comparison to the dramatic differences at the bottom of the achievement distribution: the lowest-scoring 10 percent of Korean students score, on average, .75 standard deviations higher than do the lowest-scoring 10 percent of the US student population—a truly huge difference.[6] This means that if we compare only the lowest scorers in the South Korean distribution (those in the bottom 10 percent of that country's distribution) to the lowest scorers in the US distribution (those in the bottom 10 percent of the US distribution), the typical low-scoring Korean student would outscore almost 80 percent of the low-scoring US students. This massive difference at the bottom of the two distributions goes a long way to explaining why, on average, South Koreans do so much better than US students. Even modest increases in test scores at the low end of the US distribution would significantly raise the overall US average and thereby make the United States look considerably better in international rankings.

Children who score at the bottom range of the distribution have dramatically fewer opportunities for employment in jobs that pay a living wage.[7] These lowest-achieving US students are disproportionately from low-income, minority backgrounds, primarily concentrated in urban areas.[8] An enormously important question is whether school improvement can help overcome these disparities in math achievement. For those who led the University of Chicago Charter School (UCCS), the answer was yes, and the results we present in chapter 8 provide some support for this claim.

The UCCS approach to math unfolded more slowly than did the approach described in the previous chapter for reading, which was the primary focus of school improvement during the early years of UCCS's existence. Yet, at least in outline, the general approach for improving math instruction was similar to the general approach for reading: immerse children in challenging and interesting work; adopt an ambitious schoolwide curriculum; frequently assess student learning and tailor instruction to the current heterogeneity in student skill; provide teachers with substantial learning opportunities and pedagogical support; mobilize instructional time to ensure that all children are on track for success; and engage parents in the relentless schoolwide campaign for high math achievement. As in the case of reading, UCCS leaders designed this strategy to overcome inequality in early childhood. However, as we'll see, some important differences arose between math and reading in how to enact this approach.

In thinking about how to overcome inequality in math skill, we need first to reckon with the fact that inequality in math skill starts early, before entrance into schooling.[9] In this chapter, we trace the early sources of inequality in foundational numerical and spatial reasoning that are rooted in inequality in math learning that occurs at home.[10] US preschools have not typically focused on math, which means that preschool education has done little to equalize math learning systemwide,[11] placing a large burden on K–12 schooling to cope with vast heterogeneity in students' math-related knowledge and skills.

Moreover, in elementary school, children encounter teachers who themselves vary enormously in their knowledge of mathematical concepts, how children learn math, and how to teach math concepts and skills. Working in the privacy of their classrooms with far too little guidance or information and too few opportunities to improve their instruction, teachers generate remarkably variable learning opportunities in math for their students. Unless they have systematic schoolwide strategies to overcome initial inequality, elementary schools are unable to overcome these early inequalities and may exacerbate them. The majority of high schools in the United States cope with heterogeneity in student math skills by sharply differentiating math courses; thus many students—and particularly students from low-income families—do not have access to rigorous academic math coursework during the secondary years.[12] Variation in math course–taking at the secondary level is strongly linked to variation in college attendance and success,[13] with lifelong implications for economic success. In the next section, we discuss the mechanisms that shape the emergence of inequality in mathematics achievement in the United States. In the remainder of the chapter, we describe how the model in place at UCCS attempted to address this inequality.

Sources of Inequality in Math

Let's first consider how inequality shapes children's development of math skills, beginning before they enter school and continuing through their elementary and high school experiences. We begin with recent research that suggests children develop certain fundamental math skills earlier than we had previously believed. We then investigate what happens in elementary school when teachers with various levels of mathematical expertise work autonomously to address the needs of students who enter school with high variability in their math skills. Finally, we link disparities in math achievement across economic background and race to high school tracking, which stratifies students' exposure to the mathematics required for a host of postsecondary opportunities.

Early Roots of Math Inequality

Variation in the early home and preschool experiences children have with number and spatial reasoning leads to considerable inequality in preparation for math before children enter kindergarten. The development of early skills in number sense and spatial reasoning depends on caregiver language and other aspects of caregiver instruction.[14] As in the case of reading, parents vary dramatically in the number and quality of mathematical experiences they provide their children. Consequently, gaps across race and social class in mathematical ability emerge by the time children enter school.[15] In principle, preschool could go a long way toward overcoming these early inequalities, as we have evidence that some preschool teachers are very skilled at helping very young children develop both number sense and spatial reasoning.[16] However, such teachers appear to be the exception rather than the rule, partly because mathematics learning has not historically been an explicit goal of preschool instruction in the United States. While most states now have early learning standards that specify mathematics goals for preschool classrooms—and while early mathematics learning is becoming more of a focus for teachers of very young children—making serious math learning a priority for US preschools is a long, slow process, and we still have a long way to go.

Recent research indicates not only that children are capable of learning more complex mathematical concepts at younger ages than previously thought possible,[17] but also that inequality in early exposure to such concepts is a driver for later inequality. Consequently, as we discuss further below, an ambitious approach that emphasizes not only basic skills but also problem-solving and conceptual understanding, beginning in the preschool years, has the potential to reduce economic and racial inequality while addressing the mathematical learning needs of all children across the skill distribution.[18]

The Elementary Years

The gap in math skills that emerges before children enter kindergarten incrementally increases over the course of schooling.

Teacher variation and student inequality. Recent research suggests that math instruction in elementary schools generates modest differences among children in rates of math learning during each subsequent year of schooling. It is the accumulation of these modest differences that leads to the greater inequality we see in mathematics learning over time.[19] This evidence suggests that the current approach to elementary math instruction is not powerful enough to overcome initial disadvantages rooted in the differences in children's early experiences before entering school. Moreover, several studies have found systematic differences in the quality of mathematics instruction that white and African American students receive, with inferior instruction for African American students.[20]

Teacher knowledge in math is linked to students' academic success; the more mathematics a teacher knows, the higher his or her students achieve.[21] Many elementary school teachers do not have sufficient mathematical knowledge[22] and also lack confidence in their mathematical competency; this likely shapes the amount and quality of math instruction students receive. At the same time, research suggests more effective alternatives to the traditional content and pedagogy of elementary school mathematics instruction. However, many elementary school teachers have not only limited knowledge of mathematics, but also little experience with innovative approaches to teaching mathematics, so they are often not well prepared for teaching demanding mathematics in new ways.[23] Teachers' relative lack of expertise and confidence in mathematics, combined with insufficient opportunities for professional development once in the classroom, undermines instructional improvement.[24]

The suboptimal level of mathematics knowledge among US elementary school teachers and the private, autonomous organization of teaching create a deadly combination for mathematics instruction in many urban elementary schools, likely exacerbating inequality. In this situation, teachers with limited skills are left largely on their own—without adequate training or support—to construct and implement mathematics lesson plans and assessments. Such a fragmented instructional system also likely limits instructional coherence across the grades. Given the inequality in teacher preparation, (which works heavily against poor children) and the overall low level of teacher skill in math (which results in part from a vicious cycle that ensures that the children who receive inadequate math instruction today become tomorrow's ill-prepared math teachers), expecting teachers working alone to generate good math instruction—independent of any serious guidance or support—has had disastrous results. If ever there was a need for a shared, systematic, schoolwide approach to instruction, it surely would be in mathematics. This is especially true at the elementary level, where teachers rarely specialize. In countries that do well in math, teachers often have, overall, quite modest levels of training, but a coherent system of instructional supports, coordination, collaboration, and teacher specialization compensates for the lack of individual teacher skill.[25]

Content, pedagogy, and assessment. Economic and racial inequality in math skills have also engendered debate about what kinds of math instruction children should receive.[26] One long-disputed question in mathematics education, for example, is whether skills or meanings should come first.[27] Skills-first advocates argue that proficiency in basic facts and procedures is a prerequisite for understanding meanings; hence, one should attempt to solve math problems requiring reasoning only after becoming proficient in procedures and math facts.

By contrast, believers in putting meanings first hold that procedural proficiency without understanding the underlying concepts is fragile and inflexible. They assert that teachers can use well-chosen problems to teach skills and meanings rather than simply to provide practice for methods students already know. Equally contentious debates among math educators focus on the proper scope of the elementary curriculum, the place of real-world applications, the role of paper-and-pencil computation in an increasingly technology-driven society, and the amount and distribution of drill and practice.

High School Tracking and Adult Inequality

As children move beyond elementary school (as early as seventh grade but certainly no later than by ninth grade), US schools create very different paths of courses for students, especially in math. This means that early inequality in math as a function of economic background and ethnicity is often translated into inequality in access to high school mathematics courses like algebra, geometry, trigonometry, and calculus. We have good evidence that secondary school math contributes strongly to overall educational stratification.[28] Tracking is very pronounced in math. The course sequences many US students take, as compared to those taken by students in other countries, are taught at shockingly low levels, effectively precluding students' opportunities to pursue serious mathematics in college or to gain access to colleges that offer such coursework, if they gain access to college at all.[29]

Summary

The fact that many children have poor math preparation early on and that comparatively few learn serious math in secondary school goes some way to explaining why math skills are so unequally distributed, with large implications for disparities in access to college and college-level math. This also means that many will be shut out of serious science courses, so their prospects for science, technology, engineering, and/or mathematics (STEM) careers are severely diminished. Indeed, a principal cause for the failure of many students to attain a college degree is their inability to meet mathematics requirements.[30]

Cumulatively, this evidence suggests that the deck is currently stacked against overcoming early inequality in math achievement. The organization of math instruction in elementary schools is too weak to address early gaps in mathematical learning. When teachers implement math instruction autonomously, in the privacy of their classrooms, without systematic guidance and careful articulation among classrooms, many children experience critical gaps from the very beginning of their mathematical training. As these children progress from one grade to the next, each year with a different teacher who is independently making his or her decisions about what and how to teach, these gaps continue to increase.

In addition to experiencing gaps in basic skill development, children may also fall behind in learning how to engage in critical thinking and problem-solving in mathematics. Of paramount importance is helping children learn core competencies, develop conceptual understanding, and engage in rich, meaningful problem-solving in tandem from the earliest grades. Many elementary schools are unequipped to achieve this balance due to a lack of teacher experience with this approach, combined with a lack of tools, training, and other necessary support to implement it well.

In contrast, leaders at UCCS reasoned that a schoolwide instructional system can reliably provide rigorous instruction in basic skills, conceptual understandings, and problem-solving techniques for all students. Such a system would intensify instruction in ways that can accelerate and deepen math learning for each child, and reduce economic class and racial inequality in math achievement.

A Shared Approach to Teaching and Learning in Mathematics

Leaders at UCCS reasoned that overcoming economic and racial inequality in math achievement would require a fundamental reorganization of mathematics instruction, beginning in preschool and extending through high school. This involved a strong partnership forged in 2007 between UCCS school leaders and experts from the University of Chicago's Center for Elementary Mathematics and Science Education (CEMSE).[31] CEMSE includes the authors of *Everyday Mathematics* (*EM*), a widely used elementary school mathematics curriculum. CEMSE staff, including Debbie Leslie, Andy Isaacs, and Sarah Burns, were experienced in providing pedagogical guidance to teachers who use *EM*, and they collaborated closely with UCCS leaders and teachers during this study. This chapter, on which they are coauthors, draws heavily on their experience and on interviews, focus groups, and consultation sessions involving teachers and school leaders. The model for mathematics instruction has close parallels with the model described for reading instruction in chapter 5, consisting of six organizing principles.

1. *Immerse all children in ambitious math learning.* Just as the aim of reading instruction was to enable all children to gain high levels of reading comprehension, the aim in math was similarly ambitious: to enable students to become proficient mathematical thinkers and problem-solvers.
2. *Adopt an ambitious curriculum.* Also similar to reading, UCCS faculty and staff emphasized the importance of a schoolwide curriculum tailored to

achieve those goals. However, as an externally developed program, the mathematics curriculum (*EM*) was considerably more structured and formal than the curriculum for reading. As such, it offered much more detailed guidance—and consequently less latitude—to teachers about daily instructional decisions.[32] This difference reflects the distinctive characteristics of mathematical subject matter, which requires careful attention to the scope and sequence of instruction, and also to the generally weaker preparation that elementary teachers receive in math, relative to reading.

3. *Frequently assess student learning and tailor instruction to student skill.* Frequent assessments of student skill and understanding guided instruction for math, as in reading. However, unlike reading—for which Bryk and colleagues worked with teachers and school leaders to develop an original assessment system—the math assessment system was built into the math curriculum.

4. *Provide sustained pedagogical support.* Ongoing pedagogical support was essential for both reading and math instruction. Providing shared instructional materials to autonomous teachers in no way assures a common high standard of practice, and creating a robust guidance system took on particular urgency in math, due to the high variability in teacher skills and confidence.

5. *Expanded instructional time.* Expanding instructional time appeared crucial to overcoming initial inequality. Providing more time was particularly urgent in math, where instructional time in conventional elementary schools was highly variable but typically constrained (and consistently less than the time allotted for reading).

6. *Engage parents.* UCCS aimed to provide parents frequent and detailed feedback on their children's progress and to encourage activities that parents could engage in at home to support mathematics learning.

In the remainder of the chapter, we elaborate each of these principles and conclude with a vignette that illustrates their enactment in practice.

1. Immerse All Children in Ambitious Math Learning

Recall that the broad aim of reading instruction described in the previous chapter was to ensure that all students would read with high levels of comprehension by grade 3. This required attending to children's conceptual and language development while simultaneously assuring that all students learned the basic skill of word decoding. The parallel in math is clear. The aim was to enable students to become proficient mathematical thinkers and problem-solvers, requiring that children develop the five intertwined strands of mathematical proficiency articulated by the National Research Council in its 2001 report, *Adding It Up: Helping Children Learn Mathematics*. These strands are (1) conceptual understanding, (2) procedural fluency, (3) strategic competence, (4) adaptive reasoning, and (5) productive disposition. The idea is that children should develop the skills and dispositions in tandem. They should gain automaticity in basic number facts and simple operations so that when they approach a math problem, they can focus on its meaning and think flexibly and strategically, rather than focusing on trying to recall basic facts or operational procedures. However, UCCS leaders did not regard automaticity as a prerequisite to thinking about math conceptually. Rather, just as in reading, they embraced the idea that conceptual understanding and basic procedural skills could and should develop together, through the use of varied instructional activities. To achieve these ambitious goals, UCCS leaders and CEMSE math advisors emphasized immersing children in a culture of mathematical sense-making, creating a mathematically rich environment, and promoting lively classroom discourse about mathematical ideas.

Mathematical sense-making. The UCCS model sought to invite, support, and validate mathematical sense-making through interactions between and among students, teachers, and materials. UCCS leaders held that elementary school students were too often directed to apply mathematical rules or to carry out mathematical procedures without any regard for why these rules and procedures work, or how they might be useful outside of math class. Think, for example, about the US traditional "long division" algorithm—a complicated series of steps that students typically memorize. CEMSE advisors had observed that, in conventional classrooms, if students were to ask questions about why the steps work, whether the steps could be modified in various ways, or when this procedure might be used in real life, those questions typically would go unanswered ("Don't worry about why it works; just do it"). The result was, in the view of UCCS math coaches, a troubling elementary school culture in which children learned that mathematics does not need to make sense or be relevant. A math teacher at NKO explained that UCCS used a different approach:

> When I teach math, I am teaching for the facts and the language. [For example,] I want them to know what parallel lines are; I want them to know what perpendicular lines are—I want them to know these names.

But I also want them to be able to apply what they mean in the classroom. I ask my students to look at the walls [in the classroom] and try to get them to discuss why walls might need to be parallel or perpendicular.

Mathematically rich environment. It is possible to walk into many elementary school classrooms and see no evidence—on the walls, in the desks, in conversations, or elsewhere—that mathematics is taught or learned in that classroom. By contrast, at UCCS campuses, we observed classrooms with mathematical reference materials and resources—such as number lines, number grids, and class-created graphs—on display for students to use and refer to at any time. Students had ready access to tools and manipulatives, such as calculators, measuring tools, base-ten blocks, and pattern blocks. Most of these resources were part of the schoolwide curriculum, supporting consistency and a logical progression in student activities across classrooms and grade levels. UCCS leaders embraced this approach to allow students to become increasingly proficient over time at choosing and using mathematical tools within a learning environment that valued and promoted mathematical thinking and problem-solving.

At the beginning of each school year, NKO and Donoghue teachers visited each other's classrooms in search of new ideas for organizing their mathematics tools and manipulatives to make sure that they were accessible to students. Formally scheduled visits also allowed teachers to share management strategies for using these tools in ways that were consistent across classrooms at the UCCS elementary campuses and, therefore, familiar to students as they moved from grade to grade. Students appeared to benefit from these shared systems and from continued access to the tools and resources that they found useful.

Mathematical discourse. Crucial to the model was the engagement of all children in critical discourse around mathematical ideas. When teachers allow children to grapple with worthwhile problems that have multiple solution strategies, children inevitably approach and solve those problems in many different ways. UCCS leaders and math advisors believed that carefully guided discussion of such solutions would expand children's mathematical understanding as children explain their own thinking and compare it to the thinking of their classmates. Teachers explained that children began to see how they could learn mathematics from one other. This emphasis on mathematical discourse gave teachers a window into students' thinking.

Teachers told us how they used small-group work in mathematics to help students "find their voices" during mathematics time—especially students who were reluctant to participate during whole-group discussions and activities. The goal was to make discourse a ubiquitous feature of mathematics instruction.[33] Teachers explained how they adapted strategies from their reading instruction to promote rich discussion during mathematics. For example, they adopted "turn and talk" and "think, pair, share" strategies during math lessons, which required students to discuss mathematical problems with a partner before participating in a whole-group discussion.[34]

2. Adopt an Ambitious Curriculum

Mathematical content spans interconnected strands, such as number, operations, measurement, and geometry. Many aspects of mathematical learning build sequentially, within and across strands and from grade level to grade level. The complex nature of the subject matter makes coherence and articulation of instruction extremely important, but also quite difficult, especially when teachers are expected to teach a balance of mathematical skills, concepts, and problem-solving at all grade levels. The tremendous variability in what elementary teachers know about mathematics makes quality control especially challenging. Therefore, the second guiding principle in the UCCS model was the use of a balanced, rigorous, and carefully articulated mathematics curriculum across grade levels to help address these challenges. A common curriculum creates shared language, structures, and routines and provides common teaching strategies and assessments.

UCCS leaders reasoned that the curriculum must engage students in worthwhile mathematical tasks and create predictable structures and routines that enable teachers and students to efficiently use their time. UCCS leaders also recognized that elementary mathematics in the United States had been insufficiently ambitious in the past, possibly because textbook writers anticipated limited instructional time; so the leaders resolved to choose a more ambitious curriculum.

UCCS leaders believed that *EM* was well aligned with the principles underlying the UCCS model. UCCS leaders did not claim, however, that adoption of *EM* was essential to the model, noting that other curricula that fit the model may also be suitable.[35] It seemed particularly useful to have locally available *EM* experts provide pedagogical support to UCCS teachers, ensuring that the guidance was closely aligned with their curriculum.

TABLE 6.1. Sample of grade-level goals

	Place value and notation
Pre-K	Develop an awareness of numbers and their uses Associate number names, quantities, and written numerals Recognize and use different ways to represent numbers (e.g., groups of objects or dots)
K	Model numbers with manipulatives Use manipulatives to exchange 1s for 10s and 10s for 100 Recognize that digits can be used and combined to read and write numbers Read numbers up to 30
Grade 1	Read, write, and model with manipulatives whole numbers up to 1,000 Identify places in such numbers and the values of the digits in those places
Grade 2	Read, write, and model with manipulatives whole numbers up to 10,000 Identify places in such numbers and the values of the digits in those places Read and write money amounts in dollars-and-cents notation
Grade 3	Read and write whole numbers up to 1,000,000 Read, write, and model with manipulatives decimals through hundredths Identify places in such numbers and the values of the digits in those places Translate between whole numbers and decimals represented in words, in base-10 notation, and with manipulatives
Grade 4	Read and write whole numbers up to 1,000,000,000 and decimals through thousandths Identify places in such numbers and the values of the digits in those places Translate between whole numbers and decimals represented in words and in base-10 notation
Grade 5	Read and write whole numbers and decimals Identify places in such numbers and the values of the digits in those places Use expanded notation to represent whole numbers and decimals

Coherent, articulated content. EM provides a sequence of topics and lessons across grades that integrates procedural fluency, conceptual understanding, and meaningful applications. By way of example, table 6.1 displays, by grade, *EM*'s sequence of instructional aims, or "grade-level goals," related to the topic of place value. The edition of *EM* that UCCS campuses were using during our study articulated goals like these for each mathematical topic addressed in the curriculum. The school's designers reasoned that making these aims explicit would facilitate teachers' understanding of how content develops across grades. Such understanding would promote collaboration between teachers within and across grades. They sought to ensure that all teachers were aware of the goals for each grade and had opportunities to discuss these goals in relation to the mathematical content they were teaching.

Predictable structures and routines. A common curriculum has the advantage of providing a predictable framework to help teachers organize their lessons and establish consistent instructional routines. We observed that most math lessons at UCCS followed the same template that was built into *EM* lessons. The *EM* lessons include an initial whole-class mental arithmetic warm-up task; small-group or individual work on a problem designed to introduce the key mathematical ideas of the lesson; discussion of children's solutions to the introductory problem; and practice with the key ideas of the day. Claudine Randolph, a fourth/fifth–grade teacher and math coach at the Donoghue campus, explained, "I'll start with [a] whole-class mini-lesson; then I work with smaller groups. It's the same pattern across the board [across subjects and across teachers at each grade level], where we start in a large community and then move into smaller groups."

Weaving mathematics into everyday classroom life in ways that are meaningful and personally engaging to children is challenging work. To address this, coaches and teachers told us about the "program routines"—activities that recur regularly throughout the curriculum and provide common language for children and teachers across grades and throughout the school. For example, UCCS primary-grade students used the Frames and Arrows routine, shown in figure 6.2,[36] to practice addition and subtraction rules and to analyze the number patterns and sequences that are generated. Older students continued to use the Frames and Arrows routine to explore more complicated mathematics by applying and analyzing rules such as multiplying or dividing by powers of ten or squaring. Frames and Arrows is also an example of a routine that blends skills practice (as students apply computation-based rules) with concept development and critical thinking (as children generate and analyze number patterns and functions). This routine can be adapted to teach a range of functions, from simple to complex, and becomes a familiar way for students to envision functions while also gaining fluency with number facts.

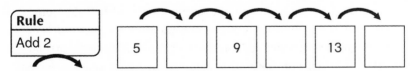

FIGURE 6.2. Frames and Arrows used with the rule "Add 2"

3. Frequently Assess Student Learning and Tailor Instruction to Student Skill

As in reading, frequent math assessments enabled teachers to determine a child's current skills, evaluate the efficacy of recent instruction, and make decisions about next steps. Teachers, coaches, school leaders, and parents became familiar with a shared system of assessments. The aim was to provide a common system to describe and support each child's mathematical development. Teachers were trained to gather and use data from a combination of sources: (1) informal, anecdotal assessment, (2) curriculum-embedded assessments, and (3) nationally normed tests.

Informal, anecdotal assessment. Teachers used students' questions and comments during whole-group and small-group instruction to develop an evolving portrait of each child's basic skills, conceptual understanding, and attitude toward mathematics. This more subjective information complemented the objective and systematic data that teachers also regularly collected about each child.

Curriculum-embedded assessment. At both UCCS campuses, grade-level teams collected, reviewed, and analyzed curriculum-embedded assessment data that they had entered into an electronic assessment management system. In grades 1 through 6 (and less frequently in kindergarten), *EM* lessons contained a daily assessment called Recognizing Student Achievement (RSA). The RSA was a specific task embedded in the lesson that teachers used to collect data on student performance. Each RSA was linked to a specific grade-level goal, and notes in the teacher's lesson guide provided benchmarks for judging whether a child was making adequate progress toward that goal.

Teachers used the RSA assessments to gauge whether students were making adequate progress and also to inform the way that they grouped students during small-group math instruction. Randolph, the math coach at Donoghue, worked with Leslie, a CEMSE leader and coauthor of this chapter, to develop an "exit slip" version of the RSA (sometimes modified from the RSA specified in the *EM* lesson) that helped her group her students. According to Randolph:

> I started using exit slips. It's a mini-quiz of whatever I taught that day. So if a child didn't get it, I would know from the exit slip and I would put them in a particular group. The kids would always complain, "I'm in this group with so-and-so." But then they'll find themselves later on with a really high group of math students in another concept. I had one

of my lowest math students working with the highest group because he successfully completed multiplication and division. He moved on and loved just the movement that would happen, which is very different from reading, where you're kind of in a group for a semester. In math, it would change every week, no matter what group you were in and what those centers would look like.

This informal, everyday effort allowed Randolph to flexibly arrange her students in ways that helped them understand which math skills they had mastered and which math skills they needed to develop further. Through mentoring sessions with Leslie, Randolph developed ways to share her approach for using RSAs to inform instruction with the teachers she was coaching.

Nationally normed, computerized adaptive assessment. Students in grades 2 through 5 at the UCCS campuses also took the mathematics (and literacy and science) portion of the Northwest Evaluation Association Measures of Academic Progress (MAP) Assessment test three times per year. MAP is a computerized, adaptive test that is nationally normed and can measure growth from administration to administration. MAP is also a good predictor of standardized achievement test scores. Tanika Island, NKO campus director, explained that James Sweet, the technology coordinator at NKO, also used the scores to create an in-house diagnostic report that included each child's MAP scores, typical growth trajectory, and projected scores, updated three times a year. Sweet also developed a predictor of the Illinois state assessment and created a visual representation of all the data that provided a comprehensive view of each individual student. Island explained, "We call it a traffic light report because each child is color coded for their progress: red, yellow, and green." We observed UCCS leaders and coaches and CEMSE advisors use this information to discuss why there might be particular strengths and weaknesses in student achievement from one testing period (or one year) to the next. They also discussed what steps—including targeted coaching for teachers—could be taken to address identified weaknesses at the classroom, grade, and/or school level.

Teachers told us how they used data to plan instruction for individuals and small groups of students. They explained how they compiled assessment data and shared the information, both formally and informally, with their school director, mathematics coaches, and grade-level teammates. Such data became the subject of teacher-principal conversations in monitoring meetings in much the same way that STEP assessment data did for reading (see chapter 5).

4. Provide Sustained Pedagogical Support

At both UCCS elementary campuses, the mathematics curriculum and assessments became a foundational part of the pedagogical guidance system, in part because *Everyday Mathematics* is designed to embed pedagogical guidance for teachers within the curriculum materials. In this way, the UCCS model for mathematics differs from the UCCS model for reading described in the previous chapter. However, neither textbooks nor assessments are self-enacting. Teachers working privately and autonomously with even the best textbook will tend to produce highly variable results. A curriculum cannot answer all questions that arise in daily practice: "Why present this concept in this way? How do I make this work for my class? For this particular student? For my teaching style? For my testing requirements? Can I change the pedagogy if I leave the content the same? Can I change the content if I use the suggested pedagogy?" Answers to these questions transform a written curriculum into enacted instruction. Ensuring a reliably high level of instructional quality required sustained coaching, reinforced by classroom observation. (In chapter 7, we provide a more detailed discussion of schoolwide organizational structures and practices that made this coordinated work possible.)

We observed UCCS and CEMSE leaders coordinating efforts to coach teachers. Promoting serious mathematical thinking—as well as fast and accurate computation—is not straightforward, especially given that many elementary teachers have limited mathematical training and confidence, and that their experience in conventional school cultures emphasizes computation to the exclusion of mathematical thinking.

Leslie led the effort to provide professional development, coaching, and consultation at UCCS to support the implementation of *EM*. Her goal was to maximize teachers' understanding of the program's approach and their effectiveness at using it to advance student learning. First, she worked with the NKO and Donoghue math coaches to train all teachers in content and pedagogy. She then worked with them to establish clear, schoolwide expectations for the use of curriculum materials and other shared tools, including assessments. Finally, she sought to promote cross-grade knowledge and practices among teachers, including content, pedagogy, classroom routines, and tools for analyzing and reporting the results of assessments. Throughout this process, Leslie and UCCS leaders and math coaches encouraged informal and formal teacher collaboration around mathematics teaching and learning, including observing in one another's classrooms, looking at students' work together, and sharing and discussing challenges and successes.

5. Expanded Instructional Time

The goals of the UCCS model were remarkably ambitious. UCCS leaders concluded that achieving these goals would require increasing, often as much as doubling, the amount of math instruction that students received in their classrooms every day. For some students, after-school and summer instruction were essential to get on track for success.

Children in typical US elementary schools receive on average forty-five minutes of daily mathematics instruction[37]—far from adequate to enact an ambitious math instructional program or to overcome economic and racial inequality in mathematics. Even more remarkable, variation across US classrooms in time allocated to math is large, suggesting that some students get far less than forty-five minutes per day.

UCCS elementary campuses expanded instructional time in a number of specific ways. The first occurred at the classroom level, where teachers led sixty- to ninety-minute daily math lessons for all students. Ample time allowed teachers to use the resources from the curriculum more fully, without having to eliminate or abbreviate lessons (as often occurs in conventionally organized schools), or otherwise limit students' exposure to the content and experiences the program specifies.

Second, UCCS scheduled math instruction before and after school, depending on children's math skill. This required coordination between classroom teachers, extended-day staff members, and instructional leaders. It was essential to train extended-day staff in the use of EM and in the assessments used by regular classroom teachers. Teachers identified areas of concern for each student using the curriculum-embedded assessment described previously; they then developed plans to address these concerns, aligning after-school and summer school instruction with classroom learning goals. The overlapping work schedules further supported collaboration between classroom teachers and extended-day staff.

Third, UCCS classroom teachers, mathematics coaches, and school leaders used analysis of student data to target summer school instruction to particular student needs. Extending instruction to the summer sent the message that all children could be successful with high-quality, conceptual mathematics instruction.

6. Parent Engagement in Mathematics Instruction

Educators at NKO and Donoghue routinely reached out to parents about the math education their children were receiving. Teachers shared homework assignments with parents, and each campus hosted family math nights to help parents understand the school's approach to mathematics education. Teachers used parent conferences to convey the school's mathematical approach, and UCCS math coaches and CEMSE advisors provided supplemental documents to help teachers with this communication. At parent-teacher meetings, campus leaders also explained how children were assessed in math at the school, district, and state levels. We describe the two campuses' distinctive approach to parent engagement in the next chapter.

An Illustrative Example

The following vignette illustrates key aspects of UCCS's instructional model. The vignette was from Erica Emmendorfer's first-grade class at NKO. It begins with children working independently on a problem; then they come together to share and discuss. The vignette ends at the conclusion of the group discussion.

As you read, consider how Emmendorfer used time, the nature of the instructional tasks, the supportiveness of various aspects of the physical and intellectual environment, the ongoing analysis of teaching and learning, and the role of discourse. We emphasize that Emmendorfer had been teaching at NKO for only two years and did not come to NKO with previous experience teaching math. She was not a math coach at NKO. Emmendorfer's practice reflected her school-based training. We'll see that she and her colleagues at NKO and Donoghue worked toward shared understandings and practices around schoolwide principles.

> On a late spring day at NKO, Erica Emmendorfer is teaching Everyday Mathematics, grade 1, lesson 9-3 to her first-grade class. Students return from lunch and, without prompting, take a quarter-sheet of paper with the day's "Math Message." (Each Everyday Mathematics lesson opens with a "Math Message," which is a problem or task that leads into the day's lesson and that children are expected to work on independently or in small groups before the teacher provides instruction on the task. It is intended to encourage children to actively work to make sense of the content, rather than passively receive it from the teacher.)
>
> Students begin working on the page independently. Some walk up to the

large 0–100 number grid posted at the front of the room. Others flip to a smaller version of this grid at the back of their math journals. Some complete the task without referring to a number grid. Erica circulates, making comments such as "Check that again" and "Can you think of anything that might help you?"

While Emmendorfer had provided a variety of tools and resources that children could use as they worked to solve the number-grid puzzle, she did not show the students any specific strategies for solving the puzzle before giving them a chance to tackle the problem on their own. Doing so would have significantly altered the nature of the mathematical task, changing it from one in which students actively engage with mathematical ideas and problems to one in which students more passively implement the teacher's demonstrated strategy.[38] Although simplification or "de-problematizing" of problems tends to be common in elementary school mathematics classrooms, it is something the teachers at the UC charter schools have worked hard to limit in their instructional practice.

After about four minutes, Erica gets everyone's attention and directs them to the large number grid posted on the chalkboard. After eliciting answers for the missing numbers on the "Math Message," she asks, "Do you guys see a pattern?" She calls on several children to describe what they have noticed and receives the following responses: "Every number ends in a 3" and "It starts with 13, then 23, then 33 and keeps going" and "We're going down each row." Erica affirms each response and clarifies it to the rest of the group by pointing it out on the number grid. As she facilitates this discussion of strategies, she scans the group, making sure that children seem to be following along. She stops a couple of times to ask particular students if it's making sense to them. When one child asks why the pattern didn't go 22, 23, 24, Erica thanks the child for the question and asks if anyone can help with it. She eventually calls the child to the number grid and has her put her fingers on the appropriate numbers in the column.

Then Erica asks: "What are we doing when we go down each column? What happens to the numbers?" Several students shout out, "Adding 10!" Erica pauses to confirm this with the rest of the class: "13 + 10 is 23. And 23 + 10 is what?"

"33!"

"And 33 + 10 is what?"

"43!"

"Good thinking!" she says. "We've noticed that pattern on the number grid before, haven't we? And now some of you used it to finish this number-grid puzzle."

Erica goes on to show a different presentation of a number-grid puzzle— this time covering a T-shaped group of numbers on an otherwise filled-in grid, as shown in table 6.2. In this type of puzzle, children are expected to use their knowledge of number sequence, number relationships, and place value to identify the covered numbers.

She explains that they can use what they know about the numbers around the missing numbers—and what they know about the patterns on the number grid—to figure out the missing numbers. She points to one of the missing numbers and asks if anyone knows how to figure out what it is. As before, she elicits several different strategies, each time validating the child's approach and prompting him or her to explain it to the other children. ("Did anyone do it a different way?" "Did that way make sense to you?" "Can you come up and show us what you did?") The class works together to fill in the remaining numbers; then Erica asks whether anyone can think of a way to check. They confirm, using the suggestions of several children: "The numbers on the top go up by 1"; "The numbers going down all have 4s at the end" (rephrased by Erica as "They all have 4 in the ones place") and "The numbers going down all go up by 10."

The number-grid puzzles lend themselves to a variety of solution strategies, and Emmendorfer sought and validated students' different strategies, thereby promoting problem-solving and mathematical discourse in tandem with basic skills. She exposed her students to diverse ways of approaching problems, with the goal of helping them deepen their un-

TABLE 6.2. A T-shaped number-grid puzzle

-9	-8	-7	-6	-5	-4	-3	-2	-1	0
1	2	3	4	5	6	7	8	9	10
11	12	13	14	15	16				20
21	22	23	24	25	26	27		29	30
31	32	33	34	35	36	37		39	40
41	42	43	44	45	46	47		49	50
51	52	53	54	55	56	57	58	59	60
61	62	63	64	65	66	67	68	69	70
71	72	73	74	75	76	77	78	79	80
81	82	83	84	85	86	87	88	89	90
91	92	93	94	95	96	97	98	99	100

derstandings about the place-value patterns on the number grid. She also sought to help them to realize, more generally, the important idea that a problem can have more than one solution or more than one way of reaching a solution.

Because there was more than one right way to get the answer, Emmendorfer was no longer seen as the repository of the "right" answer; students had begun to see how they could learn mathematics from one another. Students in Emmendorfer's math class were producing and exchanging their ideas, rather than simply responding to questions posed by the teacher. Furthermore, Emmendorfer's responses demonstrated that she was listening carefully and respectfully to the children and encouraged children to listen and respond to one another (*"Did anyone do it a different way?" "Did that way make sense to you?" "Can you come up and show us what you did?"*). Students' behaviors during discussions were equally noteworthy. We heard multiple student voices during the whole-group portion of the lesson, and all students participated actively during small-group and partner work. Most students listened to their peers' contributions, and several responded with questions or different strategies.

Organizing the School to Promote Ambitious Mathematics Instruction

Math lessons, such as the one described above, that feature mathematical sense-making, a mathematically rich learning environment, and well-orchestrated mathematical discourse, are the product of individual professional development. Even more important, Emmendorfer understood the UCCS instructional system for math and was able to work effectively within this system.

When she first started at NKO, Emmendorfer received initial training on EM and the details of the first-grade program. Her professional development did not stop with this initial training, however. At NKO, her math coach provided regular feedback to support her enactment of the six organizing principles described above, and she met with her grade-level partners at least weekly, to discuss, plan, and coordinate mathematics instruction. Furthermore, she and her colleagues engaged in monthly in-school mathematics professional development, facilitated by the lead math teacher and often with support from a CEMSE coach, which involved considerable teacher collaboration. These sessions supported schoolwide teacher learning in mathematics by focusing on a particular topic (such as discourse or higher-order thinking) or a particular collaborative activity (such as looking at math content progressions across grades, analyzing assessment data, or planning for differentiated instruction).

NKO and Donoghue teachers' work with one another, with school leaders and coaches, and with outside experts was intended to support the refinement of the UCCS model and teachers' internalization of its organizing principles. Through coaching and mentoring from campus directors, math coaches, and CEMSE staff, and through close collaboration, UCCS teachers and leaders came to recognize that engaging in the kinds of activities described in Emmendorfer's vignette required adequate time for mathematics. If time is short, discourse, exploration, and sense-making are often the first things to go. Teachers also realized the importance of a school and classroom environment that supports conceptual understanding, procedural fluency, strategic competence, adaptive reasoning, and a productive disposition, each of which is reflected in the brief segment from Emmendorfer's lesson. Most important, teachers recognized that students' ideas (even if wrong) and questions (no matter how many) encouraged wide engagement in ambitious mathematics. In the next chapter, we examine in detail how school leaders organized the school to support the instruction we have described in this and the previous chapter.

ORGANIZING THE SCHOOL TO SUPPORT AMBITIOUS INSTRUCTION

The optimal approach to school organization depends on the work teachers are expected to do.[1] If we conceptualize teaching as a highly personal and idiosyncratic craft,[2] then it makes sense for teachers to have substantial autonomy, for great variability in teacher effectiveness to be the norm, and for principals to adopt a laissez-faire approach to managing instruction, instead focusing on other aspects of school administration.[3] In this craft conception, the best hope for school improvement lies with hiring and retaining promising teachers, providing them with resources, and getting out of their way. By contrast, if we conceptualize teaching as a relatively routine activity, involving a high degree of certainty with minimal judgment or decision-making, then what naturally follows is a bureaucratic organization in which school leaders issue directives that prescribe how teachers instruct their students.

While the bureaucratic approach has a long history of competing with the laissez-faire model, it has gained increased traction among policy makers over the past thirty years amid rising concern about poor student achievement in US schools relative to global competitors. Mandatory assessments and standardized testing have become a dominant part of mainstream public schooling.[4] In its most extreme form, school leaders provide teachers with scripted curricula that dictate synchronized coverage of a specific topic on a given day or week of the school year.[5] These two approaches differ sharply with respect to teacher autonomy, but share the notion that teaching is largely an individual activity requiring little collaboration or coordination.

The University of Chicago Charter School (UCCS) model presumed an altogether different conception of teaching. In contrast to the view of teaching as either an idiosyncratic craft or a routine activity, the UCCS model conceptualized teaching as a public, professional practice in which teachers collaborate with fellow teachers, expert coaches, social workers, parents, and instructional leaders to pursue ambitious learning goals for each student.[6] As we saw in chapters 5 and 6, this model of instruction demanded much from teachers. Campus leaders expected teachers to use a schoolwide assessment system to collect and interpret data about the particular skills of individual children. They asked teachers to diagnose the learning needs of each child, to evaluate the effectiveness of recent instruction, and, in collaboration with others, to frame child-specific plans for future instruction. The UCCS model expected teachers to coordinate with social workers to identify social and emotional assets or barriers that might accelerate or impede each student's progress. Finally, teachers were to continuously share information about each child's instructional plan with parents, to stimulate instructional support at home, and to coordinate efforts across home and school.

This view of teachers' work had far-reaching implications for the school as an organization, requiring a novel conception of effective school leadership. Instead of leaving teachers alone to practice autonomously or prescribing how they should teach, effective leaders in this model were those who enabled teachers to use the instructional system to advance student learning, marshaling all available resources in relentless pursuit of ambitious goals for student achievement.[7] In this chapter, we elaborate how UCCS leaders organized the school to support ambitious classroom instruction, enhance children's social and emotional skills so they could take advantage of such instruction, and continuously engage parents as partners in this enterprise.

Supporting Ambitious Classroom Instruction

Organizing an effective school requires multiple kinds of leadership. Bryk and colleagues identify three distinct forms as particularly crucial: managerial, instructional, and inclusive-facilitative leadership.[8] They characterize the managerial dimension as "the most basic aspect of school leadership," the effects of which are most notable in their absence: "for example, a poorly run office, supply shortages, nothing starting or ending on time, poor communication with parents and staff," and other indications of disorder.[9] This dimension of leadership encompasses the traditional activities of school administration associated with the management of day-to-day school operations.

Instructional leadership, by contrast, involves deliberate action to shape instruction to increase student learning[10] (such as observation and coaching of teachers' practice, analyzing evidence of student learning, and allocating resources to support the ongoing improvement of instruction). It often involves challenging the norms of teacher autonomy and private practice discussed in chapter 3 and can therefore provoke teachers' discomfort or even resistance.[11]

For this reason, instructional leadership is often most effective when it is coupled with inclusive-facilitative actions that build a sense of shared purpose and inspire all members of a school community to rally around it. This kind of leadership emphasizes getting stakeholders such as teachers, parents, and students to "buy in" to decisions, rather than issuing directives from the top down.[12]

There is some debate as to which kinds of leadership are most essential to promoting student learning.[13] However, our reading of the literature, combined with our observations of practice at UCCS, leads us to suspect that each is important and that they are most effectively exercised in concert. Yet it is hard to imagine one person undertaking all the above activities effectively on his or her own. This was especially true at UCCS, given the unusually ambitious and demanding approach to instruction at the heart of the model.

Distributed Leadership to Support Each Child's Learning

The leaders of the UCCS developed an ambitious solution to this problem—one that distributed the above activities across multiple leaders, each with specialized roles and expertise—and then created structures to coordinate the leaders' work.[14] At the apex of this distributed leadership structure was the campus director, who focused primarily on monitoring learning for each child and ensuring the effectiveness of instruction in every classroom. Assisting the campus director were individuals in three newly configured roles: the operations director, responsible for tasks such as budgeting, facilities, and human resource administration; the lead social worker, with expertise in the social and emotional development of all students at the school; and the director of family and community engagement (FCE director), with strong ties to all families and connections with local community resources.

This leadership structure made the campus director primarily responsible for the instructional dimension of leadership, with the operations director focused mainly on the managerial aspects and the lead social worker and the FCE director primarily attending to the inclusive-facilitative dimension (especially engaging parents and developing an environment attentive to the social and emotional factors that influence learning). In contrast to schools that conceptualize teaching as an autonomous activity requiring minimal oversight, UCCS campuses were organized to provide continuous monitoring of student learning and support for teachers to advance it. The campus director closely supervised each teacher's classroom work, but also expected all teachers to meet regularly with other leaders whose expertise could help them address the challenges they might face in their classrooms. Additional leaders included literacy and math coaches for curricular support and social workers for social and emotional issues. The engagement of multiple leaders tended to make classrooms public places where several adults shared responsibility for solving emergent problems.

When we asked Tanika Island, director of NKO, to describe leadership on her campus, she confirmed that she relied on several types of leaders to run her building, each with different expertise that contributed to understanding "the total child":

> We want to gain insight about how the child's life is at home, their emotional well-being, how this might impact their academics and vice versa. The teachers oftentimes will consider the social/emotional parts of things when making decisions. So we need to hear that voice, and we need to look closely at how teachers manage [relationships with] parents. So those perspectives need to be present at the table when we are making decisions at the leadership level.

Leaders at UEI conceptualized the roles of lead social worker and the FCE director and built these into the organization of the school when Donoghue opened in 2005. Before starting as campus director at NKO, Island spent one year training with Nicole Woodard-Iliev, the director of Donoghue, to learn how to share leadership with the lead social worker and the FCE director at NKO.

Even within the domain of instructional leadership, Island relied heavily on several other external and internal leaders. For example, she relied on the work of reading experts Irene Fountas and Gay Su Pinnell (of the Ohio State University and Lesley University, respectively) to guide her efforts to continuously improve reading instruction at NKO.[15] Inside the school building, some classroom teachers had responsibilities as grade-level leaders. Still other teachers served as coaches of fellow teachers. Island selected these coaches because of their particular expertise in UCCS's instructional system for reading or math, and these coaches received extra compensation for their work.

New roles for diverse experts. The distribution of leadership changed the kinds of supports available to teachers. Tamara Gathright Fritz and Sybil Madison-Boyd, codirectors of UEI's Academic and Social Support Initiative, trained social workers and FCE directors at both campuses to support teachers in addressing specific issues arising with students and/or parents. Social workers learned to enact new roles as classroom consultants. External curricular experts, including coaches from the *Everyday Mathematics* project (see chapter 6), also supported teachers on-site. As noted in chapter 4, this approach to teacher training contrasts with the conventional approach, which typically involves teachers going off-site to attend workshops or receive training focused on more general topics.

School staff members who enacted these new roles understood that they were doing something novel to help teachers. Lo Patrick, the lead social worker at Donoghue, explained how her job at Donoghue was different than her previous social work jobs in the same district.

> Most Chicago Public Schools [CPS] social workers are seen as only serving the special education kids. My job now is just completely different from theirs. The typical [CPS] social worker is not considered part of the school in the same way as I am. One big difference would be that I'm here full time. That's not to say that there aren't some excellent social workers who have figured out how to do their special education minutes *and* do regular-education kid interventions, even when they have to visit several schools in a week. But it's hard to do what I am able to do if you're not at a school, serving general education students, for enough time. They are just not integrated into the school staff in the same way as I am. So I get to know all the staff and all the kids.

Todd Barnett, FCE director at Donoghue, explained that he took an ongoing approach to home-school engagement, unlike in more conventional schools, where the vice principal often takes on the role of disciplinarian or mediator only when an unmanageable crisis erupts at school. Barnett explained that parents were often shocked by how much he knew about what their children were doing inside the classroom. For example, when he shared with them during pick-up time a particularly exciting learning moment he witnessed their child experience in the classroom, parents would say, "You're not their teacher, how do you know?" He explained to them that part of his job was to bring accurate and timely information to parents about what was happening to students during the school day.

Barnett worked with his own small team of people—including LaTonya Maxwell, the family support counselor; and Danyelle Martin, the resource coordinator at Donoghue's parent resource center[16]—to continuously engage parents. Maxwell managed two separate parent workshops. One was specifically designed for struggling families that had trouble following up with recommended social services for their child, and the other was a social networking program that brought parents together so they could share information with one another about their children's learning experiences at Donoghue. Martin managed workshops that provided parents with training and information on topics such as the mandatory Illinois state assessment, the *Everyday Mathematics* curriculum, and the STEP assessment. Barnett, Maxwell, and Martin also organized school events, such as parent breakfasts, literacy nights, and math nights.

Barnett and Maxwell also gathered information about students informally each day by talking to teachers, visiting classrooms, and managing the extended-day program. Barnett explained that he was responsible for finding ways to support parents to use the school's instructional system to advance their children's learning in cooperation with many different people, including the campus director, the social worker, teachers, aides, peers, coaches, and specialists. He sought to develop common goals for students and coordinate action in pursuit of these goals across home and school settings. He was also responsible for helping parents forge connections with one another so that they could provide information and other types of resources through their social networks, as we elaborate later in chapter.

It was not always easy for new leaders to have novel responsibilities. As UEI's Gathright Fritz, who led efforts to reenvision the roles of social workers and parent-engagement staff, explained, "Social workers had to be trained to see themselves as professional experts about social dynamics in the classroom so that teachers would value their input about their everyday classroom work." As consultants to classroom teachers, these new leaders sought to help teachers with everyday problems like managing classroom behavior, developing positive reinforcement systems, or promoting the skills students needed for productive group work. They also helped teachers engage with parents. Campus directors also had to learn how to share power with their coleaders.

Expert teachers as coaches. As mentioned previously, teachers with curricular expertise became content-area coaches, with training and time to support their peers, especially new teachers. Teachers earned these positions by demonstrating expertise in using the instructional system to advance student learning. These positions were salaried higher or associated with stipends. Most coaches worked part time executing their leadership responsibilities and part time teaching, enabling them to learn from their practice while sharing ideas with other teachers. Literacy and mathematics coaches helped teachers use the school's instructional system and helped campus leaders target professional development to address specific needs of teachers. Coaches focused their efforts with teachers around trends that they identified during meetings with other campus leaders, such as the campus director, FCE director, and lead social worker. The campus director expected coaches to monitor classroom practice via regular classroom observations and coaching sessions and to coordinate with these other leaders when coaching teachers to address particular challenges in their classrooms.

Pushing resources into classrooms. For such coaching to work, teachers had to be willing to make their classrooms public places, accessible to observation at any time and ready for ongoing interventions and support from many different sources. Instead of sending their students out of the classroom to receive supplemental help, teachers had to be willing to support all their students in their classrooms. Woodard-Iliev discussed how the distributed leadership approach changed how teachers handled their students:

> In some schools (not like our school), when a child struggles, it might be the teacher just saying to a special education teacher, "Can you come get this child, because I don't know how to help them." So the teacher is not taking responsibility for meeting that child's needs. Everything that sort of doesn't work with the child, or when the child is struggling—it becomes some other person's responsibility: "Oh, well the social worker has to help him with that. The special education teacher has to help her with that." As opposed to what we are doing here at Donoghue, which is to *push those resources into the classroom* and give the teacher tools to first and foremost keep kids in the classroom, where they are learning from their teacher.

Campus leaders spoke frequently of "pushing in" to build teachers' capacity to address students' needs in the context of daily classroom instruction.

Collaboration toward common goals. In conventionally organized schools,

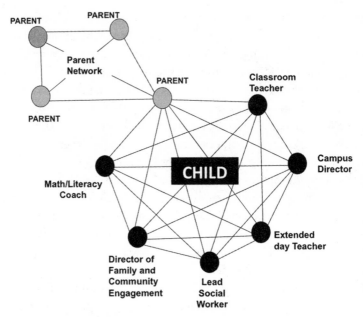

FIGURE 7.1. The potential web of collaboration to support each child's learning. UCCS leaders worked hard to align the efforts of these diverse actors to ensure that each child was on track to achieve the school's ambitious learning goals.

teachers, school clinicians, school leaders, and parents often have different goals for the same child, which can cause disagreement and tension. The UCCS model, by contrast, emphasized collaboration around a common plan for each child. Figure 7.1 shows the web of support that could emerge around a particular child as a result of collaboration among these diverse actors.[17] It also illustrates how school leaders positioned parents as partners, as well as the role of interactions among parents in advancing shared goals for students, which we discuss later in the chapter.

Professional Accountability

Mechanisms for professional accountability operated in tandem with the support for teachers described above. The UCCS campuses used annual statewide standardized test data as an indicator in an external accountability system that held each campus director responsible for student outcomes. But these statewide results arrived too late and too infrequently to be of much use to a teacher, providing no information about whether current efforts to improve practice were headed in the right direction, and whether the students sitting in front of him or her were on track to have a successful year. Therefore, leaders at the two campuses developed an internal accountability system anchored by frequent diagnostic assessments of student progress, using the tools described in chapters 5 and 6. The idea was to align the internal and external accountability systems in ways that motivated teachers to gain expertise.

A dual accountability system. Island explained that her job was on the line if her campus did not produce results for students. She worked with James Sweet, NKO's technology coordinator, to design a metric that used the computerized adaptive assessments teachers administered three times a year[18] to predict standardized test scores in the spring. She established measurable goals for improving diagnostic and summative results. UEI leaders then compared state assessment results across campuses and, together with campus directors, reported these results to the charter school's governing board. Island explained:

> Campus directors are held accountable by the governing board. We attend meetings and give updates around school performance, but twice a year we are expected to give a formal presentation around data with math and literacy. At the beginning of the year, I explained what my goals were for the year and why. Then at the end of the year, I said if I met my goals and if not, what do I think happened and what my plan is for the future.

Finally, UEI leaders made decisions regarding contract renewal and performance pay for campus directors at the end of each academic year, based in part on results from summative and diagnostic data.

These external accountability mechanisms gave campus directors an incentive not only to hold teachers accountable for the results of their own instruction, but also to cultivate a sense of collective responsibility for student learning schoolwide.[19] Island explained that as a result, veteran staff members were vested in making sure their newly hired colleagues shared their commitment to continually advance student learning. This shaped the induction of new teachers and created a "tight buffer" against any efforts to undermine this shared commitment:[20]

> The culture among teachers is so strong now, people recognize the outliers. Teachers will come to me to say, "They [a new teacher] are not fitting in. So-and-so tried to have a negative conversation with me and we don't do that. I think that they're going to be toxic to us." So we've really es-

tablished who we are and what we want to be. And when people have a tough time transitioning into that, the buffer is really tight right now.

UCCS leaders reasoned that robust systems of internal accountability that aligned individual with collective expectations would motivate and support continuous effort to achieve ambitious results for student learning.

A culture of public practice. A primary role of leaders at the two campuses was to make practice public: to upend the norm that you could spend thirty-five years teaching without anyone opening your door or scrutinizing your practice. This required sustained, deliberate action aimed at overturning the traditional norms of teaching (privacy, egalitarianism, and autonomy) discussed in chapter 3.[21] As Woodard-Iliev noted, "This is a fundamental culture shake. It can't happen without the leader saying, 'Not only are we going to do it, but this is how it's going to happen daily.'" Island explained that the director set the tone, establishing a new norm of critical dialogue focused on the results of instruction and a shared commitment to continuously moving children's achievement results forward: "It's about removing the 'This is personal' aspect of teaching and saying, 'This is really about your data. It's about what we can do to strengthen you as a teacher so that your kids will move.'" This, in turn, required building trust with teachers so that they would be receptive to instructional guidance. Island observed: "If you can get teachers to buy into that, and show teachers that you are not a 'gotcha' person, then teachers and leaders know that they are in this together."

Campus directors recognized the challenges teachers faced being constantly observed and evaluated by so many different people. The expectation that teachers' practice would be public and open to inspection at all times had the potential to heighten teachers' anxiety about failure and create pressure to perform. Teachers we interviewed acknowledged the challenges these expectations created. At the same time, they also generally appreciated the frequent observation and feedback that was the norm at the two campuses. Indeed, teachers regarded this continuous feedback cycle as a crucial element of the school's system of instructional guidance and support.

Intertwining teacher evaluation and support. In the school buildings we describe, campus directors evaluated teachers using evidence derived from the schoolwide assessment system. Teacher evaluation was not a discrete event, but rather an ongoing process in which teachers were actively engaged and were continually supported to improve. As Woodard-Iliev explained:

No one in the school should get to a conversation that's an evaluation and not have already heard everything that you're going to say to them.... It's constant communication and it's like a constant feedback loop.... For example, you're a leader and you're gathering evidence about your teachers about their practices.... When you gather evidence, you're also communicating with the teacher at the same time, figuring out what supports they need, hopefully giving them a space to tell you what those supports are. As you make some suggestions about other supports and then when the evaluation comes in, it should be both of you evaluating how all of that worked. And if it didn't work, if kids aren't where they're supposed to be, then you try the next thing, but ... [the teacher] should be able to articulate what [his or her] piece is ... if it didn't work.

As these comments illustrate, campus directors sought to intertwine teacher support with frequent and routine supervision; indeed, their credibility as instructional leaders depended on their skills in doing so. Their stated goal was to motivate teachers to seek out, rather than fear, the feedback they needed to improve their practice. Campus leaders designed this approach to address some of the problems associated with traditional evaluation systems, where the principal arrives in a teacher's classroom a few times per year to conduct a formal performance evaluation, but practice is otherwise private. Such summative evaluation is generally not based on a clear conception of good teaching that all teachers in the school share;[22] it is unlikely to be tied to objective evidence of student learning; and it is generally divorced from formative evaluations of teacher practice intended to assist teacher professional development.

The conventional practice of separating evaluation from support is partly based on the traditional view of principals as managers rather than instructional leaders.[23] Indeed, in many districts, a virtual firewall still exists between the practices of teacher evaluation and professional development, to protect teachers from capricious decisions by supervisors not knowledgeable about instruction. UCCS leaders believed that an effective school must replace fear of capricious decisions with confidence in an objective and fair system of guidance, improvement, support, and evaluation.

Organizing Pedagogical Support

Campus and UEI leaders established a set of mutually reinforcing organizational structures, norms, and practices that supported both students and teachers to achieve the school's ambitious learning goals. A schedule of formal meetings coordinated supports for both student learning and teacher development at each campus. A weekly leadership team meeting and a quarterly monitoring meeting focused on evidence of student learning. These meetings provided venues for the analysis of student learning aggregated at the classroom, grade, and school levels. The goal was to calibrate teachers' expectations of students and leaders' expectations of teachers, so as to set and maintain a high norm for all. These meetings provided occasions for collective problem-solving as well as for deploying resources (such as coaching for teachers and tutoring for students) in key areas of need. In addition, leaders simultaneously engaged in ongoing informal activity that strategically reinforced the work that occurred in more formal settings.

Leadership team meeting. The leadership team met twice a month and included the school's senior leaders, members of the special education team, all subject-specific coaches, and all full-time subject-specific teachers. Woodard-Iliev explained the work of this team and the rationale for its composition:

> We're the group of people in the building who interact with everybody in the building. . . . So I expect and want that group to be on the same page about what we're looking for, what we're trying to achieve, and how we support both kids and teachers in getting there. [The team exists] so that we have a place to talk about what's happening in the building. Who needs support? Where? Who in the team is going to provide that support? How are we going to provide it? And how can we each support that?

When discrepancies arose between the performances of students in different classrooms within the same grade level, discussions during the leadership team meeting probed for explanations and generated possible solutions. Woodard-Iliev described how she worked with the leadership team and teachers to set goals each year:

> For me, as the leader, this is about buy-in, this is about setting expectations, and we revisit it every year: Did the kids achieve it? Was it too easy? Do they need to do more? Do they need to do it [at all]? Is it right? What's missing? Okay, fifth-grade teachers, what do the fourth graders need to do that they didn't do before they came to you? Do second

graders really need to make "how to" books again? They did it for eight weeks in first grade. They don't; it's too easy. No, we're not doing that again. . . . The only way to [evaluate your progress] is if you have your leadership team and you have all your teachers and you have all this data out [and then you can ask questions like]: What happened when you did this thing across the grades?

By comparing evidence of learning across grades, the campus director sought to promote instructional coherence that would result in cumulative learning for students over time. An explicit aim was to ensure that instruction in one year built on what was learned the year before, with no significant gaps in learning.

Classroom monitoring meetings. While leadership team meetings examined data at the campus level, monitoring meetings focused on data about each student in each classroom. The campus director and the lead social worker convened monitoring meetings three times a year with each classroom teacher after each STEP and mathematics interim assessment cycle. During the monitoring meetings, the campus director and the lead social worker discussed with each classroom teacher the reading and mathematics trajectories of each student in the class. Sources included data from the STEP assessment; computerized adaptive assessments that predicted standardized test scores in the spring; everyday teacher observation records; writing samples for literacy; and Recognizing Student Achievement (RSA), progress check, and quarterly interim assessments for math. Teachers also provided data about each student's social and emotional well-being. Literacy and mathematics coaches, literacy specialists, special education teachers, and additional social workers joined monitoring meetings when needed to mobilize support for struggling students.

Informal interactions. Informal interactions between campus leaders and teachers around everyday problems of practice undergirded these formal meetings. As Woodard-Iliev explained:

In some ways the formal structures—such as monitoring meetings that happen three times a year—are a formal representation of what goes on informally every day. . . . [For example,] when the instructional leader meets with the leadership team and the classroom teacher and goes over each student in a particular class, and decides how to coordinate resources around each child's needs, they are doing something formally that they do constantly informally during their everyday interactions.

She also discussed the type of information that she, as campus leader, needed to have in order to effectively monitor student learning and how her conception of instructional leadership differed from conventional understandings of most principals:

> There are a lot of people [other principals] who know about instruction but they don't know their kids. So they'll look at a number and go, "My kids are at this such-and-such percentile." But that's a different definition of . . . an instructional leader . . . [To me, an instructional leader's role is to be] aware of what instruction is needed for each kid in each classroom.

Woodard-Iliev distinguished between instructional leadership as a generic activity focused on aggregate student performance and what she considered to be her main mandate, which was to help teachers discover what instruction was needed for each student. According to Woodard-Iliev, instructional leaders need detailed knowledge of how to apply the school's instructional system to each child. Tools such as the STEP assessment helped the school's senior leaders access detailed information about every student. The campus director, the lead social worker, the FCE director, subject experts, classroom teachers, tutors, and extended-day staff were all expected to draw on specific knowledge of each student's progress and challenges, both academic and socio-emotional, in both formal and informal conversations about students' learning.

Aligning resources to meet student needs. The autonomy and authority campus directors possessed gave them the capacity to turn on a dime to mobilize time and other resources to meet student needs. After collectively analyzing diagnostic assessment data in the ways described above, campus leaders might assign students to receive targeted tutoring, additional instructional time, after-school or summer programs, counseling, and/or mentoring. In extreme cases, campus directors would respond more aggressively to trends emerging from assessments. For example, at one campus, the director asked the literacy coordinator to provide additional small-group reading instruction to the children furthest behind, doubling the amount of such instruction the children received. In another case, the director divided two classes of struggling third-grade students into three classes, with parent support, in April of the school year. This enabled small class sizes and more intensive intervention and supports for students furthest behind. In essence, the careful analysis of diagnostic data, in combination with the authority to make decisions based on these data, meant that campus directors could and did take corrective action before it was too late.

Academic and Social Supports to Enhance Learning

Children's social and emotional skills provide a foundation for later success in schooling and beyond. Children who regularly attend school, show up on time, work hard on assignments, meet deadlines, collaborate smoothly with peers and adults, and respond adaptively to evaluative feedback experience considerable advantages later in life. These skills help adults get and retain jobs, pay rent on time, maintain a mortgage, keep out of trouble with the law, and more.[24] Weak social and emotional skills undermine connections with teachers and peers and risk disengagement from academic learning, with negative implications for adult success.

However, children arrive at school with different levels of development in the kinds of social and emotional skills required to be successful at school. Some children are more ready than others to begin the disciplined work of concentrated learning in a classroom setting because of individual challenges ranging from health problems to family issues.[25] In the following section, we show how UCCS leaders mobilized resources to provide each student the support needed to take advantage of ambitious classroom instruction.

Tailoring Support for Students

Both leaders and teachers emphasized the importance of knowing their students. They not only sought to know their students academically, but also to know each student's social and emotional assets and challenges. This knowledge helped them intervene as early in development as possible to prevent small social or emotional problems from becoming big problems that might interfere with academic progress. Directors at both campuses explained that they obtained this information via the set of formal structures (such as monitoring and leadership meetings) and informal activities (such as regular, informal observation of students) we have been describing. They emphasized the importance of new leadership roles—especially those of lead social worker and FCE director, which gave increased power, legitimacy, and responsibility to the work of supporting students' social and emotional development and engaging families, respectively.

The campus director expected the lead social worker and the FCE director to track the social, emotional, and academic development of all students, not just those assigned to special education. To accomplish this, the lead social worker and the FCE director attempted to map resources available at the school to the needs of each child and to align these resources with the supports each child was receiving at home. Each used different methods to track the supports students needed. Patrick, the lead social worker at Donoghue, explained that she made a list of needs for each student that she continually updated. She had two main categories that she used for her lists, including instructional supports and child developmental supports. Barnett, the FCE director at Donoghue, similarly developed schedules for children that included an array of supports tailored to meet different needs, particularly for students in the extended-day program.

As an example, table 7.1 provides the daily schedule of support designed for Jared Townson,[26] a fourth grader at Donoghue. There were different options during the extended-day period that Barnett and Patrick considered when planning Jared's schedule. Barnett explained that Jared was a very active boy, who appreciated frequent exercise and had a special talent for drawing. He was reading at the expected STEP level, but he struggled with his writing. His math skills were on target. At home, his mom worked full-time cleaning houses. She left early in the morning and came home late in the evening. His family qualified for free lunch. Barnett, in consultation with Patrick, created the schedule we see in table 7.1 for Jared, taking into account school and home considerations.

Because of his mom's full-time work schedule, Jared participated in early-bird and extended-day programming every day of the week and Saturdays, which allowed him to get three meals a day at the school during the week. He also received homework support before school on Monday, Wednesday, and Friday and after school on Tuesday and Friday. To build on his considerable skill in art, he had art classes on Tuesday after school, Thursday before school, and Thursday during the school day. Because of his struggles in writing, Jared had a one-on-one session with his teacher five days a week in the classroom and special tutoring sessions on Mondays and Wednesdays after school in writing. His after-school tutor began her day at 1 p.m., in the classroom, working with the teacher to align tutoring after school with the writer's workshop activities that occurred during the regular school day. To channel his energy and stay focused during learning times, Jared had some form of exercise every day in addition to PE. On Monday, he had martial arts after school. On Tuesday, he had open recreation before school. On Wednesday, he participated in the Bike Club. On Thursday, he had a dance class during school. On Friday, he had open recre-

TABLE 7.1. Schedule of support for Jared Townson, fourth grader at UCCS

	Monday	Tuesday	Wednesday	Thursday	Friday
Early bird					
7:00–7:30	Homework help	Open recreation	Homework help	Art class	Homework help
7:30–8:10	Breakfast	Breakfast	Breakfast	Breakfast	Breakfast
Regular day					
8:15–8:45	PE 8:20–9:00	Tribes	PE 8:20–9:00	Tribes	PE 8:20–9:00
8:45–9:00	PE	Mini lesson	PE	Mini lesson 8:45–10:15	PE
9:00–10:45	Guided reading	Guided reading	Guided reading	Dance 10:20–11	Guided reading
10:45–11:00	Math mini lesson	Math mini lesson	Math mini lesson	Music 11–11:40	Math mini lesson
11:00–12:15	Math	Math	Math	Art class 11:40–12:20	Math
12:20–12:55	Lunch/recess	Lunch/recess	Lunch/recess	Lunch/recess	Lunch/recess
1:00–2:00	Science/social studies	Science/social studies	Science lab	Science/social studies	Science/social studies
2:00–3:00	Writer's Workshop	Writer's Workshop	Writer's Workshop	Writer's Workshop	Writer's Workshop

(continued)

TABLE 7.1. Continued

	Monday	Tuesday	Wednesday	Thursday	Friday
Extended day					
3:00–3:05	Transition	Transition	Transition	Transition	Transition
3:05–4:05	Boys' Mentoring	Homework help	Tech Club	Etiquette class	Homework help
4:10–4:30	3rd meal plan	3rd meal plan	3rd meal plan	3rd meal plan	3rd meal plan
4:30–5:15	Martial arts	Art class (drawing)	Bike Club	Piano lessons	Tech Club
5:15–5:50	Tutoring	City Year (recycling)	Tutoring	City Year (community service)	Open recreation
5:10–6:00	Tribes	Tribes	Tribes	Tribes	Tribes
Saturday					
10:00–11:00	Group discussion				
11:00–12:00	Academic enrichment				
12:00–12:30	Lunch				
12:30–1:00	Tribes				
1:00–2:00	Fitness/recreation				

ation after school, and on Saturday, he had fitness and recreation. Finally, Jared participated in a schoolwide curriculum called Tribes that helped students learn pro-social skills, such as how to communicate clearly with peers and manage conflicts, two times a week during the school day (on Tuesday and Thursday) and every day in extended day and on Saturdays. Barnett explained that Jared's schedule reflected a composite of supports, designed to maximize his academic success. Barnett explained, "There are many possible ways of setting up a kid's schedule. Also, it changes as the year progresses. So this is something that gets worked out, changed again over time." Rather than working with three or four possible templates, the FCE director and the lead social worker explained that there were many different possible schedules that shifted over time, across the course of the school year, depending on emergent issues and each student's development. At face value, this individualizing effort would appear to be hopelessly complicated administratively. However, the new leadership roles and already established monitoring and leadership meetings streamlined and supported this process. UEI and campus leaders explained that giving new leaders hybrid roles also eased the coordination burden and reduced the cost of extended-time programming.

Mobilizing Extended Time

More time before, during, and after school was required to provide the diverse range of supports needed for students. We witnessed how UCCS leaders and designers expanded the school day to include an "early-bird" morning program from 7 to 8 a.m., an after-school program from 3 to 6 p.m., and an extended regular school day from 8 a.m. to 3 p.m. The school week expanded to include Saturday programming from 10 a.m. to 2 p.m. and thirty more days in the school year, including two weeklong academic camps. Efforts to extend learning time during and after school more than doubled learning opportunities for students who needed supports outside of the regular school day. For example, Donoghue students who participated in all extended learning opportunities received 1,361.5 more instructional hours than the typical CPS student in the 2009/10 school year.[27] At Donoghue, efforts to extend the school day were further supported by the community school initiative that CPS implemented during the time of our study. Barnett provided leadership during extended programming after school and on Saturdays, in part supported by the community school initiative.

However, adding more instructional time, while necessary, does not appear sufficient to close gaps in learning.[28] Rather, as we saw in chapter 2, it seems necessary to align extended instructional time with core academic goals and to organize such time around each child's individual needs to accelerate learning.[29] The challenge facing the FCE director and the lead social worker was therefore to align resources across the regular school day and extended time to support the learning of each child. Accomplishing this required creative staffing and training solutions, as discussed in chapter 4.

These included overlapping tutors' and extended-day staff members' schedules with the regular school day, to provide shared teaching time between tutors and classroom teachers, and providing training sessions for after-school tutors to learn regular-day instructional routines. New leaders also took on new responsibilities that in conventionally organized schools would be outsourced to others with less authority. For example, instead of hiring an after-school director, the campus director assigned Barnett to run the extended-day programming for the school. This allowed Barnett to draw on knowledge he gained from his leadership activities during the school day to inform his leadership role after school. This staffing design enabled children to experience more comprehensive interventions, coordinated across the regular-day and after-school programs.

Supporting Teachers to Advance the Socio-emotional Development of Their Students

The lead social worker and the FCE director also supported teachers in their classrooms, to help circumvent trips to the office for disciplinary violations, suspensions, and special education referrals. Their engagement might be triggered by teacher requests, observations in the hallway, follow-up efforts after incidents that occurred during the after-school program, or repeated disciplinary events. UEI experts provided these leaders guidance that informed their participation in monitoring and leadership meetings and their support for teachers in their classrooms. Island explained that teachers sometimes requested that the FCE director or the lead social worker "push in" and "just eyeball a kid." Patrick told us she made an effort to frequently observe classroom dynamics so that she could provide more tailored guidance to teachers and support for students: "I try to be in classrooms a lot so I can witness their struggles."

Academic and Social Support System (AS3) meetings. When a child was struggling, the campuses provided an option to convene a special meeting with parents, teachers, experts and leaders to quickly intervene, without the bureaucratic burdens associated with more formal special education referral processes. This meeting was called the Academic and Social Support System (AS3) meeting. Gathright Fritz provided training and coaching. Parents, teachers, academic coaches, or campus leaders could request AS3 meetings, which were held twice per week. Patrick emphasized the importance of proactively intervening on issues large and small before considering formal referrals to special education:

> The process is very much *proactive*; it's designed to assist students who are struggling. It's not a pipeline to special education [as is often the case in traditional schools]. It's much broader than that. For example, one student was struggling with getting to school on time. The classroom teacher had tracked the attendance records that showed chronic tardiness. So, LaTonya [the family support counselor] really worked with the student's mom to help with the organization at home and make a plan for the morning, so that there *was* a morning routine. This helped all the kids get to school on time—the student's mom had several younger children as well.

AS3 meetings always included the social worker, the campus director, the subject-area coaches, the child's parent, the classroom teacher, and, depending on the issue at hand, other staff members, such as the FCE director or after-school tutors. Liz Brown, the lead social worker at NKO, explained that parents were positioned as shared problem-solvers in the AS3 process, helping to create and evaluate suggested solutions.

Barbara Williams, founding codirector of the NKO campus, designed the AS3 process with Bobby Durrah and piloted it in CPS schools prior to the establishment of UCCS, as discussed in chapter 3. The process aimed to ensure that students received whatever academic and social supports they required to take advantage of ambitious classroom instruction.[30] Later, Gathright Fritz worked with practitioners at UCCS campuses and her UEI colleagues to design an online interface, called the AS3 Clinical Case Management System (CCMS)[31] to coordinate and support the use of student data to inform each stage of the AS3 process.

Helping teachers manage peer relationships among students. UEI experts also trained lead social workers to help teachers develop skills for managing peer relationships among students. They often did this by observing classroom dynamics and then consulting with teachers to provide guidance on how to improve students' interactions.[32] Campus directors, in turn, encouraged teachers to rely on lead social workers for their expertise.

In the following example, Patrick describes how she supported a teacher who requested help when students were disrespectful toward their peers in her classroom:

> A teacher asked me to help her manage the way students were treating each other, hoping to put a stop to ongoing verbal harassment among students. It became disruptive, just having so much back-and-forth put-downs with each other. I came into the classroom to help. I tried to do a combination of me modeling some assistance with that, and then also talking with the teacher, because I want the teacher to be able to handle this after I leave. If the kids can do it [interact better] when I'm there, that's great, but if they can't, then it's not that helpful.

When teachers solved classroom problems with social workers, they gained new knowledge about how to shape dynamics in their classrooms and create environments conducive to learning. They were no longer isolated in their private, autonomous classroom, but part of a network of adults working in concert toward shared goals.

Observing students in varied school settings. Peer social dynamics such as those described above are notoriously difficult to monitor because they change frequently across locations and over time. For example, they unfold not only in classrooms, but also in hallways, after-school activities, and in neighborhood and community settings. The lead social worker and the FCE director gathered information on these dynamics throughout the year, working with teachers to understand students' social networks and their consequences for student learning. As Patrick explained:

> I'm generally around the school, checking out the dynamics of each set of kids—because even though I know the kids, they're in new groups every year, and new classes every year. So, checking out the dynamics of that teacher with that group of kids is really a big piece of what I do. And I'm out on the playground doing the same thing, and in the lunchroom.

By observing students from one social setting to the next, one classroom to the next, and one grade to the next, the lead social worker developed an understanding of peer connections that helped her support teachers and parents to solve problems for children.

By comparing student behavior across settings, the social worker and the FCE director also helped the teachers think about the reasons for student behavior. For example, Patrick described how she used multiple sources of information to work with a teacher who was dealing with ongoing disruptions from one student:

> The teacher was frustrated and sent the kid to the office. So I first went to observe the kid and see what it looks like for that child in that classroom, and sort of get my own opinion on it. I also check in with the teacher about what's going on, what she thinks might have set off this type of behavior. And then I have a similar conversation with the parents as well. I get a sense of what different people's perspectives are on the problem. I also ask the student, although they sometimes have a hard time articulating it. If that kid's an angel everywhere else, then I also try and figure out what's going on by talking to the other teachers as well.

By observing student behavior in different settings, Patrick sought to uncover the causes of the behavior that concerned the teacher. This informed her consultations with a particular teacher and her efforts to support the student to succeed in multiple settings.

Engaging Parents

Partnerships between parents and teachers matter—not just during a crisis or when a student experiences serious learning difficulties, but also for providing "concerted cultivation"[33] of valuable cognitive, social, and behavioral skills required for success in school and, ultimately, in the modern labor market. Consequently, in contrast to the sporadic engagement typical in conventionally organized schools,[34] UCCS educators sought continuous engagement with parents to coordinate supports for learning.

Senior Leadership Responsible for Parent Engagement

Unlike many schools that hire part-time parent liaisons or junior staff to manage parent engagement, UCCS campuses made parent engagement the responsibility of full-time senior staff, who could provide the leadership necessary to build a strong alliance with parents.[35] As we have seen, the FCE director had administrative authority, a full-time appointment, and a mandate to coordinate parent engagement in instruction. The following description, from our field notes of pick-up time after school at

Donoghue, illustrates the coordinated, continuous engagement that campus leaders sought with parents.

> Barnett was out in the front of the Donoghue building at pick-up time, engaged in a discussion with Joelle's[36] mom about her daughter's math struggles in class earlier that day. Patrick joined the conversation, to weigh in on Joelle's recent social troubles with bullying. Then, Patrick caught the attention of Woodard-Iliev just as she finished checking in with another parent, and asked her to provide some insight about possible next steps for supporting Joelle.

In contrast to many school pick-up experiences that involve a hurried baton pass between the teacher and the parent, we observed administrators and teachers self-consciously exploit pick-up time to solve problems with parents, similar to the one witnessed with Joelle's mom. Their goal was to make visible each student's progress beyond the closed doors of the classroom, providing parents and all school staff with opportunities to align academic and social supports across home and school settings. Barnett explained that parents were more trusting when they learned how much all staff members knew about their particular child's everyday experiences.[37]

Setting common goals and coordinating support for each child was challenging because staff members were situated in different contexts, as were parents. For example, some staff interacted with children in the classroom, while others might observe them in the hallways and playgrounds, or in before- or after-school settings. Likewise, different members of families often played different roles in the child's life. The FCE director had the responsibility of mapping out who the important people were at home and school for each student. Barnett told us:

> I work together with Nicole [Woodard-Iliev] to align all of the adults that come into contact with or support the kids. That includes home. I take on supporting parents—and when I say parents, I should say families, because it's grandmothers, it's aunts, it's uncles, it's grandfathers. I talked to a grandmother last night who was picking up her grandkids. So we know who to go to [to discuss a child's well-being]. But if you don't take the time to get to know the different people in the family and what their roles are and how they support their kids or the grandkids or nieces and nephews, then you can't shift what happens for kids.

Gathering such fine-grained details about each child's family and home environment was not something the FCE director did alone, or all at once. Rather, Barnett explained that collecting this kind of information was an ongoing challenge for all staff members. His role was to compile and track this information so that he and other leaders could use it when making decisions at the school level. Barnett explained that the team approach they used to solve problems made a difference for parents:

> The success in our model of parent involvement is really not about any one person. It's really about the team of people that are reaching out to include the parent, not just at [an] initial meeting, but throughout the school year. Some parents certainly are overwhelmed at first. But after we get in the middle of it and people are throwing out all these great ideas and people are being very supportive, parents quickly realize, "Wow, this is great. Where else could I go and get five people all coming to the table to help me and my kid?"

Creating a Culture of Continuous Engagement

While parents can be observed talking with teachers at many schools, what struck us as different at UCCS campuses was the ongoing interaction that parents had with a range of leaders at each campus every day, before, during, and after school. Barnett explained why continuous interactions mattered:

> When parents come in [to talk to campus leaders about a concern], they are talking to people who have been engaging with them all year long, about their child. We still have parents that come in and maybe they are irate—and sometimes rightfully so. But what matters is what has already happened, before they had their concern.

From Barnett's perspective, continuous engagement with parents created a social foundation to support collaboratively addressing difficult issues that might arise with children throughout the year.

To prevent small challenges from becoming big problems, Barnett encouraged frequent communication between teachers and parents, actually requiring teachers to call parents regularly, as we discuss below. He explained that the classroom teachers routinely called parents to touch base; for example, to say how well a child did on a recent assignment.

However, the purpose of the FCE director role was to do more than just increase traditional parent-teacher exchanges. Rather, it was to encourage parents to interact continuously with both the teacher and also other staff members about their child's progress: "It's really much more of an ongoing relationship. It's not that, 'Okay, I'm coming in here to talk to this school person that I don't know and I've never talked to before.'" Establishing routines for ongoing contact with parents laid the groundwork for this relationship.

Setting expectations for parent engagement. Barnett described how leaders used their authority to mandate continuous parent engagement. He and the other Donoghue leaders first set an example by publicly reaching out to parents in many different informal and formal ways. Next, Barnett, Woodard-Iliev, and Patrick told staff to follow their lead, requiring teachers to make weekly calls home; participate in drop-off, pick-up, and check-ins; and schedule brief informal meetings with parents.

Barnett observed that staff members, once they began practicing it, experienced advantages that convinced them to continue reaching out to parents.

> Our network—our staff network—is always expanding. It's not just one person reaching out to parents. It's not just me. It's not just Nicole [Woodard-Iliev]. But all of the staff, the after-school staff, the classroom teachers—everybody is making that kind of effort with parents. We told them to. It wasn't a staff training. I mean, it really was just a mandate. We do it by example, and, fortunately, everybody has bought into it. I think some people were skeptical at first and said, "Where am I going to find time to call all of these parents?" But when they started to do it, they saw the behaviors of the students were more consistent and it was positive. It definitely gives them more credibility with parents and it makes the relationship a lot different. Parents began to approach staff in a different way. It's not perfect, but it is the direction we need to go.

Claudine Randolph, a classroom teacher and math coach at Donoghue, explained how she worked with parents in her classroom:

> I share with parents pretty much whatever they want to know. Our parents are pretty informed because they know how we work. They learn about it from all different staff. So they'll call and ask about their child's status and assessments and what we're going to do next. I had

a really good relationship with my past [students'] parents. They really knew everything that was going on. *They* want evidence too, so we'll give them a writing portfolio so they can see progress in their child's writing. And we'll show them math assessments and math information. So it's not just about a final grade, but: "Here's the progress or the process too." It's like a constant informational stream.

Randolph explained that she communicated with parents both electronically and in person. For example, she described how she used e-mail to create classroom forums. However, she emphasized that she used electronic communication as a supplement to, not a substitute for regular, in-person conversation:

The parents all get our class e-mail. So a lot of parents will e-mail back and forth and ask each other and us. If something gets started on e-mail, I will always later finish the conversation with the parents in person, so that they know before the report card comes out what's happening.

Coaching teachers to engage parents. Teachers were sometimes anxious about contacting parents about difficult problems, and vice versa. At UCCS, the lead social worker was often engaged to provide teachers and parents with the necessary supports. For example, we observed lead social workers Liz Brown at NKO and Patrick at Donoghue coaching teachers to work through difficult issues with parents, during both formal encounters (such as parent-teacher conferences) and informal check-ins (such as phone calls home, or in person at drop-off and pick-up). Patrick explained, "There definitely are teachers who are more stressed out about having to call a parent. There are teachers who come to me and say, 'How do I bring this up to a parent?' And I would problem-solve with them and talk about how you could do that." Randolph explained, "I just go directly to the social worker and say, 'I have no idea how to reach this child. Help me figure this out so I can have the conversation with the parents so that they know.' I hate for parents to be surprised."

Teachers working with the lead social workers were able to rehearse potentially difficult interactions with parents, which helped build the skills they needed to step outside their comfort zone and engage a broader range of parent interactions than they would otherwise. Patrick explained that she also provided teachers with a safe place for them to vent their frustrations: "Teachers know they can come to me and vent, but then also after they've vented, they'll be able to get some ideas, or just a different perspective from me, which I think helps them. Because they can vent about it, and I'll understand, it *is* really difficult, and also help them figure out a way to get through the rest of that day, week, month . . . year." At the same time, Patrick also helped teachers reflect on their immediate responses to frustrating interactions with students or parents, helping them gain emotional distance and providing an alternate perspective:

> I do a lot of reframing with teachers and staff. I do think it helps them. . . . Teachers are able to be more thoughtful about how they discuss what happened in their classrooms [with parents and with other teachers]—because later, when we're in meetings, working through problems, and I'll say, "Well, let's look at the data—does that happen [the child's behavior disrupting classroom learning] *at times*, or on certain occasions, versus every day." And they'll lessen it, and they'll [say], "You're right [the disruptions were not occurring all the time]." So I do think it helps teachers step back, after they have had a chance to vent, and use data instead of emotions to discuss what happens in their classrooms.

Teachers at both campuses confirmed that this kind of support from the lead social worker and the FCE director changed the way they approached parent engagement, helping them ground conversations with parents in evidence and work collaboratively toward shared goals.

Managing expectations. A key challenge in promoting a culture of continuous engagement between staff members and parents was managing expectations. As Barnett observed:

> To me it's about managing expectations of both parents and of the school faculty. If it's not managed correctly, it's a setup for the parents, because they may take something and run with it, but not have the support they need to accomplish it. But if there's the right set of expectations and it is clear there's the right kind of support, parents can definitely meet expectations. But you just have to be more thoughtful. Also there can be problems with the expectations that the parent has of the teachers. It's really having those kinds of constructive conversations and putting people in the best possible situation to succeed. That is at the heart of my job. It takes time. It's not an easy thing to do, but when you can manage expectations, you can really change things for children.

Barnett explained that teachers sometimes expect parents to accomplish tasks at home that parents do not have the support to complete. Parents, too, sometimes have unrealistic expectations about what teachers can do in their classrooms. Campus leaders worked hard to calibrate these expectations.[38]

Helping Parents Help One Another

One result of UCCS leaders' efforts was the emergence of a group of parents who were knowledgeable about the instructional system. The hope was that these "core parents" would take initiative to share information with other parents and become a resource for one another, extending the capacity of school leaders and broadening the support available to all parents.[39] Referring to STEP, Barnett explained, "It's our goal to help parents to understand how formative assessment works because they're our best allies." He explained that during PTCO meetings at the school about assessment, he witnessed certain parents stepping forward to offer advice to other parents who were struggling to understand how assessment worked.

School leaders explained that when parents helped one another understand the assessment system, activities at home and school became more aligned. This, in turn, motivated parents to persevere through barriers they might face at home when supporting their child's academic work. Leaders at the two campuses also believed that building expertise among parents about the instructional system would increase trust and collaboration between home and school because parents would have a better understanding of teachers' and school leaders' goals for students.

Barnett also sought to promote a parent culture where parents motivated one another to support their children at home.[40] He elaborated:

> The perfect example of the kind of parent exchanges that we are trying to encourage took place in the office one morning between two dads. One of the dads was a single dad who had a little guy in kindergarten, and he talked to his child's teacher every week, meeting with her, and making sure homework was done, making sure his child was ready for school and on time and in his uniform. The other dad in this story was frustrated because his kindergarten daughter was really struggling. The two dads struck up a conversation. The frustrated father said, "My little girl is really struggling. They're telling me that she's not working hard and she's not trying and she's not really talking yet." The other dad turned around to him and said, "You know, what you have to do is work

with her every night. If your wife isn't going to do it, you have to do it, and that means you sit down and you do her sight words with her. You need to sit down and you read her guided reading book with her and you make sure her homework is done every night. You can do this—I do it every night—you can do this, but you have to do it for her."

For Barnett, the two key mechanisms in the story relayed above were the sympathetic relationship between the two dads and the constructive encouragement that the frustrated dad received from his peer. Underlying that was a third mechanism, which was the strong relationship that the active father had been able to forge with the classroom teacher, so that he could give specific advice to the frustrated parent. Barnett viewed these reinforcing networks across home and school as potent resources to support each child's learning.

Paying for an Ambitious Elementary School

The organizational model we describe in this chapter is novel in part because it entailed expanded mobilization of people and time. We've described the extensive use of instructional coaches in literacy and math and the creation of a new leadership role, the director of family and community engagement. Unlike typical CPS schools, each UCCS campus had a full-time social worker. Staffing these roles costs money. Moreover, we have described in the preceding chapters how teachers spent considerable time individually assessing their students; yet someone else had to take over the classroom during these assessments, and such persons had to be paid. Extended-day and extended-year activities also required extra staff. How did UCCS find the resources to support these roles and activities, and how much did this version of elementary schooling cost? We interviewed UCCS leaders and obtained documents that provide some answers to these questions.

Many have asked about the cost of running the UCCS and how this compares to per-pupil spending for typical elementary schools serving demographically similar students. This is an important question, but one that is difficult to answer with precision. According to information we obtained from UEI, UCCS spent $11,260 per student for the 2010/11 school year (the year for which we have the largest number of student test scores for our lottery study).[41] This figure, which represents an average of spending across all four campuses (two elementary, one middle, and one high school), is very close to publicly reported average per-pupil spending (for elementary and secondary schools combined) by the Chicago Public Schools that same year. However, it is considerably less than spending in other large urban disticts (most notably New York City).[42]

Yet such comparisons are not terribly meaningful (and can actually be misleading) because of the way in which publicly reported per-pupil spending figures for CPS and other large districts are calculated (by simply dividing total exenditures by the number of students in the district). This method of determining per-pupil spending does not tell us very much about how districts actually allocate these dollars (for example, what percentage of funds per pupil are spent at the school site versus how much is spent on central office administrative costs). Indeed, what schools actually receive per pupil is often substantially lower than these publicly reported figures, since large urban districts typically take several thousand dollars per pupil for central office costs, loan repayment, capital costs, and other overhead costs. In short, such figures typically include "large numbers of costs that don't reach the school house door."[43]

By contrast, we have a much clearer picture of how UEI actually allocates funds to UCCS and what percentage of this is spent on school-level versus central adminstrative costs. As mentioned previously, UCCS spent $11,260 per pupil in 2010/11. This figure includes an average of $6,344 per pupil in local funding from CPS ($5,873 and $7,341 per pupil for the elementary and high school campuses, respectively) as well as funding from federal and state sources. It also includes $314 per pupil in central administrative costs (such as human resources, budget, and operations management provided by UEI). Finally, it includes $2,885 per pupil in funds from private sources (such as foundations and individual donors), which UCCS leaders raised to support key aspects of the model, such as the full-time social worker roles and the extended-day and extended-time programs. UCCS attempted to minimize the cost of these programs by relying on community residents (who were not certified teachers) to staff aspects of the extended-day programs. In sum, while the costs of running the UCCS are similar to those for other large urban districts (and are in some cases actually lower), such comparisons must be made with caution due to the ambiguity surrounding publicly reported district spending figures.

UCCS leaders emphasized that certain novel aspects of the schooling model described here were made possible by creative allocation of funds received from CPS. To support the position of director of family and com-

munity engagement, UCCS leaders reallocated funds that would otherwise have supported the more conventional position of vice principal. A
grant that supported the community schools initiative also supported the
position of FCE director. UCCS teachers—who are of course employees of
CPS—were paid on the same scale as CPS teachers in regular schools. However, they were, on average, less experienced, so the overall teacher payroll
was lower than would otherwise be the case. Moreover, the school day at
UCCS was longer than the school day in CPS generally, allowing teachers
time to meet to devise individualized instructional plans. In sum, UCCS
raised outside funds and reallocated available funds whenever possible
to support key novel aspects of the model. Per-pupil expenditures were
significantly higher than in regular Chicago public elementary schools,
though still less than in the public elementary schools of other large urban districts.

A key question, however, is whether additional per-pupil funding
would be needed to expand this model to many more schools. If UCCS
relied on experienced or highly trained teachers, for example, we would
worry that widespread expansion of the model would be impossible without correspondingly widespread increases in the skill of the teacher labor
market. However, as noted previously, UCCS teachers were, on average, less
experienced than the average teacher in CPS, and UCCS denied that their
teachers were unusually well trained or highly skilled when they began
their employment at UCCS. Instead, UCCS leaders emphasized the importance of on-the-job learning that enabled teachers to become proficient in
using the schoolwide instructional system we have described.

For one important contributor to the success of the model, however,
it is difficult to calculate the per-pupil cost. The University of Chicago's
Urban Education Institute functioned as a small urban district, oversee-
ing the recruitment and training of leaders for each campus, assisting
in fundraising, and mobilizing considerable intellectual resources to
plan and oversee the work. UEI included exceptionally well-trained educators who provided what Cohen and Moffitt have called "infrastructure" that enables schools to benefit from ideas, practices, and tools
found useful more broadly.[44] It is hard to quantify the cost of such infrastructure, though its presence strikes us as essential to the creation
and sustenance of the model. We consider the problem of expanding
infrastructure for effective schooling in the final chapter, highlighting
the unfulfilled potential of universities as partners in the expansion of
effective schooling.

In the next chapter, we assess the effect that the UCCS model described in chapters 5, 6, and 7 had on student achievement in reading and math. The results provide convincing evidence that UCCS students learned substantially more than they would have had they not attended the school, and that these impacts persisted through the middle school years.

PART III

IMPACT AND IMPLICATIONS

CHAPTER 8 THE IMPACT OF ATTENDING AN AMBITIOUS ELEMENTARY SCHOOL

In this chapter we ask how attending the type of school we have described in this book influences the learning of those who attend. This is a causal question, and it is typically difficult to answer causal questions about school attendance. However, the University of Chicago Charter School (UCCS) tended to be oversubscribed, enabling school leaders to base admission decisions on a randomized lottery. While creating a fair opportunity for families to gain admission, the lottery also ensured that those who won the lottery and therefore were offered a seat at the school were statistically equivalent to those who lost the lottery and therefore were not offered a seat. This means that any reliable difference between those who won and those who lost the lottery cannot be explained by preexisting differences but rather must have arisen from the opportunity to attend UCCS. By following the children through elementary and middle school, we were able to assess whether any initial impact of attending the school persisted. Although the lottery-based studies pose some methodological problems of their own, we can make a convincing case for valid causal inference based on these data. The results provide clear evidence that students who won the lottery and were thus able to attend the school learned substantially more than they would have had they lost the lottery and therefore were unable to attend the school. These impacts persisted and in fact increased through the middle school years.

Readers who are not interested in how we designed and implemented the statistical analysis can skip to the final section of this chapter, "Implications for Educational Equality." For those who are interested in the analysis, please read on!

Among those who applied to UCCS each year from 2005 to 2010,[1] students were randomly designated as "lottery winners" (and offered a seat) or "lottery losers" (i.e., those who were put on a waiting list in case a seat opened up in the future). As a result, there should be no systematic differences in observable or unobservable characteristics between lottery winners and lottery losers, and the lottery losers can serve as a statistically equivalent comparison group for the lottery winners. In the literature on program evaluation, the impact of assignment to a new program is called the intent-to-treat (ITT) effect. However, not all students who won the lottery actually attended the charter school, and some who lost the lottery were ultimately offered a seat and did attend the charter school. Thus, assuming that UCCS was effective, the ITT effect understates the impact of actually having attended the charter school. Using now-standard methods, described below, we can estimate the impact of actually attending the school on those whose attendance was caused by winning the lottery. This is called the complier-average causal effect (CACE).

Grade Distribution of Lottery Winners and Losers

Before assessing the impact of attending UCCS, we have to clarify a few more details. Our lottery study is not really a single study but rather a fleet of independent studies. In fact, the analysis we now present summarizes results from twenty-three distinct lotteries. Within each lottery, all applicants had the same probability of winning. However, that probability depended on which of the two campuses the parent preferred, the year the parent applied, the age of the child, and whether the child had a "priority status." Let's consider each of these in turn.

Parental preference. On their application, parents could indicate whether they were interested solely in the NKO campus or solely in the Donoghue campus, or whether they would accept admission at either school. Parents who were solely interested in one school or the other faced a reduced probability of winning the lottery. In contrast, expressing a willingness to attend either school enhanced the probability of winning the lottery. To see why, consider the case in which a child's name was selected on the day of the lottery but the preferred campus was already fully enrolled. If the parent had restricted his or her interest to that school, the child would not have won the lottery. In contrast, if that child's parent had expressed a willingness to enroll in either school, the child would have been offered admission to the school that was not yet filled. Because the probability of admission depended in this way on parent preference, we subdivided all students who applied for admission according to their parents' preferences.[2]

Application year and age. Each year, the school invited new parents to apply for admission. If the number of applications exceeded the number of seats available in a particular grade, the school held a lottery. Because the number of seats available and the number of parents applying varied across years and grades, the probability of winning the lottery varied as well. Hence it is essential to subdivide all applicants by the year in which the lottery was held and the grade for which the parent applied.

Priority status. The school gave priority to some students who lived near the school and others who had siblings already in the school. Such students were automatically admitted unless there were not enough seats to accommodate them, in which case a special lottery was held to decide on admissions. In this case, the probability of winning the lottery would depend on how many slots were available and how many families with the same priority applied. We therefore subdivided the sample by priority status in our analyses.

We emphasize that our analysis does not include any students who were automatically admitted because of their priority status; nor does it include any students who were denied admission because there were no seats available at UCCS in a particular year or grade.[3] For every student in our sample, the probability of being offered a seat in the charter school was neither 0 nor 1.0. Let's call this set of students the "lottery sample." We were able to match 91.2 percent of the lottery sample to their Chicago Public Schools (CPS) test files, and of those, more than 95 percent produced at least one test score.

Table 8.1 describes the "analytic sample": those in the lottery sample who were matched to their CPS data and who produced at least one test score. The table classifies the twenty-three lotteries according to the lottery year (2005–10); by the grade to which the child applied (pre-K/3 is preschool for three-year-olds; pre-K/4 is preschool for four-year-olds); by priority status; and by parent preference. Two of the lotteries were restricted to children who had a sibling already at the campus, six were restricted to children who lived in the local attendance zone of one of the campuses; and the remaining fifteen were labeled "general" in that families applying in those lotteries had no priority.

To understand the table, consider the third row: fifty-four children entered the lottery for kindergarten in 2005. Of those, ten won the lottery and were offered seats at UCCS, and forty-four lost. As the table shows, the

TABLE 8.1. Sample of students by lottery

Lottery year	Lottery grade	Priority status	Preference	Lottery losers	Lottery winners	Total lottery applicants
2005	Pre-K/3	General	Single school	6	2	8
2005	Pre-K/4	General	Single	10	9	19
2005	Kindergarten	General	Single	44	10	54
2005	Grade 4	Sibling	Single	2	2	4
2006	Pre-K/3	General	Both schools	6	8	14
2006	Pre-K/4	General	Both	12	2	14
2006	Kindergarten	General	Both	36	21	57
2006	Grade 2	General	Both	17	1	18
2007	Pre-K/4	General	Both	9	2	11
2007	Kindergarten	General	Both	30	17	47
2007	Kindergarten	General	Single	19	2	21
2007	Kindergarten	Attend zone	Single	2	10	12
2008	Kindergarten	General	Both	15	29	44
2008	Kindergarten	Attend zone	Single	3	6	9
2008	Grade 2	General	Both	16	3	19
2008	Grade 2	Attend zone	Single	6	1	7
2008	Grade 3	General	Both	17	1	18
2010	Grade 2	General	Both	23	2	25
2010	Grade 2	Attend zone	Single	1	3	4
2010	Grade 3	General	Both	22	1	23
2010	Grade 3	Attend zone	Single	1	2	3
2010	Grade 4	Attend zone	Single	1	3	4
2010	Grade 4	Sibling	Both	2	1	3
Total				300	138	438

largest lotteries were general lotteries for seats in kindergarten. For example, in 2006, fifty-seven children entered the general lottery; of those, twenty-one won and thirty-six lost—that is, were assigned to the waiting list. The general lotteries for kindergarten seats in 2007 and 2008 were also comparatively large. Few seats were available in grades after kindergarten, which is why the numbers winning seats in those lotteries is small. Overall, 438 students are in the analytic sample, 138 of whom won the lottery and 300 of whom lost the lottery and were therefore placed on the waiting list. Twelve of the lotteries consisted of parents who would accept admission to either of the two schools (labeled "both schools"), while eleven of the lotteries consisted of parents who would accept enrollment at only one of the two schools. (We do not specify in table 8.1 which of the two schools was preferred in each of these eleven lotteries, although we do account for these differences in our statistical analyses.) The table makes clear that the number of applicants as well as the probability of winning varied greatly across the lotteries. The probability of winning was typically highest in pre-K or kindergarten, when there were lots of seats to fill. In later years, few places became available and the chances of winning diminished accordingly.

Grade Distribution of Test Scores

Because children entered the school in different years and different grades, they varied in the number of test scores they produced. Table 8.2 shows how this happened. The first four columns describe the lottery just as in table 8.1. The next columns give the number of students who provided data in each grade. (Note we combined data from grades 6, 7, and 8 because of the comparatively small number of scores in each of these grades.) To see why the available test years varied by lottery, let's look at two examples. Consider the third lottery—the fifty-four who applied for admission to kindergarten in 2005. Of those, fifty-two produced a test score in 2009, when we would expect to see those children in grade 3, the first grade in which CPS students are tested. These same students produced fifty-three test scores in 2010 (when the students were in grade 4), fifty test scores in 2011, and forty-nine test scores in 2012.[4] Compare this group to those in the 2008 general lottery for kindergarten. These students produced forty-four test scores in 2012, when they were expected to be in grade 3. They could have produced no more test scores for our analysis because our data collection terminated in 2012. So the blank cells in table 8.2 represent year-grade combinations when it was impossible for us to obtain test score data.

Missing Data

Data that are unavailable because our study ended do not impose any bias on our analysis. However, we had to be concerned about other reasons for missing data. We might worry that those who lost the lottery were particularly likely to seek other schooling options outside of CPS—including,

TABLE 8.2. Tested grades for multiple lotteries: The analytic sample

Lottery year	Lottery grade	Priority status	Preference	Grade 3	Grade 4	Grade 5	Middle (6, 7, 8)
2005	Pre-K/3	General	Single school	8	7		
2005	Pre-K/4	General	Single	18	17	17	1
2005	Kindergarten	General	Single	52	53	50	49
2005	Grade 4	Sibling	Single		3	2	7
2006	Pre-K/3	General	Both schools	14	3		
2006	Pre-K/4	General	Both	14	11		
2006	Kindergarten	General	Both	56	55	47	4
2006	Grade 2	General	Both	16	15	16	33
2007	Pre-K/4	General	Both	11	2		
2007	Kindergarten	General	Both	44	45		
2007	Kindergarten	General	Single	21	19		
2007	Kindergarten	Attend zone	Single	12	12		
2008	Kindergarten	General	Both	44			
2008	Kindergarten	Attend zone	Single	9			
2008	Grade 2	General	Both	17	18	18	
2008	Grade 2	Attend zone	Single	7	6	6	
2008	Grade 3	General	Both	18	18	17	17
2010	Grade 2	General	Both	25			
2010	Grade 2	Attend zone	Single	4			
2010	Grade 3	General	Both	22	20		
2010	Grade 3	Attend zone	Single	3	2		
2010	Grade 4	Attend zone	Single		4	4	
2010	Grade 4	Sibling	Both		3	3	
Total				415	313	180	111

for example, private schools or suburban schools. In this case we would expect that those losing the lottery would be less likely to attend CPS, and thus we would not see their test scores. There is, however, no evidence that this was the case in our study: we were able to match 91.8 percent of lottery losers and 91.0 percent of lottery winners to their CPS data, and the fractions of each group who produced at least one test score were nearly identical (96.2 percent of lottery winners and 95.5 percent among lottery losers).

Likelihood of Attending UCCS

If all the lottery winners had attended UCCS and none of the lottery losers had, we could observe later outcomes of both groups and calculate the difference between them within each lottery, then average these differences. This would reflect the average causal impact of attending UCCS.

Things are more complicated in the real world: 79.3 percent of the lottery winners did in fact decide to attend UCCS while 20.7 percent did not, reflecting the fact that families had schooling options for their child other than UCCS and that some moved residence, making attendance at UCCS inconvenient or impossible. Moreover, 26.8 percent of the lottery losers attended UCCS as well. This is not surprising. Lottery losers were placed on a waiting list. If new seats opened up after the lottery, or if some lottery winners decided not to attend, those wait-listed students were offered seats at UCCS. The fact that some lottery winners did not attend UCCS while some lottery losers did attend is known in the statistical literature as "noncompliance" with random assignment.

Noncompliance makes the analysis of randomized lottery data more complicated than it otherwise would be. Under noncompliance, and assuming that UCCS is more effective than the alternative, the average difference in outcomes between lottery winners and lottery losers—that is, the ITT effect—within a lottery underestimates the impact of attending the charter school for those who actually attended. If UCCS was effective, a lottery winner could benefit only by actually attending the school, but only 79.3 percent did; hence 20.7 percent of the lottery winners did not receive whatever benefit UCCS may have produced. Moreover, a lottery loser could benefit from UCCS if that child gained access to the school, as 26.8 percent of the lottery losers did. Thus, the mean difference between lottery winners and lottery losers (the ITT effect) is in reality a mean difference between two mixed groups—each group contains some who did and some who did not attend the charter school. Of course, a significantly positive ITT effect gives good evidence that the charter school was effective; it's just that the size of that effect is an underestimate of the effect of actually attending.

Statisticians have developed methods to estimate the impact of participating in a program on a subgroup of students known as "the compliers"— those whose participation was actually determined by random assignment.[5] This effect is called the complier average causal effect (CACE). We can easily estimate the size of this subgroup by calculating the difference between the proportion of lottery winners who attend (79.3 percent) and the proportion of lottery losers who attend (26.8), yielding 52.5 percent. In a simpler experiment—for example, one that had a single lottery—we could estimate CACE as ITT/0.525. Given that we have a multiplicity of lotteries, the analysis is slightly more complicated, because we have to average the lottery-specific CACE effects to obtain an overall average effect. Moreover, we have data on impacts in each grade from 3 through 8, and we are reluctant to assume a priori that the impacts are the same in every grade.

Analytic Approach and Results

ITT model. We standardized test scores within grades to have an overall mean of 0 and standard deviation of 1.0 in CPS schools. Our results were similar for math and reading, so we created a "mean achievement variable" that is the average of the two and called it "achievement."[6] Our main strategy was to estimate the ITT impact on achievement for students tested in grade 3, grade 4, grade 5, and "middle grades" (combined data from grades 6, 7, and 8). We combined the middle school grades because the sample sizes at these grades were not large enough to support separate, stable statistical analysis. Our primary approach uses a two-level hierarchical linear model with time-series data nested within students, controlling for fixed effects of the twenty-three lotteries described in table 8.1. This approach analyzes all data simultaneously and ensures that all comparisons are restricted to lottery winners and lottery losers within the same lottery. For student i in lottery j at occasion t, the outcome is Y_{tij}, where $t = 1$ is the first occasion during which the child produces a test score, $t = 2$ is the second occasion, and so on. No child produced more than four test scores. According to our model, the outcome depends on whether the student won the lottery ($T_{ij} = 1$) or lost the lottery ($T_{ij} = 0$) and the child's grade (indicators G_{3tij}, G_{4tij}, G_{5tij}, $G_{mid,tij}$ at grades 3, 4, 5, and middle, respectively), according to the model

$$Y_{tij} = G_{3tij}(\gamma_{30} + \gamma_{31}T_{ij}) + G_{4tij}(\gamma_{40} + \gamma_{41}T_{ij}) + G_{5tij}(\gamma_{50} + \gamma_{51}T_{ij})$$

$$+ G_{mid,tij}(\gamma_{mid0} + \gamma_{mid1}T_{ij}) + u_j + r_{ij} + e_{tij} \tag{8.1}$$

so that γ_{30}, γ_{40}, γ_{50}, γ_{mid0} are means for lottery losers at grades 3, 4, 5, and middle, respectively, and γ_{31}, γ_{41}, γ_{51}, γ_{mid1} are ITT effects at each of those

TABLE 8.3. Unadjusted and fitted mean achievement for lottery winners and lottery losers

	Grade 3	Grade 4	Grade 5	Middle (Grades 6, 7, 8)
A. Unadjusted means (standard errors in parentheses)				
Lottery winners[a]	.451	.333	.371	.582
Lottery losers[b]	.273	.118	.205	.122
Mean difference	**.178 (.088)**	**.215 (.110)**	**.166 (.110)**	**.460 (.151)**
B. Fitted means				
Lottery winners[a]	.496	.393	.419	.631
Lottery losers[b,c]	.250	.098	.187	.098
Mean difference	**.246 (.095)**	**.285 (.114)**	**.232 (.114)**	**.533 (.159)**

[a] n = 138 lottery winners produced 276 test scores.
[b] n = 319 lottery losers produced 778 test scores.
[c] Lottery losers produced slightly more test scores on average than did lottery winners because (a) the probability of winning the lottery declined sharply for lotteries for grades after kindergarten, as fewer seats are open in UCCS after kindergarten; and (b) these later lotteries produced more test scores because testing begins at grade 3 (see table 8.2).

grades. Here u_j is a fixed lottery effect, capturing unmeasured differences in achievement between the twenty-three lotteries; r_{ij} is a random child effect capturing unmeasured child-specific achievement differences and having variance τ^2; and e_{tij} is an occasion-specific random error having variance σ_e^2.

ITT results. Results are summarized in table 8.3. For comparison, the top panel (panel A) displays the simple, unadjusted means for lottery winners and lottery losers; these do not account for the lottery to which a student applied. The bottom panel (panel B) provides the estimates based on fitting equation (8.1) (these estimates are conventionally called the "fitted" means), which does adjust for the lottery to which each student applied.

The unadjusted means (panel A) and the means we obtained by fitting equation (8.1) (panel B) are qualitatively similar in table 8.3. The main difference is that the mean differences between lottery winners and losers are a bit larger after adjusting for the lottery to which students applied. We discovered that this difference is explained by parent preferences. Parents whose interest was confined to a single campus had, not surprisingly, lower probabilities of winning the lottery than did parents who would accept either of the two campuses. Moreover, the children of the more-selective parents scored higher on average in reading and in math than did the children of the parents who were willing to accept either school. This was not because one of the two campuses was more effective than the other; in fact, we can find no evidence that the two campuses are differentially effective. Rather, the smaller differences in the top panel of table 8.3 reflect what statisticians call "selection bias." The results in the bottom panel are more credible because they reflect the correct classification of parents; subdividing lotteries by parent preference is crucial to obtaining unbiased inferences about the impact of attending UCCS. The results in the bottom panel of the table are stable when the lotteries are correctly defined, even when we employ alternative ways of analyzing the data.[7]

Using the results that correctly adjust for student preference, we first tested the omnibus hypothesis that there was no impact of winning the lottery at any grade level; that is, H_0: $\gamma_{31} = \gamma_{41} = \gamma_{51} = \gamma_{mid1} = 0$. We reject this null hypothesis, $\chi^2(4) = 12.55$, $p = .014$.

Next, we tested the omnibus hypothesis that all grade-specific impacts were equal; that is, H_0: $\gamma_{31} = \gamma_{41} = \gamma_{51} = \gamma_{mid1}$. The test approached the conventional 10 percent level of significance, $\chi^2(3) = 5.89$, $p = 0.12$, leaving some doubt concerning heterogeneity of impact by age given the relatively low statistical power of this test.

Under the hypothesis that impacts are constant over grades, the best summary is the average impact. We estimate the average impact to be 0.324 in standard deviation units, $se = 0.106$, $p = .003$. There is no evidence that impacts varied across grades 3, 4, and 5; however, the middle school grades (6, 7, 8) seemed to produce a significantly higher impact than the others: difference = 0.280, $se = .109$, $p = 0.010$. If we accept this conclusion, two impact estimates are of interest. The first is for elementary grades 3, 4, 5 combined: estimate = .253, $se = 0.101$, $p = .011$ The second is the impact of the middle school grades (6, 7, 8 combined): estimate = .553, $se = .159$, $p = .001$. Figure 8.1 displays these results.

The outcome on the vertical axis ("mean achievement") is the standardized mean achievement score; that is, the average of the math and reading achievement scores standardized to have a mean of 0 and a standard deviation of 1.0. Black represents lottery winners and light gray represents lottery losers.

CACE model and results. Thus far, we have described the impacts of winning the lottery versus losing the lottery. As mentioned earlier, winning the lottery increases the probability of attending UCCS by about 53 percent, on average, across lotteries. Almost a fifth of the winners did not attend UCCS, and about a fourth of the losers did attend UCCS. This means

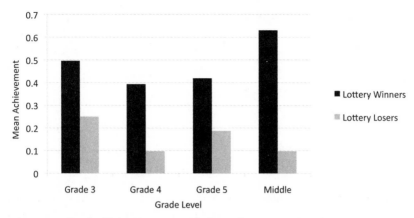

FIGURE 8.1. Graph of intent-to-treat results by grade

that the ITT effects significantly underestimated the impact of actually attending UCCS. We now use the method of two-stage least squares to estimate the impact of attending UCCS on those induced to do so by having won the lottery.

Our theoretical model parallels that of equation (8.1) but now uses actual attendance at UCCS as the causal variable:

$$Y_{tij} = G_{3tij}(\delta_{30} + \delta_{31}A_{ij}) + G_{4tij}(\delta_{40} + \delta_{41}A_{ij}) + G_{5tij}(\delta_{50} + \delta_{51}A_{ij})$$
$$+ G_{mid,tij}(\delta_{mid0} + \delta_{mid1}A_{ij}) + v_j + s_{ij} + \varepsilon_{tij} \tag{8.2}$$

where $A_{ij} = 1$ if student i applying for admission in lottery j attended UCCS in the year after the lottery and $A_{ij} = 0$ if not; v_j is a fixed lottery effect; s_{ij} is a random child effect capturing unmeasured child-specific achievement differences; and ε_{tij} is an occasion-specific random error. Directly estimating equation (8.2) would produce a biased estimate of the impact of attending the school if those who chose to attend differed from those who did not in ways that predict future achievement. However, we can use the random lottery result as an instrumental variable to identify the causal effect of attending UCCS on the "compliers"; that is, those induced to attend by virtue of winning the lottery. The intuition behind the instrumental variable strategy is that to some significant extent, part of the variation in attending UCCS is explained by winning the lottery, and this component of attendance generated by random assignment is not confounded with child or family characteristics that predict school choice. Hence, we can substitute the predicted value of attending as a function of winning or

TABLE 8.4. Impact estimates by grade

Parameter	ITT impact (standard error)	CACE (standard error)
Grade 3 impact	0.246 (0.095)	0.404 (0.192)
Grade 4 impact	0.283 (0.114)	0.580 (0.222)
Grade 5 impact	0.232 (0.114)	0.511 (0.220)
Middle-grade impact	0.533 (0.159)	0.957 (0.319)

losing the lottery into equation (8.2) to estimate the impact of attending on those induced to do so by having won. We estimate this predicted value by estimating, within each of the twenty-three lotteries, the probability of attending for lottery winners ($T_{ij} = 1$) and lottery losers ($T_{ij} = 0$); that is,

$$\Pr(A_{ij} = 1 | L_j, T_{ij}) = T_{ij} * \Pr(A_{ij} = 1 | L_j, T_{ij} = 1) + (1 - T_{ij}) * \Pr(A_{ij} = 1 | L_j, T_{ij} = 0) \quad (8.3)$$

where L_j indicates the lottery to which the student applied. To estimate these probabilities, we substitute the corresponding sample proportions based on the data in table 8.1. We substitute this predicted value of A_{ij} into equation (8.2) to obtain an estimate of CACE: the impact of attending UCCS on achievement for those who were induced to attend by winning the lottery.

Our estimates of equation (8.2), based on this procedure, are displayed in table 8.4, along with the ITT results by comparison. Point estimates of the CACE impact—that is the impact of attending on those induced to do so by winning the lottery—are 0.404, 0.580, 0.511, and 0.957 for students in grades 3, 4, 5, and middle, respectively. As anticipated, these impacts tend to be larger than the ITT impacts. The average CACE impact is 0.613, $se = 0.22$, $p = .004$. A close look at the data, lottery by lottery, suggests that the large CACE impact estimate for the middle grades is driven largely by the kindergarten cohorts and particularly the kindergarten cohorts of 2006–08, who produced most of the "middle grade" data. Note, however, that the middle-grade impact has a large standard error (0.319) because of the comparatively small sample of middle-grade test scores.

Implications for Educational Equality

The central finding of our analysis is that those induced to attend UCCS by winning the lottery learned substantially more in reading and math as registered on the Illinois state assessment than they would have had they lost the lottery and hence not attended. Our best estimates of the size of the average impact range from 0.40 standard deviations in grade 3 to 0.96 standard deviations in the middle school grades (table 8.4), with a mean impact of 0.61, se = 0.21. We can say with 95 percent confidence that the true average impact lies between 0.20 and 1.00, with the most plausible values in the neighborhood of 0.61. These impacts apply to the "compliers"; that is, those who were induced to attend UCCS by winning the lottery. We estimate this group to be about 53 percent of the sample. (The noncompliers are those who would find a way into the school whether or not they won the lottery and those who would choose not to attend regardless of whether they won the lottery). Our data give us no information on how those noncompliers would be affected by attending the school. It therefore makes sense to figure out who the compliers are.

To take a closer look at the compliers, we examine the data from grades 3 through 5. This includes the majority of our sample, and impact estimates are very similar over these three grades. Confining our examination to these students is conservative because it excludes the middle-grade test scores for which our impact estimate is large but more uncertain. Let's now consider the students in these grades who were induced to attend the charter school, based on winning the lottery; these are the students who give us causal information. For these students, we estimate the average impact of attending the charter school to be 0.50, half a standard deviation. How would these students have fared had they not won the lottery and hence not attended the charter school? We estimate that the average achievement score of this group (averaging across reading and math) would be approximately 0.09.[8] To put this number in context, the average achievement for all white students in Chicago in grade 5 in 2011 was 0.75 and the average achievement for all black students in Chicago was −0.16.[9] Hence, the mean of .09 achievement for our control group (the compliers who lost the lottery) is 0.25 higher than the average for black students in Chicago and about 0.66 lower than the mean for whites in Chicago. We can therefore estimate that winning the lottery and hence attending the school would yield, on average, a score of 0.09 + 0.50 = 0.59 units. This would place the compliers who won the lottery and hence attended the school about 0.16 units lower than the Chicago white mean. We might then say that, for this subgroup, attending the school reduced the gap between them and the white mean by 0.50/0.66 = .76, or 76 percent. This is a remarkable result, implying a large reduction in racial inequality. It is also conservative, because our average estimate including middle school test scores is 0.61.

The results just described say something about the students to whom our results apply: African American students in Chicago, who would score on average about 0.25 higher than the mean for Chicago's African American students, even if they had lost the lottery and hence not attended the school. However, these results also say something important about how much these students benefited. If a typical complier in our study had lost the lottery and hence did not attend UCCS, we estimate that that student would score at about the 26th percentile of the white distribution. In contrast, winning the lottery and hence attending UCCS would place that student at the 44th percentile of the white distribution.

Our results also show that the gap between UCCS and non-UCCS students grows during middle school. We know this because the average impact of attending UCCS in the middle grades, though uncertain, is statistically significantly higher than the average impact of attending UCCS in the elementary grades. This point deserves some elaboration. By the time they reach grade 6, students in our lottery sample who attended UCCS had moved to middle school. Our results show that the gains made in elementary school carried over into the new middle school. We learned through interviews that UCCS staff provided counseling as students considered what middle school to attend. Specifically, the staff counseled UCCS students to apply for the best available middle school—often a magnet middle school or a selective exam school. Of course, if these students learned a great deal during elementary school, the counselors had a realistic basis for recommending that students attend a demanding (and perhaps selective) middle school. This suggests that part of the enhanced impact of attending UCCS during the elementary grades resulted from the fact that enhanced learning and counseling combine to increase the chances that UCCS students would attend a good middle school. While we have no direct data to test this proposition empirically, it is clear that the impact of having attended UCCS persists and in fact increases after students leave elementary school. This finding is a counterexample of the frequent finding that initially favorable effects of new interventions fade out in subsequent years.[10] In the next chapter we consider the implications of these results for those who seek to improve elementary schools on a broader scale.

CHAPTER 9 PRODUCING KNOWLEDGE FOR SCHOOL IMPROVEMENT

Our book began by posing a paradox. Extensive research reviewed in chapter 2 suggested that increasing the amount and quality of schooling has large potential to reduce inequality in educational outcomes. Yet despite decades of school reform aimed at reducing achievement gaps, inequality in education is large and perhaps even increasing.[1]

Despite sweeping changes in school resources, regulation, and accountability over the past several decades, the basic organization of teachers' work in elementary schools has remained remarkably stable. In most elementary schools, teachers work largely in isolation in the privacy of their own classrooms, with little access to timely, objective evidence about how well their children are learning and with little guidance on how to solve instructional dilemmas.[2] We have called this organization of teachers' work, aptly described by Lortie forty years ago,[3] the "private, autonomous" approach. We have argued that in schools where teacher skill is highly variable, where staff turnover is high, where neighborhood conditions are challenging, and where hard-pressed families with few resources struggle to support their child's academic goals, the private, autonomous approach is not likely to be reliably effective. But even under more favorably resourced conditions, this approach appears to produce great heterogeneity in student learning. Chapter 3 provided a case study suggesting how difficult it can be to overcome this conventional organization of teachers' work in urban schools serving low-income minority children.

An Alternative Model

The educators whom we interviewed and whose work we observed for
five years adopted an approach to the organization of instruction that
sharply contrasts with the private, autonomous model. The school's designers reasoned that early inequality in academic skills cannot be solved
by a collection of isolated teachers, no matter how motivated or skilled
they might be. Rather, the designers envisioned a school that would provide a sequence of instructional experiences that would ensure that each
child got on track and stayed on track for success in high levels of reading comprehension and mathematical reasoning. The remarkable heterogeneity in children's skills when they enter school posed challenging
design problems for enacting such coherent instructional sequences for
each child, the solution for which required a sustained collaborative effort
and a schoolwide instructional system.

We have devoted most of the pages of our book to describing in some
detail the principles that enliven this alternative approach and the practices that flow from those principles, so there is no need to repeat that
description here. We have called this alternative a "shared, systematic"
approach because the entire school staff embraced a common strategy
for assessing student outcomes; planning, enacting, and evaluating instruction; and mobilizing social and parental support. We describe this
practice as "shared" in two senses of the word: strategies and tools for
instruction, assessment, and mobilizing broader support for students
were shared by the entire staff; and the classroom came to be a space
that was open to observation by colleagues and school leaders rather than
the private domain of the individual teacher. Central to this alternative
approach was the overarching aim of ensuring that every child was on
track for academic success. To pursue this aim, teachers and school leaders sought to closely monitor the progress of every student, to develop
explicit instructional plans for each child, and to allocate extended time
to ensure that no child fell behind.

The designers of this school had based the system of curriculum, assessments, and instruction in part on scientific research on learning and
teaching. Yet for reasons described in chapter 2, we know that scientific
research is not by itself a guide to the construction of a powerful school.
To build a powerful school requires expert judgment on how to combine
scientific findings with insights from practice to produce reliably good
teaching within a supportive school organization. We described how this

worked in detail in chapters 5 through 7. School leaders sought to mobilize expert teachers to assist all teachers, novice or experienced, in enacting the desired instruction within a school culture where all adults were accountable for children's outcomes. School leaders also emphasized the importance of mobilizing social supports and parent engagement.

Explaining the Impact of the School on Student Learning

Chapter 8 shows that students who won a randomized lottery between 2005 and 2012 and as a result attended the University of Chicago Charter School (UCCS) learned dramatically more in reading and math than they would have had they lost the lottery and hence been unable to attend the school. These students were all African American and predominately from low-income families living on the South Side of Chicago. While these students were not on average as disadvantaged as the typical African American child in Chicago (see chapter 8 for details), we can be reasonably sure that if these students had not won the lottery and hence not been able to attend the school, they would have scored far lower on average than white students in Chicago. For these students, our best estimate is that attending the UC Charter School eliminated most of the gap between them and typical white students in Chicago.

How are we to understand these striking results? We reason that the model of school leadership and instruction described in this book was sufficient to produce the substantial gains we have documented in chapter 8. We choose the word "sufficient" with care. Our interpretation is that the collection of ideas and practices we have described, taken together, produced the impacts on student learning that we have observed. We don't know that each element of the model was essential because our study design cannot isolate the unique contribution of any particular element of the model. It is possible that certain components were not necessary or even that some elements actually undermined the effectiveness of the school. Nevertheless, to learn that an approach composed of an identifiable set of coherently linked elements was sufficient to dramatically reduce racial and social inequality strikes us as exceptionally important.

There is a key caveat. We cannot estimate the extent to which the practice of the educators in the school we have studied fully conformed to the model as articulated by those we interviewed. A rigorous study of the consistency of implementation of the model as it has been described to us would have required a comprehensive sampling of classrooms and

very extensive observation in those classrooms. We did not have the resources to conduct such a study. So it may be that some elements of the
model were not strongly present in practice or that important practices
not in the model helped produce the impact we see. This is a problem that
researchers call "mis-specification" of causation, and it cannot be ruled
out. What we can say is that multiple repeated, independent interviews
of practitioners at the two campuses produced remarkable consistency
regarding the aims, strategies, and organization of the work. Moreover, in
many visits to the two campuses, we observed numerous practices consistent with the model. We have highlighted these findings from interviews
and observations in chapters 5 through 7. It is clear that what people
told us and what we saw were consistent with the notion that these two
campuses operated under a distinctive model of school leadership and
instruction, though we cannot rule out the possibility that implementation of the model was variable and that important aspects of the work not
described as part of the model were operating and producing good results.

With this caveat in mind, we hope that our articulation of the model
in some detail will assist others who are struggling to create powerful
schools. Adopting this model in theory would of course be much easier
than making it work in any particular setting. A great deal of hard work
will, in any instance, be required to create a school organization that effectively challenges deeply ingrained notions of teaching as a personal craft,
carried out largely in solitude. Our work suggests that it will not generally
be a simple matter to identify a cadre of committed teachers, train them
for leadership roles, and find a way of compensating them for their enhanced contributions. The organization of this kind of school contradicts
widely practiced routines of school life. For example, providing teachers
with time and space to carefully assess their students individually and
to meet in teams to generate instructional plans requires dedicated staff
cooperation time and individualized assessment tools not readily available in most schools. Novel practices—such as integrating a social worker
into the leadership team of the school and hiring a director of family and
community engagement to mobilize parents around specific instructional
support for their children—require careful planning and implementation
by school leaders who are often pressed for time and resources. Flexibly
using after-school time and summers to assure that students are on track
complicates the problem of school management. Routinely analyzing formative assessment results and supplying teachers with timely feedback
calls for training that schools usually don't provide.

Questioning School Reforms That Target Teachers in Private,
Autonomous Classrooms

Thinking about how to create a powerful school based on this experience
makes us reflect on the history of school reform in a new way. School
reform efforts have generally involved some combination of supplying
resources, regulating inputs such as teacher training and certification,
aligning curricula with standards, and using accountability and market
pressures to create incentives. These strategies can affect who is hired,
what resources they have, what they are expected to teach, and how hard
they work. The implicit assumption is that smart, hardworking people
with adequate resources and the right incentives will figure out how to
put in place the instruction that students need.

Reflecting on our research for this book, this implicit assumption
seems incorrect. What our society now expects schools to do is extraordinarily complex and uncertain. In an economy that puts a premium
on knowledge rather than routine labor, we want all students of all backgrounds to become engaged in various forms of higher-order thinking,
as exemplified by reading with high levels of comprehension, expressing
sophisticated ideas in writing and speaking, using mathematical ideas
in scientific reasoning, and more. Unfortunately, the knowledge about
how to make these things happen—particularly for more-disadvantaged
students—is not widespread. Hence, better resources and hard work, while
essential, are not sufficient.

Ensuring that all children learn at a high level would be challenging
enough if teachers, like physicians, could assess the needs of one child at
a time and then prescribe and enact a treatment regime for each child.
However, if we really want to achieve the ambitious goals now expected
of schools, we must, in effect, expect teachers to assess a whole collection
of students who are heterogeneous in background and skill and then to
enact instruction that is correctly calibrated to the development of each
child—while managing the entire collection of students. Moreover, that
work must be coordinated across grades and subject areas. Success would
require a clear understanding of how children learn at various stages,
what each child currently knows, what instruction is most essential, and
how to maximize learning opportunities for twenty-five or so students
simultaneously.

If this reasoning is correct, it is not enough to hire the right people,
buy the right textbooks, and use accountability policies and incentives to

motivate hard work. A huge challenge looms: the challenge of producing and disseminating the knowledge needed to capitalize on resources and incentives in order to create and sustain outstanding teaching within the organization of the school. Past reform efforts have fallen short, at least in part, because they were not based on knowledge about how to organize reliably effective schools. The findings we present in this book suggest that school leaders and teachers need to know what students know, what instruction children need, and how to organize everyday life within the building to provide that instruction. Put bluntly, past reforms have left in place an approach to school organization that leaves teachers alone to solve problems that no individual can actually solve and that the policy makers themselves do not understand.

The Role of the University in School Improvement

Having concluded that lack of knowledge is a key missing link in school improvement, we might then ask about the potential contribution of universities. We can trace many contributions of universities to the schooling we have described in this book. Developmental scientists have uncovered how inequalities in children's early experiences create the basis for later inequality in academic skills. We described these contributions in chapters 5 and 6, and they are important because they help us define the challenges that must be met in ensuring equal access to learning at school. Researchers at the Ohio State University conceived the "balanced literacy" program that the two campuses used, and the faculty at UCCS assessed children's literacy skills using the STEP assessment developed at the University of Chicago's Center for School Improvement (the forerunner of the current Urban Education Institute—see chapter 5). The University of Chicago Mathematics Project generated the mathematics textbooks whose use is described in chapter 6. Scholars from a variety of disciplines have contributed to the thinking of UCCS leaders regarding instructional leadership and social support and parent engagement (chapter 7). Universities trained all the teachers and leaders we interviewed. Universities have contributed extensively to the knowledge that has become useful to the school we have studied and to the practice of schools throughout the nation.

These contributions, in our view, are quite different from the conventional notion of "knowledge transfer" widely heralded in US universities. One problem with this conventional notion is that schools and school districts are not organized systematically to learn from research; nor are researchers primarily incentivized to interact with practitioners in a way that would clarify the potential applications of what researchers know.

However, an even more fundamental problem is that a great deal—perhaps most—of the knowledge we need to make schools reliably effective is stored in the minds of expert practitioners. That is one of the primary lessons we have learned from writing this book. Leading practitioners have remarkably coherent, detailed, and nuanced understandings of how to organize their work. They are experts at combining information from many sources to respond to an array of unpredictable scenarios that arise daily. Samples of interviews quoted in this book barely scratch the surface of the insights school people shared with us. Moreover, intensive daily interactions among these educators has generated a remarkably consistent view of "the work" and how one "pushes" to get it done. Unfortunately, expert practitioners, immersed in their challenging work, have little time to write down what they know so that others might learn from it, scrutinize it, modify or add to it, or systematically test it in new settings. The problem of "scaling up innovations" can be understood from this point of view partly as a problem of making research available to practitioners, but more profoundly as the failure to capitalize on what practitioners know.

Fortunately, making implicit ideas explicit, writing about them, scrutinizing those ideas, testing them, and revising them are exactly the habits that make scholars successful. Indeed, this is the work scholars are trained and paid to do. Researchers, in their search for originality, want to know what has been tried and what is currently known about many aspects of student learning, teaching, school organization, teacher labor markets, and policy options. They have time and incentives to read about what has been tried in other districts, states, or nations and can promote conversations with practitioners, who care deeply about these issues.

Hence, we see in our experience in preparing this book a strategy for addressing the knowledge problem that has thwarted serious school reform. Our work encouraged researchers and practitioners to work together, over long periods of time, to clarify and make explicit promising ideas about how to organize and sustain effective teaching and learning. Our experience suggests such interactions will produce novel questions for research, while sharing new ideas and findings on a broadened scale.

We conceived this book as the product of a practitioner-researcher collaboration where knowledge grew out of a long-term, dynamic process. Within this kind of collaboration, researchers and practitioners can work together to make the elements of expert practice explicit and visible, enabling others to learn and to disagree and to revise. Consequently, expert practitioners become more self-conscious about their theories of action and, presumably, more effective in carrying out those theories in practice. At the same time, the uncertainties and potential contradictions that emerge as problems of practice can help frame novel research questions and thereby propel the work of scholars. The more explicit the model of schooling practice, the more amenable it will be to revision, based on new research findings, and the more potential researchers will have for framing new research questions. As a result, schools and school systems will then become more capable of using and contributing to research.

This vision, while idealized, may nonetheless strike many readers as a description of what already happens. Many university researchers work closely with expert practitioners now.[4] An important question arises: How can researchers intensify this dynamic process such that the university-school partnership becomes a powerful engine for school improvement with a focus on educational equality?

In our view, professional incentives support researchers to frame compelling empirical questions, use rigorous methods to answer them, and write up the results in peer-reviewed journals. This labor will help make practitioners more expert, more articulate, and more capable of changing schooling for the better. The synergies embedded in the dynamic process we have described can drive success for both groups.

These ideas suggest a much more active role for the research university in contributing to school improvement. A cascading series of opportunities could result. Universities might run local schools not because universities will ever run more than a small fraction of schools, but because doing so creates a ready opportunity to form collaborations between expert practitioners and scholars. Universities might seek to base the practice of the schools they run on the best available knowledge, while using the experience in those schools to reveal expertise. Universities might base their practitioner-training programs on the instructional practices in the schools they control and might train prospective teachers in those schools or closely affiliated schools.[5] Developmental scientists at the university might scrutinize the instructional models in place and frame new questions for research. Organizational sociologists and labor economists might be consulted to frame policies for personnel and management of local schools. Joint seminars might debate questions of interest to both. Researchers deeply engaged in school improvement might convince local policy makers to roll out new initiatives in ways that enable them and others to learn from the experience. Local policy makers might induce researchers to evaluate new innovations. Instead of serving as sites for researchers to run studies, schools and school districts might develop the capacity to collect and use information in more rigorous ways while collaborating with researchers who then have access to fresh evidence for publication.

These ideas may sound Pollyannaish, and we have not enumerated the host of problems that can crop up whenever researchers and practitioners try to collaborate. Political sensitivities, data security, potentially unfair distribution of rewards and benefits from research, disruption of school routines, and many other difficulties arise, and we are acutely aware of these. The larger question, however, is whether we might expect universities to systematically and intensely produce the knowledge required to create ambitious schools for the children who are currently least likely to receive effective schooling.

In sum, our experience working on this book has encouraged optimism about the potential power of school improvement, while underscoring the challenges facing those who seek to create and sustain ambitious schools. The challenges go beyond finding skilled people, motivating them, and putting in place good curricula. These elements are certainly important; but we also face a knowledge problem. We need to know much more about how to create and sustain powerful schools, and we argue that universities have a compelling role to play in producing the knowledge needed to do so.

School Improvement and the Problem of Infrastructure

Is starting a new charter school the only way to build an ambitious school? We remain agnostic about the particular form of governance that might best support the ambitious elementary schools that many children depend on for successful development. Networks of charter schools may be powerful equalizers, but so may networks of outstanding public schools.[6] What seems to matter most is that adults in the ambitious schoolhouse work relentlessly toward the success of every child, and that those adults have access to the knowledge, resources, incentives, and tools that can enable them to realize this commitment.

We argue that ambitious schools—whether they be charter schools or traditional public schools—require certain key kinds of authority. The 1996 Illinois Charter Schools Law gave the University of Chicago the authority to adopt new curricula; reshape teacher evaluation and professional development; make decisions about hiring, promotion, and termination of staff; and reshape and extend instructional time. Without such powers, the instructional model and school organization described in this book would not have come to fruition. One might therefore conclude that promoting new charter schools is the solution to the problem of improving schooling and reducing educational inequality.

However, we adopt a different view. It is true that charter school laws have enabled educators to create a number of highly effective schools, particularly for low-income minority children.[7] We regard this as a pioneering contribution to educational research and improvement. A great deal can be learned from these schools, and we hope readers will learn from our book. But it does not necessarily follow that creating a very large number of charter schools will produce powerful schooling on a large scale, or that relying on conventional public schools cannot produce such powerful schooling at scale.

Research to date suggests that charter schools are, on average, no more effective than are regular public schools.[8] What seems clear is that charter schools are more variable in their effectiveness than are their regular public school alternatives. Hence it is quite plausible that the primary effect of replacing regular public schools with charter schools would be to increase heterogeneity of school quality and therefore not to reduce inequality.

Advocates of school choice often claim that competition among charter schools and between charter and regular public schools generates incentives to learn what works best. Weaker schools would go out of business, and the strong survivors would supply increasingly high-quality teaching. In this view, schooling would then become an efficient market, and competition would reveal powerful school practice. There is, however, considerable uncertainty about the prospects of relying on market mechanisms to improve schooling, even among its advocates.[9] One major question is whether individual charter school operators have the capacity to create truly effective schools on a large scale. The need for knowledge looms large.

Infrastructure

To judge whether any large-scale school reform strategy is likely to be effective, it makes sense to consider what Cohen and Moffitt called the "infrastructure" for school improvement.[10] The authors reason that nations that share a common curriculum and a common examination system create a powerful infrastructure for preparing prospective teachers, designing pedagogy, promoting professional development of incumbent

teachers, and evaluating their performance. Knowing what to teach focuses one's thinking on how to teach. In contrast, in a system where school
governance is highly decentralized (as it is in the United States), teacher
educators have great uncertainty about what curriculum prospective
teachers will teach. Cohen and Moffitt conclude that teacher educators
are then less able to provide strong training in instruction. Within each
state and district, a wide array of vendors will sell professional development programs geared to a variety of curricula, and purchasers will generally have little objective information about how well these programs
work. In order to evaluate programs of instruction within a state or district, testing companies will avoid devising curriculum-specific tests and
instead produce generic, norm-referenced tests that may be insensitive to
local improvements in instruction. Textbook writers will want to sell to a
broad market of buyers who use widely varying curricula; as a result, the
textbooks may cover a wide range of topics superficially rather than reflect
a focused, coherent plan of study. Teachers working with weak training,
varied levels of skill, and high levels of autonomy will use these tests and
texts in highly variable ways. Hence, a system with weak infrastructure
and high teacher autonomy will tend to generate considerable heterogeneity in student outcomes.

When the infrastructure for school improvement is weak, we reason
that it is far more difficult to create an effective school than it should
be. Just as each teacher is required to invent his or her own instructional
system within a culture of autonomous teaching, those who wish to create a powerful school will operate largely on their own within a system
of weak infrastructure, each putting together an idiosyncratic combination of curriculum, student assessment, professional development, and
teacher evaluation.

But Cohen and Moffitt note that strong infrastructure need not be nationwide. Effective school districts, charter school management networks,
and networks of comprehensive school reform programs can each provide
infrastructure to support local school organization.

The two school campuses in our book were rich in infrastructure: they
were run by the University of Chicago's Urban Education Institute, which
was directed by Timothy Knowles, the past deputy superintendent for
Teaching and Learning at Boston Public Schools and a gifted leader. The
initial design of these schools was led by noted Professor Anthony S. Bryk,
a leading educational researcher who went on to become the president
of the Carnegie Foundation for the Advancement of Teaching; by his distinguished colleagues Sharon Greenberg and Marvin Hoffman; and also

by Sara Spurlark, a legendary South Side school principal. Leading the pedagogical guidance system in math was Debbie Leslie, a leader at the University of Chicago's Center for Elementary Mathematics and Science Education, which publishes *Everyday Mathematics*, among the most widely used math texts in the nation. Yes, the infrastructure for school improvement was rich!

Powerful infrastructure involves institutional support that allows educators to use relevant knowledge. By supplying knowledge, resources, and tools, infrastructure is the antidote to a decentralized system in which each school creates its own organizational model from scratch and each autonomous teacher invents his or her own idiosyncratic approach to teaching math or reading.

But how can powerful infrastructure become available to countless schools that must be effective if we are to successfully tackle educational inequality? Cohen and Moffitt describe collections of regular public schools and charter schools that have, at times, developed the capacity to support coherent schoolwide systems of instruction. Such schoolwide systems integrate curriculum, professional development, formative assessment, and teacher evaluation with the aim of producing reliably powerful sequences of instruction across the grade levels. Ideally, a school operating with strong infrastructure could put into place an instructional system akin to that described in this book by capitalizing on what is known rather than taking on the arduous process of constructing such a system anew. How to foster infrastructure that supports powerful schools is an important question that is beyond the scope of this book.

Taking Exemplary Practice to Scale

Our book is about the conception, design, and impact of a novel school. The critical reader will ask what bearing this inquiry has on the problem of improving existing schools. In thinking about this question, our colleague Michael McPherson has suggested an analogy with the work of John Rawls, who famously worked hard to describe a just society. While some regarded his project as utopian, Rawls believed that those who struggle daily against injustice would benefit from having in mind a clear vision of the ideals for which they are struggling. That essentially captures our view. Those who designed, revised, and sustained the school we have described here have produced useable knowledge about the reliable provision of powerful teaching. We conclude that if certain aspects of school organization and instruction are in place, children who are currently faring quite badly will do remarkable work. These results provide a compelling argument in favor of struggling to ensure that those aspects of schooling are in place for those students.

Researchers have asked, "Are these kids, who face challenges economically, in their neighborhoods, and sometimes in their homes, capable of achieving at high levels academically?" Our reading of the research and our experience studying UCCS lead us to conclude that this question has been answered. Another question then arises: "How hard are we willing to work and how much are we willing to pay to ensure that children who have been underserved achieve at high levels?" We like this question better. The children are ready. Are we?

Chapter 1

1. The majority of the randomized lottery studies have identified especially effective charter high schools and middle schools (Abdulkadiroglu, Angrist, Cohodes, et al. 2009; Angrist, Pathak, and Walters 2013; Dobbie and Fryer 2009; Abdulkadiroglu, Angrist, Dynarski, et al. 2011). Bloom and Unterman (2014) provide convincing evidence based on randomized lotteries that innovative, small, non-charter public high schools in New York have quite dramatically increased graduation rates and college attendance among low-income students. Such studies of elementary schools are comparatively rare, but see Dobbie and Fryer 2011.
2. See Merseth 2009.
3. See Borman, Slavin, et al. 2007; Cohen and Moffitt 2009.
4. Payne 2008.
5. Cohen and Moffitt 2009.
6. Heckman and LaFontaine (2010) study historical trends in high school graduation rates; Reardon (2011) describes historical trends in test scores.
7. Neal 2006.
8. Heckman and LaFontaine's (2010) estimates of graduation rates do not include GED recipients for reasons they describe in detail; see also Murnane 2013. Ginder, Kelly-Reid, and Mann (2015) describe college graduation rates.
9. In 2009, 78 percent of students at NKO and 82 percent of students at Donoghue qualified for free or reduced-price lunch.
10. Sybil Madison-Boyd, Tamara Gathright Fritz, and Marvin Hoffman were also members of the design team that created the concept for Donoghue.
11. Lortie (1975) vividly describes this approach to the organization of teaching—one that remains largely in place (Johnson 2015).
12. Newmann, King, and Rigdon 1997; Elmore 2004, 2005a, 2005b.
13. Angrist, Imbens, and Rubin 1996.
14. This inference is based on a reading of the studies cited in note 1.
15. Past research suggests that, on average, charter schools produce results that are similar to those of public schools; see Gleason et al. 2010. Charter schools and public schools presumably vary in their effectiveness, but they appear to vary around a similar average. In contrast, rigorous studies of *particular* charter schools (see note 1) show that those specific schools produce large positive effects. How can charter schools, on average, be similar in their effectiveness to public schools while every charter school producing specific evidence is highly effective? The simplest explanation is that we

do not see the results of the ineffective charter schools. While many charter schools conduct lotteries and therefore have potential to produce unbiased evidence of their effectiveness, only a few produce and publicize the results. This raises the question of whether selective reporting and subtle forms of publication bias are censoring what we know about specific charter schools. This is not to disclaim the credibility of the results we do see; instead, we point out concerns regarding the social process whereby research evidence about school effects comes to public attention. Our approach has been different. We have been committed from the outset to test the model we describe here. Moreover, we spelled out the theory of action behind the school campuses we describe *before* we saw any results.

16. Borg 2003; Mour 1977; Zeuli 1994.

17. Cohen and Moffitt 2009.

18. Readers familiar with *Organizing Schools for Improvement* will notice a strong conceptual alignment between the "five essential supports" for school improvement that Bryk, Sebring, Allensworth, et al. (2010) articulate in their book and the three imperatives of the UCCS model we elucidate in ch. 3. This speaks to the common intellectual roots of both projects in more than fifteen years of work at the University of Chicago under the leadership of Anthony S. Bryk.

19. Duncan and Murnane 2014 also includes a description of the model we study and connects this work with other efforts nationwide. We also take inspiration from Merseth 2009, which provides an in-depth view of the inner workings of five high-performing Massachusetts charter schools, analyzing factors that likely contribute to their success.

20. See, however, Gill et al. 2007; see Merseth 2009 for a notable exception. For reports on remarkably effective charter schools, see Abdulkadiroglu, Atila, et al. 2009; Angrist, Pathak, and Walters 2013; Dobbie and Fryer 2009; Angrist, Dynarski, et al. 2010; Angrist, Dynarski, et al. 2012; and Abdulkadiroglu, Angrist, et al. 2011.

21. From 2008 through 2012, we collected several sources of data. Included were twenty-two semistructured interviews about instructional and organizational practices at each campus, ranging from forty-five minutes to two hours, and ten focus group interviews with teachers, instructional coaches and school leaders at both schools. We asked about teaching, leadership, reading, social supports and extended-day programming. Focus groups lasted between forty-five and ninety minutes. We conducted eleven site observations, each spanning multiple days for two to four hours. We convened eleven workshop sessions, three prior to submitting the book for publication. During these sessions, we elicited feedback on specific chapters of our book. Participants included teachers and school leaders at each campus, UEI leaders, and other University of Chicago colleagues and stakeholders.

22. We describe this three-phase consultation process in detail below.

Phase 1. To identify the guiding principles for the model, we met with twenty-two campus leaders, instructional coaches, and classroom teachers at both campuses, and we conducted semistructured interviews. We structured the protocol to solicit details about practices across multiple domains. We also collected hard-copy and online documents produced by leaders, subject specialists, and classroom teachers at the school. These documents were used for administrative purposes, to guide classroom functioning, and for communication with parents.

TABLE 1.1. Overall participation in data collection at UCCS campuses

	Total	NKO	Donoghue	Other	Time frame
Overall data collection					
Total number of interviews	22	7	13	2	2008–12
Focus groups	10	5	5	0	2009
Number of focus group participants	34	19	14	1	2009
Site observations	11	5	6	0	2008–11
Overall study participants	39	20	16	3	2008–12
Feedback events					
Workshop sessions	11	–	–	–	2008–09
Presubmission feedback events	3	–	–	–	2010
Chapter feedback sessions	8	2	4	2	2009–13

To analyze the data from this first phase of work, we transcribed the interviews and coded the transcriptions and the accompanying hard-copy documents for common patterns that revealed guiding principles for the model across the two campuses. We sorted coded material to note patterns and relationships; identify confirming and/or disconfirming evidence during subsequent data collection; and gradually elaborate a set of generalizations that were consistent with the patterns discerned from the data. We wrote analysis memos around identified themes. We then drafted two preliminary instructional chapters about reading and mathematics practices in classrooms, as well as five other chapters linking organizational supports to everyday instruction in leadership, parent engagement, teacher training, extended-day programming, and academic and social supports. We conducted feedback meetings where different groups of authors and practitioners met together to critically examine preliminary drafts and to provide feedback about how the underlying principles of the model were described.

Phase 2. During the second phase of data collection, we conducted ten focus groups organized around specific topics—including reading, mathematics, leadership, parent engagement, and academic and social supports—to further specify the components of the model and work toward a coherent version of the underlying guiding principles of each component of the model. We also conducted eleven field visits to confirm our understanding of the different underlying principles and seek examples of practices at the school, so that our readers could begin to envision how the campuses were configured.

During this second analysis period, we transcribed the audio recordings of the focus-group meetings and the field notes, coded the data for patterns, and revised all chapters in the book accordingly. We also reached out to past faculty and practitioners who had designed the foundational work for the UCCS campuses, as well as current faculty, researchers, and practitioners who were developing new iterations of the model. Our participants included people from the Urban Education Institute, the Center for Elementary Mathematics and Science Education, and the Committee on Education at the University of Chicago. We asked participants to provide feedback regarding our findings.

Phase 3. As the UCCS campuses are uniquely embedded in the university community, we also completed a third phase of work, reaching out to university stakeholders to clarify the model, check the identified guiding principles, and confirm our developing understanding of the model. To accomplish this third phase of work, we conducted two three-day workshops, with forty-five participants who participated in eleven different moderated sessions, focused around each component of the model. In the sessions, we used our preliminary analysis and written drafts of the model as a baseline for discussions between teachers, literacy coaches, school leaders, clinical and research faculty, donors, community stakeholders, and all authors working on the book. We also presented the work at the University of Chicago Workshop on Education to the broader university community, including undergraduate students, graduate students, clinical and research faculty across disciplines, and researchers and practitioners engaged in the larger Chicago community.

In addition to our analytical goals, these different workshop sessions also served collegial aims to share findings and bring together school practitioners and university faculty, students, and community members who were engaged in educational research. We sought to forge ties between the practitioners at the charter campuses and the university community in order to inform researchers about everyday conditions in schools and to give practitioners feedback about their emerging model of instruction. We analyzed audio recordings of meeting notes through a process that included transcribing selected sections of audio recordings of meeting notes, affixing codes to transcripts, and gradually elaborating a set of generalizations that were consistent with the patterns discerned from the data.

In tandem with all three phases of qualitative data collection, we also conducted a comprehensive literature review of each component of the model, linking theory with practice to describe how the organization of schools shapes outcomes for student learning. Because of our iterative feedback activities with practitioners and researchers throughout all three phases of the study, we were able to repeat the cycle of analysis several times, with different types of stakeholders, to ensure that we captured the model components and to link our findings with broader research concerns in the literature. Our various engagements promoted deliberation about the state of current knowledge, articulated key unanswered empirical questions, and, over time, reduced uncertainty about the key issues and important elements of the UCCS model we describe in this book.

Chapter 2

1. Excerpt from President Lyndon B. Johnson's commencement speech at the University of Michigan, May 22, 1964.
2. See Gamoran and Loveless 2003.
3. Reardon 2011.
4. See Neal 2006. One explanation emphasizes continued discrimination in the labor

market. Neal does not deny the existence of discrimination in the labor market, but he shows that the market provides strong incentives to obtain degrees—and these incentives are even stronger for minority youth than for white youth. Hernstein and Murray (1994) argue that once civil rights laws eliminated legal barriers to educational access, the remaining gaps between racial and ethnic groups then reflected real differences in intellectual ability and that these differences are inherited. Three kinds of evidence refute this argument. First, as Dickens and Flynn (2006) show, black-white gaps in IQ test scores have substantially diminished over time, "faster than genes can travel." Second, studies show that black-white gaps in IQ are small to negligible when black children raised by white parents are compared with white children raised by white parents (Nisbett 1998). This finding gives interesting new support to the claim that IQ tests measure cultural capital rather than some kind of culture-free, innate intelligence. Third, the passage of civil rights laws did not eliminate barriers to equal opportunity. A large body of social science evidence refutes this assumption (see Loury 2002).

5. Wilson 1987.

6. See, for example, Hart and Risley 1995 and Huttenlocher, Haight, et al. 1991. It is likely that unequal schooling has contributed significantly to inequality in outcomes. Highly educated parents transmit their own educational advantage to their children by providing effective instruction at home. Those children then pass down to their own children similar benefits of home instruction. Such an intergenerational accumulation of inequality would be most pronounced when school quality and home-instruction quality are positively correlated, as all research suggests they are. However, for any given generation, variation in cognitive skills is explained far more by variation in home environments than by variation in schooling environments.

7. For example, we see that the impact of attending school is significantly greater on mathematical knowledge than on reading literacy, simply because most children learn less about math at home than they do about language and reading. See Cooper et al. 1996; Bryk and Raudenbush 1988; Alexander, Entwisle, and Olson 2001.

8. See Heath 1983; Huttenlocher, Haight, et al. 1991; Peterson and McCabe 1992; Hart and Risley 1995; Huttenlocher, Vasilyeva, et al. 2002; Rowe et al. 2009.

9. McLoyd 1998.

10. Klibanoff et al. 2006; Levine, Suriyakham, et al. 2010.

11. Ramani and Siegler 2008; Levine et al. 2012; Tracy 1987.

12. Coleman et al. 1966.

13. See Carneiro and Heckman 2003.

14. McCarton et al. 1997; Schweinhart, Barnes, and Weikart 1993.

15. Dreeben and Barr 1988; Nomi and Raudenbush (2017).

16. A similar argument can be made with respect to other ethnic achievement gaps, such as the gap between Hispanics and whites.

17. Morrison 2000; Morrison and Connor 2002.

18. Oreopoulous (2006) provides parallel evidence about the powerful impact of compulsory schooling during adolescence.

19. See review by Carneiro and Heckman 2003.

20. Schweinhart, Barnes, and Weikart 1993.

21. See review by Carneiro and Heckman (2003).
22. Raudenbush and Eschmann 2015.
23. Camilli et al. 2010.
24. Gibbs 2010.
25. Raudenbush and Eschmann 2015.
26. See review by Krueger (2003).
27. Entwisle and Alexander 1992; Downey, von Hippel, and Broh 2004; Alexander, Entwisle, and Olson 2001, 2007a, 2007b; see review by Raudenbush and Eschmann (2015).
28. Alexander, Entwisle, and Olson 2007a.
29. Jacob and Lefgren 2004; Allington et al. 2010.
30. See review by Cohen, Raudenbush, and Ball (2003).
31. Chetty, Friedman, Hilger, et al. 2011; Nye, Konstantopoulos, and Hedges 2004.
32. Nye, Konstantopoulos, and Hedges 2004.
33. Gordon, Kane, and Staiger 2006.
34. Kane et al. 2013.
35. Chetty, Friedman, and Rockoff 2014; Chetty, Friedman, Hilger, et al. 2011.
36. See Hong and Hong 2009.
37. Finn and Achilles 1990; Krueger and Whitmore 2001.
38. Krueger and Whitmore 2001.
39. For a discussion, see Cohen, Raudenbush, and Ball 2003.
40. Stecher et al. 2001.
41. See Cohen, Raudenbush, and Ball 2003 for a detailed discussion.
42. Clotfelter, Ladd, and Vigdor 2005.
43. Goldhaber and Brewer 1997; Hill, Rowan, and Ball 2005.
44. Raudenbush, Fotiu, and Cheong 1998.
45. Stigler 1990.
46. Ma 1999.
47. National Reading Panel 2000.
48. Chall 1983a, 1983b.
49. See Morrison 2000 and discussion in "Age-Cutoff Studies," above.
50. National Research Council 2004.
51. Ma 1999.
52. Le Corre and Carey 2007; Le Corre, Van de Walle, et al. 2006; Mix 2008; Wynn 1990, 1992.
53. Parsons 1959; Heckman and Krueger 2003; Dreeben 1971.
54. Raudenbush and Kasim 1998.

Chapter 3

1. See "A Proposal to Establish a Center for School Improvement: A Collaboration between the Department of Education, University of Chicago, Department of Research and Evaluation, Chicago Public Schools, and National College of Education," June 14, 1989, provided to the authors by Sharon Greenberg and Anthony S. Bryk.
2. The historical discussion in this chapter draws on both formal, in-depth interviews and informal conversations with the leaders and founders of this early work, as well

as unpublished documents such as grant proposals, internal project memos, and annual reports to external funders.

3. CSI chose to work in the "bottom quartile" of CPS schools, in which typically less than 25 percent of students were achieving at national norms. The majority of students in these schools were low-income African American children living in racially isolated neighborhoods. The schools were racially segregated and staffed by the system's least well-prepared teachers. See Hess 1995, 17–19.

4. CSI was unique among school reform organizations at that time for its focus on improving classroom instruction—especially on enhancing teachers' pedagogical skill and supporting principals to lead instructional improvement in their buildings. Chicago was then in the midst of a dramatic local school reform movement, set in motion by the Illinois state legislature in 1988 via the Chicago School Reform Act. The latter mandated the creation of local school councils to empower parents and community members with dramatically increased decision-making authority over their neighborhood schools (e.g., the power to hire and fire school principals), while greatly reducing the authority of the district's central administration. Most school reform organizations at the time were focused almost exclusively on issues of school governance, management, and control (e.g., training parents to serve in newly empowered roles and helping principals undertake a host of new responsibilities that were no longer the purview of the central office). See Bryk, Sebring, Kerbow, et al. 1998; Hess 1991.

5. The modern school reform movement has its origins in the early 1980s, with the publication of an alarming report, "A Nation at Risk," which famously warned of a "rising tide of mediocrity" in American schooling that threatened the nation's prosperity and security (see National Commission on Excellence in Education 1983). This spawned two successive reform efforts, frequently referred to as the first and second waves of US school reform. The first wave, in the early 1980s, involved a largely top-down effort by state legislatures to raise standards for teachers and students to assure excellence in student performance. Beginning in the late 1980s and early 1990s, a second, more bottom-up wave of reform followed, this time focused on "restructuring" schools at the building level. This second wave, led by educators and professional organizations rather than state legislatures, focused on the professional empowerment of teachers and emphasized school-by-school structural change. For example, its proponents called for the adoption of school-based management, especially giving teachers a stronger voice in decision-making and planning at the school-building level and encouraging teachers to collaborate to develop school improvement plans in which teachers felt invested and about which they had a sense of ownership. It also encouraged experimentation with alternate forms of school organization to improve teaching and learning (such as block scheduling and team-teaching) and with new roles for teachers (such as mentor and lead teacher roles). During this same time, other voices argued that the main impediment to quality schooling in the United States was an excess of bureaucracy and centralized control that discouraged innovation and quality. For example, Chubb and Moe (1990) argued for dramatically overhauling the public school funding and governance system and replacing it with a market-driven funding approach that would give parents greater choice over the schools their children attend and schools greater autonomy over decisions at the

building level. Neither wave of reform resulted in large-scale improvements in teaching and learning.

6. The initiative was entitled "Urban School Development: Literacy as a Lever for Change"; see Bryk, Rollow, and Pinnell 1996. The initiative drew upon Marie Clay's work to develop the Reading Recovery intervention for struggling readers (1991; for later elaborations of Clay's ideas, see 2001, 2005a, 2005b). It also drew heavily on the work of Fountas and Pinnell, with whom Bryk and colleagues were collaborating and exchanging ideas (Fountas and Pinnell 1996; see also 2001, 2009, 2010) and the principles of the Literacy Collaborative model for improving reading and writing instruction; see also Pinnell et al. 1995. A unique contribution of CSI's initiative was to take the latter scholars' ideas and adapt them for application in urban schools, where they had not previously been implemented.

7. The literacy coordinator was responsible for helping teachers develop the skills required to enact the literacy instruction we have described, including the conceptual understanding of the reading process this approach to literacy instruction requires. The coordinator's role included introducing and modeling new techniques for instruction and assessment, designing professional development for groups of teachers, and providing coaching and mentoring for teachers on an individual basis.

8. The assessment, which we discuss in detail in ch. 5, measures students' progress from the beginning of reading skill acquisition—including both phonics-related skills and the ability to read for meaning—until they gain basic proficiency in reading comprehension, reflecting expectations for students' skill development from kindergarten to the end of grade 3.

9. CSI leaders developed the design principles for AS3 in partnership with staff members Barbara Williams and Bobby Durrah. Williams codeveloped and led CSI's parent and community engagement and its social support efforts in network schools; she later became codirector of the NKO campus, with Marvin Hoffman. After the establishment of NKO, Bryk collaborated with Tamara Gathright Fritz and Denise Nacu to develop a web-based tool, the Clinical Case Management System, that would make AS3 referrals more evidence based—a need Gathright Fritz had identified at NKO.

10. CPS administrators created this policy for select schools in the 1970s as a response to concerns about safety in neighborhoods suffering from violence, drug, and gang activity, but the Chicago Teachers Union (CTU) lobbied to give all schools the opportunity to adopt the policy. While it was intended to enhance campus safety, the policy had unintended negative consequences for schools because it severely constrained time for teacher professional development.

11. For many years, CPS had the shortest school day and year in the nation. However, after a major battle with the CTU in 2012, CPS and the CTU signed a new contract extending the school day and eliminating closed campuses. Whereas the typical elementary school day was previously approximately five hours and forty-five minutes long (usually from 9 a.m. to 2:45 p.m.) due to the pervasiveness of closed-campus policies, the 2012 contract stipulated that elementary students receive a seven-hour school day and that teachers work, on average, seven hours and forty minutes per day. It also established that all Chicago elementary schools would have recess and all teachers a duty-free lunch period.

12. See Louis, Kruse, and Bryk 1995. The idea that teaching should be a profession rather

than a craft was gaining ground in the research and reform literature at this time as part of a broader national conversation about the need to improve teaching and teacher education. This conversation included increasing calls for the "professionalization" of teaching, beginning in the late 1980s. (For example, see the 1986 report by the Carnegie Forum on Education and the Economy and its Task Force on Teaching as a Profession, "A Nation Prepared: Teachers for the 21st Century." "Tomorrow's Teachers," a report published the same year by the Holmes Group—a consortium of deans of prominent schools of education—addressed similar themes.) There was also growing interest at this time in the idea of teacher "professional community," an idea Bryk was helping to develop; see Louis, Kruse, and Bryk 1995. Bryk, Greenberg, and Spurlark were also influenced by their observations of highly effective urban school districts such as New York City's District 2 under the leadership of Anthony Alvarado; see Elmore and Burney 1997. Finally, they were influenced by the Reading Recovery and Literacy Collaborative models, in which the enactment of a shared, public practice and reflective dialogue on its effectiveness played a vital role in the development of teacher expertise.

13. Lortie 1975 provides the classic account of these occupational norms and their impact on the teaching profession. For related discussions, see Bidwell 1965; Rosenholtz 1989; Little 1990; Stoll and Seashore 2007. These analyses illuminate some of the persistent cultural obstacles to meaningful change in the organization of teachers' work. There is a related literature on the need to "reculture" schools and the cultural obstacles to reform in urban schools, including how the culture of teaching marginalizes those who attempt to reform or lead improvement in their schools; see Datnow 1998; Fullan 1999; Hargreaves 1994; Muncey and McQuillan 1996; Payne 2008; Sarason 1996. Our analysis in this section also draws on the conceptual framework for the Information Infrastructure System project, led by Anthony S. Bryk and Louis Gomez, which aimed to improve urban school practice via new tools and social practices that directly challenged these traditional norms; see Bryk, Gomez, et al. 2005.

14. For a discussion of the architectural origins of this structure, see Tyack 1974, 44–45.

15. Recent policy efforts have attempted to bring questions of effectiveness into the practice of teacher evaluation, but these have been extremely contentious. Notable among these is President Obama's Race to the Top initiative, which rewarded states for tying teacher evaluation to evidence of student learning. This issue was a central point of debate in a systemwide teachers' strike in the Chicago Public Schools in 2012.

16. This conventional scenario has been slowly changing over the past twenty-five years under the weight of the standards and accountability movement, which has called into question the traditional "loosely coupled" organization of elementary schools and increased pressure on elementary school principals to improve instruction in their buildings. For a discussion of this transformation, see Elmore 2002; Mehta 2013. However, these changes have been controversial and slow to take root, partly because of the way in which they challenge the traditional occupational norms of teaching; for example, see Hubbard, Mehan, and Stein 2006. The recent adoption by most states of Common Core State Standards represents a further step in the direction of creating a more tightly coupled educational system. For a discussion of this change in relation to the Common Core State Standards as well as the backlash against it, see Porter et al. 2012; Rothman 2011.

17. See Rollow and Bryk 1995.

18. See Moultrie 1992; Rollow and Bryk 1995; Bryk, Sebring, Kerbow, et al. 1998, 93–148; Comer 1980, 1992; Useem et al. 1997. Rollow (1998, 34) suggests that the tendency for urban schools to be dominated by authoritarian principals may be a response to the chaotic and unstable conditions in many inner-city school communities. A principal is regarded as successful in such contexts if he or she can bring a sense of safety and order to a school, regardless of the impact (or nonimpact) on instruction.

19. For historical discussions of the expectations on principals and how they have changed over time, see Cuban 1988; Hallinger 1992.

20. See Rollow and Bryk 1995.

21. Rollow 1998; Anyon 1995; Lipman 1998, 2002, 2004; Payne 2008.

22. For example, see Datnow, Hubbard, and Mehan 2002; Hargreaves 1994; Hubbard, Mehan, and Stein 2006; Miller 1998; Payne 2008; Louis 2007.

Chapter 4

1. See "Proposal for Center for School Improvement/North Kenwood Charter School," submitted to the Chicago School Reform Board of Trustees in October 1997, provided to the authors by Sharon Greenberg and Anthony S. Bryk.

2. Bryk left the university in 2004 for a position at Stanford. The university initially established UEI in 2005 as the Urban Education Initiative, which included CSI, but renamed it the Center for Urban School Improvement, or USI. In 2008, the university changed UEI's name to the Urban Education Institute and created a more centralized administrative structure for this work, appointing Knowles as the Lewis-Sebring Director of UEI. The new institute included the Consortium on Chicago School Research (later renamed the University of Chicago Consortium on School Research), the Urban Teacher Education Program, core functions of USI, and the University of Chicago Charter School.

3. For several years after the establishment of UCCS, until roughly 2010, UEI maintained a network of CPS schools, in which staff from the charter school participated. Via this network, UCCS staff received coaching and other professional development support to help them learn and enact the ideas about instruction, school organization, and broader support for student learning that we outline in this chapter.

4. Our discussion in this chapter draws on two main sources of evidence: (1) interviews conducted in 2001 with Bryk, Spurlark, Greenberg, and colleagues aimed at clarifying the big ideas animating their work in its founding phase; and (2) a series of interviews, focus groups, and observations at the two campuses from 2008 to 2012, focused on understanding how the second wave of school and UEI leaders (especially Knowles, Woodard-Iliev, and subsequent campus directors) developed, refined, and systematically implemented these ideas at the two campuses. There is a gap in our qualitative data of about seven years (2001–2008), during which efforts to refine and develop the model continued, but about which we have less direct evidence. However, we discovered a high degree of alignment between the ideas the founders were pursuing in the early stages of this work and the words and actions of the practitioners we observed and spoke with at the two campuses from 2008 to 2012. This suggests that the period for which we lack direct qualitative data (2001–2008) was primarily devoted to refining and further developing these early ideas. This process

entailed clarifying the roles, practices, structures, and routines—including support from UEI—required to enact these ideas.

5. For example, the Donoghue campus had a director of family and community engagement from its inception in 2005, whereas this role was not established at NKO until a few years later.

6. Not all CPS charter schools have attendance zones, which are designated at the discretion of the Board of Education, and the idea is somewhat controversial. The NKO campus did not have an attendance zone when the school was first established. However, all four of the current UCCS campuses now have such zones, which is unusual for charter schools in both Chicago and the nation.

7. Most CPS elementary schools at this time served students in pre-K through grade 8.

8. CPS has moved in recent years to make these conditions more widely available. For example, in 2004, CPS created two new categories of schools ("performance" and "contract") that, like charter schools, have increased flexibility and autonomy over critical issues such as budgeting and staffing.

9. When hiring teachers, UCCS leaders sought individuals with some prior experience and philosophical agreement with the instructional systems at the two campuses, or with similar instructional approaches. They also sought teachers eager to participate in a school model where all members enact a common practice. Of additional importance was hiring teachers interested in taking on leadership roles that might involve supporting the professional development of both their own colleagues and teachers visiting from other CPS schools.

10. In addition to drawing on the work of Gay Su Pinnell, Irene Fountas, and Marie Clay discussed in ch. 3, Bryk and colleagues were also influenced by research on "authentic achievement" by researchers at the Center on Organization and Restructuring of Schools (CORS) at the University of Wisconsin–Madison, with whom Bryk had collaborated to investigate a series of studies of "restructuring" schools in the early 1990s. Extrapolating from an analysis of criteria for significant adult accomplishments, CORS researchers defined authentic student achievement as work involving the "construction of knowledge, through disciplined inquiry, to produce discourse, products, and performances that have meaning beyond success in school" (Newmann and Wehlage 1995, 11). For additional analysis of student work in reference to these standards, see Bryk, Nagaoka, and Newmann 2000. See also Cohen, McLaughlin, and Talbert (1993), whose ideas also influenced the school's founders.

11. Research in Chicago elementary schools emerging around the time of NKO's founding validated this critique of the relative merits of interactive versus didactic instruction (Smith, Lee, and Newmann 2001). Based on test scores from more than one hundred thousand students in grades 2 through 8, and surveys from more than five thousand teachers in 384 Chicago elementary schools, this research demonstrated that the use of interactive (rather than didactic) teaching methods was associated with more learning in both reading and mathematics for students in CPS.

12. Lesnick, Hart, and Spielbeger (2011) found that students at the Donoghue campus in the 2009/10 school year participated in more than one hundred of these different programmatic combinations. The goal of both campuses was to provide extended programming for 100 percent of students and their families; however, the resources to fully support this work were not fully in place. During the time period when we

collected data for this project, more than 85 percent of students at Donoghue participated in programming that extended learning time, while 50 percent of NKO students participated in extended programming. School directors and teachers worked closely with parents to provide financial support to families of students who required extra academic or social supports during extended-day programming. At Donoghue, parents contributed on a sliding scale to the cost of the extended-day program. Fundraising efforts were directed toward resolving the funding constraints that restricted the full implementation of extended-day programming.

13. Weick 1976; Meyer and Rowan 1977.

14. For examinations of the distinctions between internal and external accountability and the relationships between them, see Newmann, King, and Rigdon 1997; Elmore 2002, 2004, 2005b.

15. The base funding for this came from the Community Schools Initiative of CPS, initially funded by a three-year grant from the Illinois State Board of Education using a combination of private and federal funds, with matching contributions from CPS enabled by gifts from corporate donors. CPS's Renaissance 2010 initiative, under which Donoghue was initially established, gave all new schools such community school funding. In addition, UEI also received a grant from Chase Bank to more fully fund "early-bird," extended-day, and summer school programming at Donoghue. The latter campus served a somewhat more disadvantaged population of students than NKO, making the extension of instructional time—and the community school mission more generally—especially vital. See "A Community School for Chicago's Mid-South Side Sponsored by the University of Chicago," an October 2004 proposal to the Chase Foundation, provided to the authors by Timothy Knowles.

16. The FCE director was also responsible for outward-facing activities such as community outreach and external partnerships. However, we limit our discussion to the FCE director's work inside the school and how this supported teachers, parents, and other school staff to achieve ambitious learning goals for students.

17. As discussed in a previous note, the Donoghue campus began with additional grant funding to support its mission as a community school, which the school's designers used to more fully fund innovative features such as the parent resource center.

Chapter 5

1. See Clark and Foster 2005; Raz and Bryant 1990; White 1982; Wells 1985; Velting and Whitehurst 1997.

2. Bowey 1995; C. E. Snow, Burns, and Griffin 1998; Borman and Hewes 2002; Borman, Hewes, et al. 2003; Slavin and Madden 2006; Parrila, Kirby, and McQuarrie 2004.

3. Rayner et al. 2001.

4. National Reading Panel 2000. Importantly, research studies with reasonably valid causal inferences supported each key approach.

5. See Chall 1983b.

6. See Chall 1983a and 1983b for further discussion of the stages of reading development.

7. Barbarin et al. 2006; Hart and Risley 1995; Chall 1983a, 1983b.

8. See C. E. Snow 2010. "Academic English" is defined here as the language of instruction in school and the language of academic discourse. See Heath 1993 and Laureau 1989, 2003 for differences in language learning at home across social class and race.

9. Chall 1983a, 1983b.

10. Huttenlocher et al. 1991; Hoff-Ginsberg 1991; Hart and Risley 1995; Haden, Haine, and Fivush 1997; Weizman and Snow 2001; Goldberg 1989; Azevedo 2007.

11. Some might argue that it is not just exposure to academic English but also other kinds of cultural advantages that middle-class parents provide for their children. For example, childrearing practices such as "concerted cultivation" (Lareau 2003) include regular exposure to cultural resources such as museums, participation in enriched learning environments outside of schooling, and continual training for children in how to intervene on their own behalf in institutional settings. A central component to these cultural advantages is that they also encourage communication between children and their parents (ibid.), increasing overall exposure to academic English.

12. Connor, Piasta, et al. 2009; National Reading Panel 2000; Rayner et al. 2001.

13. See Morrison 2000; Morrision and Connor 2002.

14. See C. E. Snow, Burns, and Griffin 1998; Sulzby and Teale 1987; Taylor and Strickland 1986; Teale and Sulzby 1987.

15. Parents who practice concerted cultivation actively synchronize their child's schooling experiences with home advantages (Lareau 2003). Middle-class parents in Lareau's studies interacted with teachers and other middle-class parents in order obtain detailed information about their child's schooling experiences, so as to better customize their child's learning experiences at home (Lareau 1989, 2003; Lareau and Shumar 1996). More-advantaged students also tend to maintain their school-year gains, especially in literacy, through the summer months, while more-disadvantaged students tend to lose ground in both literacy and math. See review by Heckman and Krueger (2003).

16. See Useem 1992; Lareau 1989, 2003; McGhee Hassrick and Schneider 2009; McGhee Hassrick 2007; Horvat, Weininger, and Lareau 2003; Cucchiara and Horvat 2009.

17. Chall 1983a, 1983b; Ogbu 1999; C. E. Snow, Burns, and Griffin 1998; Ehri 1997; Wilson and Rupley 1997.

18. The balanced literacy approach is founded on ideas developed in New Zealand (New Zealand Ministry of Education 1996); in the Early Literacy project at the Ohio State University (Fountas and Pinnell 1996); and in the work of Reading Recovery, an intensive early intervention program for struggling readers (Clay 1987; Pinnell 1989).

19. The essential idea is to provide a *balance* of "reading to, with, and by" children, and to vary the proportion of these activities over time as each child's skills develop. *Reading to, with, and by Children* is a classic book by New Zealand educator Margaret E. Mooney (1990), a pioneer of the balanced literacy approach.

20. Gay 2000; Ladson-Billings 1994; C. Lee 2007; Moll et al. 1992; Perry 2003.

21. Tatum 1997.

22. Barr and Dreeben (1991); Gamoran, Nystrand, et al. (1995); Hallinan and Sorensen (1983); and Sorensen and Hallinan (1986) describe the rationale and uses of within-class ability grouping. Critics reason that within-class grouping reduces opportunities for the teacher to interact with each group, reduces opportunities for peer interactions across ability levels, and may promote unequal learning opportunities for different groups (Macintyre and Ireson 2002; Oakes, Gamoran, and Page 1992; Tach and Farkas 2006). Hong and Hong (2009), using national survey data and sophis-

ticated causal inference methods, find that homogeneous grouping helps lower-skill students when combined with adequate instructional time but is harmful when instructional time is limited.

23. See Fountas and Pinnell 1996, 2001, 2009, 2010.

24. Connor, Morrison, et al. 2007.

25. See Kerbow and Bryk 2005; Kerbow, Gywnne, and Jacob 1999. Currently more than seventy-five schools across the nation have adopted this system of assessment to guide their instruction. The components of the assessment delineate how each task in the assessment system is organized by STEP level. Many of these tasks are similar to other early literacy assessments contained in DIBELS, the Early Reading Screening Inventory (ERSI), the Developmental Reading Assessment (DRA), and the Texas Primary Reading Inventory (TPRI). However, the explicit combination of these tasks in developmental sequence is unique to the STEP assessment and is organized on both a theoretical and an empirical basis.

26. Figure 5.2 is from Bryk and Kerbow 2006.

27. All the lower-grade students in the school received literacy instruction during the same three-hour block of time—from 8:30 to 11:30 a.m.—except for Teyona's students, who received their literacy instruction in the afternoon so that she could coach other teachers during the literacy block. When Teyona was observing or meeting with other teachers during the morning literacy block, an additional teacher was teaching math to her students.

28. Quarterly literacy analysis meetings took place either during the 3–4:30 p.m. time block dedicated for collegial work at the end of the school day or during the regular meeting and planning time that was built into teachers' instructional day, when their students were at lunch or with a specialist such as the art, physical education, or foreign language teacher. During this time, children in the literacy coach's classroom were taught by another full-time teacher who team-taught with the literacy coach.

29. Frazier and Morrison 1998. Clark and Linn (2003) find that decreasing learning time is strongly related to diminishing student knowledge integration around complex concepts.

30. See Alexander, Entwisle, and Olson 2007a, 2007b; Downey, von Hippel, and Broh 2004; Borman and Boulay 2004; Stone, Engel, and Nagaoka 2005; Roderick, Jacob, and Bryk 2002.

31. C. E. Snow, Burns, and Griffin 1998; Pearson and Fielding 1991; Pressley 1998; National Reading Panel 2000; Pinnell et al. 1995.

32. Pearson and Fielding 1991; Pressley 1998; National Reading Panel 2000; Pinnell et al. 1995; C. E. Snow, Burns, and Griffin 1998.

33. Clay 1991; D. A. Snow 2001; Liberman and Shankweiler 1985; Vellutino and Scanlon 1987; Lundberg, Frost, and Petersen 1988.

34. Ravitch 2001; Rayner et al. 2001.

35. Several recent interventions have extended the school day, week, and year with some success (Merseth 2009). Several of these ambitious programs have resulted in gains in reading test scores, especially for disadvantaged students (Gettinger 1984; Henig 2008; Woodworth et al. 2008; Cooper et al. 1996; Alexander, Entwisle, and Olson 2001; Clark and Linn 2003; Farmer-Hinton 2002). However, the extra demand that extended work hours place on teachers might cause teachers to burn out. While new work arrangements are currently being implemented in some schools, these work arrangements require contracts that demand a longer work day, a longer work week, and a longer work year (Henig 2008; Woodworth et al. 2008; Kolbe, Partridge, and O'Reilly 2012). But further evidence suggests that simply extending instructional time is not sufficient in and of itself (Aronson, Zimmerman, and Carlos 1999; Haslem, Pringle, and Adelman 1996; Karweit 1984). While extending time is controversial, over the past five years, it has rapidly become a central component for many new urban school reforms. Effective schools also share other characteristics, including strong leadership; high expectations of student achievement; and safe and orderly classroom and school management (Pressley et al. 2004; Wharton-McDonald, Pressley, and Hampston 1998). Similarly, recent evidence about "no excuses" charter schools further supports the importance of extended instructional time, a school culture of high expectations that includes a relentless focus on student outcomes and aligned external and internal accountability structures and systems (Angrist, Dynarski, et al. 2010; Merseth 2009). Literacy interventions that have included these reforms (such as Success for All, Literacy First, and Literacy Collaborative) and charter schools that implemented schoolwide reforms (such as KIPP) did improve certain literacy skills such as word reading and phonological awareness. However, even with school-level changes and additional literacy instruction, schools still had difficulties raising the vocabulary and reading comprehension skills of all students (Tivnan and Hemphill 2005; Angrist, Dynarski, et al. 2010).

36. Boulay et al. 2010. Research on the effectiveness of after-school programs is inconclusive. Most conventionally organized schools that add more learning time do not show student gains. However, according to the Expanded Learning Time Initiative (http://www.mass2020.org/elt-initiative), five particular activities did increase student learning during extended instructional time: focusing on a few key goals; continuously assessing student progress; allotting time for teachers to collaborate; and allotting time for teachers to provide high-quality enrichment programs that build academic and social and emotional skills show evidence of boosting student achievement. While these findings indicate that simply extending time is not sufficient, they do suggest that extended instructional time that is aligned with core academic goals and organized around each child's individual instructional needs can improve academic progress. Extending the literacy period to include diagnostic instruction emerges as a critical component in this process. Reading interventions that do not include this component have less long-term impact. For example, students participating in an extended ninety-minute literacy block of direct literacy instruction in the Success for All intervention experienced reading gains (Borman and Hewes 2002; Borman, Hewes, et al. 2003; Slavin and Madden 2006). However, some students still lagged behind in comprehension when they reached third grade (Slavin and Madden 2006), suggesting that more is required than an extended class period to accelerate the rate of literacy learning. While programs such as Success for All do require more literacy instruction time, they also require that teachers use a script to systematize instruction, which provides a common system of instruction but not the diagnostic flexibility needed to address variability in student learning. The delivery of diagnostic instructional regimes is a central component to the University of Chicago Charter School model.

37. For other recent urban schooling reform efforts, see Borman and Hewes 2002; Borman, Hewes, et al. 2003; Slavin and Madden 2006; Henig 2008; and Woodworth et al. 2008.

Chapter 6

1. See Park 2013.
2. Data from figure 6.1 is based on findings from Programme for International Student Assessment 2012.
3. See Snyder and Dillow 2011.
4. Hanushek, Peterson, and Woessmann 2013; A. Duncan 2013.
5. Loveless 2013, 2014.
6. Park 2013.
7. Rivera-Batiz 1992; Murnane and Levy 1996; Levy and Murnane 2004. As low-skill manufacturing jobs increasingly move to developing nations, developed nations depend more strongly on high levels of human capital to compete in sectors of the economy that generate, organize, and use knowledge and data (de la Fuente and Ciccone 2003). Especially important are skills in math, science, and engineering. In the recent past, the United States has relied heavily on importing mathematically skilled workers from countries with less-productive economies, but as these economies develop and more countries—particularly China and India—invest in their tertiary education systems, competition will grow for such international students.
8. Moreover, students in urban schools make up the overwhelming majority of high school dropouts in the United States. While large and medium-size cities have only 20 percent of high schools enrolling more than three hundred students, these cities share 60 percent of high schools with the nation's lowest graduation rates (Balfanz, Legters, and Jordan 2004). Race matters: since the early 1990s, the National Assessment of Educational Progress (NAEP) has documented enormous gaps between the mathematics achievement of white and black students (Rampey, Dion, and Donahue 2009; Vanneman et al. 2009).
9. Sarnecka and Lee 2009.
10. National Research Council 2009.
11. V. E. Lee and Burkam 2002; Levine, Suriyakham, et al. 2010.
12. Gamoran and Mare 1989; Nomi and Allensworth 2008.
13. Adelman 1995; Horn and Kojaku 2001; Allensworth et al. 2010a.
14. Levine, Suriyakham, et al. 2010; Gunderson, Ramirez, Levine, et al. 2012; Gunderson, Ramirez, Beilock, et al. 2013. The attitudes adults have toward math can shape their children's attitudes as well: children of parents who are anxious about math are more likely to develop their own anxieties (Maloney et al. 2015).
15. For example, Jordan, Huttenlocher, and Levine (1992) find that young children from families with more limited economic resources have lower levels of mathematics achievement than their more affluent peers. Other researchers who have found similar results include Klibanoff et al. (2006); V. E. Lee and Burkam (2002); and Saxe, Guberman, and Gearhart (1987).
16. Klibanoff et al. 2006.
17. See G. J. Duncan, Dowsett, et al. 2007. Examples include ordinality, comparing the size of varied sets, being able to name and compare shapes, and conceiving how an object would look if rotated.
18. Fortunately, a broad consensus has been emerging about school mathematics—a consensus that is reflected in documents such as the "Curriculum and Evaluation Stan-

dards for School Mathematics" from the National Council of Teachers of Mathematics (1989), which was endorsed by every major organization in both mathematics and mathematics education, and the National Research Council's *Adding It Up: Helping Children Learn Mathematics* (Kilpatrick, Swafford, and Findell 2001). These documents call for balancing skills and meanings; broadening the elementary school curriculum to include not only arithmetic, but also geometry, algebra, data analysis, and probability; increasing attention to problem-solving and applications; updating the curriculum, especially in computation, to take account of advances in technology; balancing group and individual work; and increasing discussion in mathematics classes.

19. For example, Fryer and Levitt (2006) found that African American children enter kindergarten behind white children and that the gap increases by roughly 0.1 standard deviation per grade through third grade. They note, "If this trend were to continue, by the tenth grade, Blacks would be one standard deviation behind Whites—a number consistent with prior research" (250). See also Jones, Burton, and Davenport 1982; Phillips, Crouse, and Ralph, 1998; Phillips 2000.

20. Bodovski and Farkas 2007; Mix, Huttenlocher, and Levine 2002; Lubienski 2002; Flores 2007. Flores explains that "African-American and Latino students are less likely than White students to have teachers who emphasize high-quality mathematics instruction and appropriate use of resources" (2007, 32). Flores also found that African American and Latino students were more likely to have less-qualified, less-experienced teachers, with lower expectations for their performance. In addition to these differences in teachers, they were also less likely to receive equitable per-student funding (Flores 2007).

21. Hill, Rowan, and Ball 2005; Hill, Ball, and Schilling 2008.

22. Wu 2011; Ball 1990; Ball, Hill, and Bass 2005; Ball, Thames, and Phelps 2008.

23. See Ball 2000; Ma 1999.

24. Beilock 2010.

25. Lampert et al. 2010.

26. Debates about these issues have come to be known as the math wars. Unfortunately, the math wars' polarizing rhetoric has obscured many areas of substantial agreement. Both sides, for example, agree that students need both skills and meanings—and that one doesn't come first. Both sides agree that students must memorize their basic facts and that problem-solving is important. But the arguments continue and are often particularly strident with respect to students in urban schools.

27. Colvin 1993; Schoenfeld 2004; Kuhn and Dempsey 2011.

28. Nomi and Allensworth 2008; Nomi and Allensworth 2010; Allensworth, Takato, et al. 2010b; Raudenbush, Rowan, and Cheong 1993.

29. Nomi and Allensworth 2008; Nomi and Allensworth 2010; Allensworth, Takato, et al. 2010a; Raudenbush, Rowan, and Cheong 1993.

30. Bryk and Treisman 2010.

31. When the UCCS NKO campus first opened in 1998, school leaders adopted a math curriculum different than *Everyday Mathematics* (*EM*). They began using *EM* in the 2000/01 school year. The Donoghue campus used *EM* from the beginning, when they opened their doors in the 2005/06 school year. In the 2007/08 school year, the University of Chicago received a grant to fund CEMSE math support for Donoghue and NKO, as

well as several neighborhood Chicago Public Schools. Debbie Leslie and Sarah Burns from CEMSE began working with NKO and Donoghue teachers in fall 2007 as part of this grant.

32. For example, as we discuss in the previous chapter, the reading model offered teachers a framework and set of guiding principles to organize their instructional decisions (such as criteria for determining appropriate books for the various reading activities that comprise the balanced literacy approach). However, it allowed teachers significant latitude to make choices within that framework over the specific books they might select for each of these activities—which teachers might vary depending on the season, student interest, etc.

33. See Hill, Rowan, and Ball 2005; Hill, Ball, and Schilling 2008.

34. See Hill, Rowan, and Ball 2005; Hill, Ball, and Schilling 2008.

35. For these purposes, the leaders chose the *Everyday Mathematics* curriculum produced by the University of Chicago, as noted previously. This curriculum has been rigorously evaluated with favorable results (Waite 2000). However, we are not asserting that the key ideas behind the UCCS model require the specific choice of *Everyday Mathematics*, as other curricula may be suitable as vehicles for following the five key principles laid out in this chapter.

36. Figure 6.2 is from *Everyday Mathematics*, McGraw-Hall Education.

37. Engel, Claessens, and Finch 2013.

38. See Stigler and Hiebert 2009.

Chapter 7

1. Rowan (1990) argues that different conceptions of teaching imply different approaches to school leadership. Drawing on contingency theory—a class of behavioral and organizational theory that contends there is no single "best" way to design or lead an organization—Rowan argues that an approach to leadership that is effective in one set of conditions or circumstances may not be effective in others. Also see Rowan, Raudenbush, and Cheong 1993.

2. Lortie 1975; Bidwell 1965.

3. Institutional sociologists have argued that this conception of instruction—as highly individual and not amenable to either standardization or reliable external evaluation—has given rise to a common form of school organization they describe as "loose coupling." In loosely coupled school organizations, the work of administrators is only weakly connected to the "technical core" of the organization (the work of teaching), which is itself weak and uncertain. Consequently, administrative activity functions primarily to buffer the technical core from external scrutiny. As Elmore (2000) observes, "Administration in education, then, has come to mean not the management of instruction but the management of the structures and processes around instruction." For classic discussions of schools as loosely coupled organizations, see Weick 1976; see also Meyer and Rowan 1977.

4. The laissez-faire approach to school leadership has a long history, but has fallen out of favor since the rise of the standards and accountability movement, beginning in the late 1980s. The latter have brought demands on principals to create more "tightly coupled" organizations and act not simply as building managers, but also as instructional leaders; see Elmore 2000.

5. See Milner 2013.

6. The leadership model we examine in this chapter bears some similarities to what Rowan (1990) originally called the "commitment" or "organic" strategy of school design, which relies on teachers' expertise and collective problem-solving (rather than top-down controls) to coordinate and manage teachers' work. It requires the expansion of teacher authority and leadership, as well as lateral patterns of communication that facilitate collegial dialogue; collective problem-solving; and the sharing of information, expertise, and professional advice. However, the UCCS model implies a stronger role for the campus director as an instructional leader who both supports teachers to develop their expertise and holds them accountable for advancing student learning.

7. See Miles and Frank 2008.

8. Bryk, Sebring, Allensworth, et al. 2010, 61–64.

9. Ibid., 61.

10. Calls for leaders to take more concerted action to improve classroom instruction have been at the heart of school reform efforts in the United States for roughly three decades. For a discussion of this transformation, see Elmore 2000.

11. See Elmore 2000; Hubbard, Mehan, and Stein 2006.

12. See Bryk, Sebring, Allensworth, et al. 2010, 61–64. Others have called this "transformational" leadership; see Sergiovanni 2000.

13. See Goddard and Miller 2010.

14. This approach is characterized in the research literature as "distributed," "collaborative," or "shared" leadership. For a discussion of these various terms, their diverse meanings in the literature, and the mechanisms by which collaborative or distributed leadership may advance school improvement, see Heck and Hallinger 2010, 4. This approach to leadership activity involves strategic, coordinated action to improve student learning on the part of multiple school professionals—including teachers—and involves both collaborative decision-making among these multiple actors and shared accountability for student learning.

15. As a teacher, Island and the whole NKO staff had received training in the Literacy Collaborative model, a program based on the work of Fountas and Pinnell (1996, 2001, 2009, 2010).

16. As described in ch. 4, Donoghue's parent resource center was staffed by a full-time parent coordinator and offered programming for parents before, during, and after school.

17. For related work, see Miles and Frank 2008.

18. The adaptive assessment in use at NKO was the MAP (Measures of Academic Progress) assessment, developed by the Northwest Evaluation Association. See ch. 6.

19. For further discussion of the distinctions between internal and external school accountability, see Elmore 2004; Newmann, King, and Rigdon 1997.

20. For a detailed case study of how a strong sense of shared mission can encourage conformity in relation to shared professional norms, see Raywid 1995. Bryk referred to the school described in this study, Metro Academy, as a model for the strong professional culture he hoped would develop at NKO.

21. For discussion of the cultural transformation involved in implementing new norms of public practice, see Stein, Hubbard, and Mehan 2004.

22. Teacher evaluations have historically been pro forma (Rowan and Raudenbush 2016).

23. Cuban 1988; see also Fink and Resnick 2001. For analysis of the cultural difficulties that arise from attempting to combine the traditionally separate activities of teacher evaluation and professional learning, see Stein, Hubbard, and Mehan 2004. See also Hubbard, Mehan, and Stein 2006, 136–81, which examines the challenges faced by principals in San Diego in their effort to make the transition from bureaucratic manager to instructional leader, including learning how to evaluate teacher practice and provide meaningful feedback to help teachers improve.

24. Parsons 1959; Heckman and Kautz 2012. Cognitive skills as measured on standardized tests only explain 25 percent of labor market success; see Bowles, Gintis, and Osborne 2000; Raudenbush and Kasim 1998.

25. For example, health or physical problems might affect social and emotional skill development for some children, including such things as asthma, seizure disorders, vision or hearing challenges, attention deficit disorders, or childhood injuries. Other difficulties influence a child's social interactions, such as shyness, stuttering, speech delays, communication difficulties, interaction impairments, or autism. Another category includes emotional challenges, such as anxiety, depression, bipolar disorders, and aggression difficulties. Experiences such as abuse, trauma, domestic violence, and family upheaval can also impede students' readiness to learn. Such difficulties are related to both individual-level factors (such as genetic makeup and temperament) and environmental risk factors at birth and throughout early childhood. See Blair and Scott 2002; Hibel, Faircloth, and Farkas 2008; Tomlinson 1982; Mehan, Herweck, and Meihls 1986.

26. This is a fictitious name.

27. See Lesnick, Hart, and Spielberger 2011, which compares the learning opportunities of Donoghue students in 2009/10 with those available to students in a typical CPS school day (which ran from 9 a.m. to 2:30 p.m.) and school year (which did not include summer school).

28. See review by Raudenbush and Eschmann (2015).

29. Massachusetts 2020 2011; Slavin and Madden 2006.

30. Nationally, at least 77 percent of schools employ academic and social support personnel, representing a sizable investment. See Brener, Martindale, and Weist 2001. Schools generally utilize a team approach to academic and social support provision, including both school-based and district-level personnel. These teams have a unique genesis in schools and from their inception have been tied to special education services under the Individuals with Disabilities Education Act (IDEA, 1997). Chalfant, Pysh, and Moultrie (1979) introduced the concept of school-based social support teams as a means of servicing students prior to the special education referral process. These teams—often known as problem-solving or pre-referral teacher assistance teams—began to increase in public school systems across the country and are now a regular part of the landscape of schools. This increase is due to many reasons. According to Schrag and Henderson (1996), the over-referral of students to special education had become a national problem with the introduction of special education legislation in the late 1960s. The fact that assessment and services were available to students only through special education proved to be costly and time consuming, thus revealing the need for pre-referral support structures. These teams also began to be commonplace for many schools when mainstreaming and inclusion occurred and general education teachers needed assistance in meeting the diverse needs of

the students in their classrooms. Lastly, as many legal cases propagated across the country challenging the validity of many special education placements (particularly for low-income, minority students of color and English as a Second Language students), public school districts realized the need to create an intervention and documentation structure for students en route to special education assessment. In later years, these teams have been utilized to provide support services outside the realm of special education. However, many teams operate solely as pre-referral teams for students en route to special education placement. UCCS designers viewed the lack of a more preventative focus as unfortunate because they saw this narrow definition of academic and social support as a missed opportunity to leverage valuable resources to support teaching and learning in the general education environment, thus lessening the need for more costly interventions later. They regarded this traditional pre-referral function as a model ill equipped to provide services to the vast majority of students who need them.

31. Developed by the Information Infrastructure Systems team at UEI, the Clinical Case Management System (CCMS) was a technological tool designed to aid school staff in identifying issues that impede teaching and learning and in their efforts to provide academic and social support for students. The provision of specified interventions for students represents a unique challenge for schools, since needed diagnostic data as well as tracking and communication efforts are often uncoordinated. The CCMS was modeled after the Academic and Social Support System (AS3) process discussed earlier. To aid this process, the CCMS provided instant access to multiple forms of data assembled in comprehensive and developmental student-, class-, and grade-level profiles. Schoolwide trends were also accessible in the tool. Additionally, data were longitudinal, allowing the team to make well-informed decisions about student, classroom, and possibly teacher needs. The training in evidence-based decision-making provided by the leaders of UEI's Academic and Social Services Initiative, along with site-based technical support, provided users with a template for how best to use the CCMS data in their decision-making process. With a better understanding of the issues at hand, the AS3 teams were well positioned to fully utilize their expertise in designing appropriate interventions. The dynamic student data offered by the tool introduced a new level of efficiency and evidence-based practices for school staff. The CCMS also supported the planning and documentation of student interventions as well as student response to intervention, which supported oversight and accountability for administrators. Communication tools embedded within the CCMS aided in the exchange and coordination of information between school staff.

32. See McFarland 2001 for the importance of peer effects on teachers.

33. Lareau (2003) coined the phrase "concerted cultivation" to describe the way middle-class families support their children's academic trajectories. G. J. Duncan and Murnane (2014) use the phrase to describe what they assert is necessary for children to develop the complex cognitive, social, and emotional skills needed to complete college and compete for knowledge jobs.

34. Accomplishing such continuous engagement is particularly challenging in urban schools. G. J. Duncan and Murnane (2014) show that increasing residential isolation by income concentrates struggling urban families in schools that generally do not have the capacity to coordinate and support their needs; they also provide supporting research that suggests teachers in isolated, high-poverty schools face classrooms with

more students with mental health and behavior issues (G. J. Duncan and Magnuson 2011), greater numbers of students coping with mobility strains (Raudenbush, Marshall, and Art 2011), and more immigrant students, many of whom speak little English (Schwartz and Stiefel 2011). They explain that such highly impacted classrooms demand highly skilled teachers, supported by schools that provide higher levels of academic, social, and familial supports. However, they summarize research suggesting that many schools serving low-income students do not have the resources and supports needed to attract, mentor, train, and retain effective teachers. See Jackson and Bruegmann 2009. As a result, most often, schools serving low-income students have a disproportionate number of novice teachers. See also Reardon and Bischoff 2011.

35. See Noguera 2003; Griffith and Smith 2005; Reay 1998; Lareau 2003; Walker et al. 2005; Vincent 2000. For minority parents, see Puma et al. 2005; Payne 2005; Lightfoot 1981.

36. Joelle is a pseudonym.

37. See Bryk and Schneider 2002. Levels of social trust are lower in urban schools that teach predominantly African American and Latino children, not only because resources that can solve problems are scarce in such schools, but also because minorities—African Americans in particular—have the lowest amount of social trust when compared with other racial groups; this is partly due to a long history of racial discrimination (see Wellman 1993; Feagin and Hernan 2000). The lack of social trust in organizations that serve minorities is tied to greater, more durable historical trends of racism. As Payne writes, "Being in a vulnerable position makes people circle up all their little resources. They're looking over their shoulder. Sociologically, we should regard the capacity to trust as a marker of social privilege" (2005, 7). Because trust between teachers and minority parents is so strained, they often have misperceptions of one another that can cause conflict. For example, Lightfoot explains that teachers may interpret the lack of participation of minority parents as apathy and disinterest regarding their child's educational progress, rather than "the inability to negotiate the bureaucratic maze of schools or as a response to a long history of exclusion and rejection at the school door" (1981, 100).

38. See Bryk and Schneider 2002 on the importance of aligning mutual expectations for the development of relational trust in schools.

39. Small (2009) argues that organizations that serve children also provide parents with "unanticipated" social resources that can help them help their children. For example, parents who attend meetings or participate in daily routines at their child's day care center gain many opportunities to meet other parents who can share with them information and resources that they might not have access to elsewhere. The social networks that originate from organizational affiliation provide parents with many different types of resources. Lareau (1989) finds that school-based connections among middle-class parents helps create home advantages for children. For specific discussion of the configuration and effects of school-based social networks among middle-class parents, see McGhee Hassrick 2007, McGhee Hassrick and Schneider 2009; Horvat, Weininger, and Lareau 2003.

40. Coleman (1988) explains that the strength of social norms, such as ambitious academic goals and aspirations for children, depends on social closure among parents. He argues that the connections parents share with the parents of their children's friends creates intergenerational closure that allows them to jointly monitor and reward child behavior that is aligned with ambitious academic goals and aspirations.

41. University of Chicago Charter School Audit Report for Fiscal Year 2011, provided by the Urban Education Institute (copy available from the authors).

42. See Cornman, Keaton, and Glander 2013.

43. Timothy Knowles, personal communication.

44. Cohen and Moffitt 2009.

Chapter 8

1. Those who applied during these years produced test scores starting in grade 3. Thus, our test-score data were collected from 2008 to 2012.

2. Preferences were not observed for all parents. We compared the children whose preferences were missing to those whose preferences were observed and found that those with missing preferences were statistically similar to those who were willing to attend both schools. We therefore treated the parents with missing preferences similarly to those willing to accept both schools. We also reanalyzed the data with the missing preference group treated as a separate category; the results were very similar to those presented in the tables in this chapter.

3. The exclusion of such students has no bearing on the validity of causal inferences we draw in this chapter. However, it does constrain generalizations we make to those who participated in a valid lottery.

4. Two of these students produced test scores in grade 7. These students were originally placed in grade 1 rather than kindergarten despite the fact that they entered the kindergarten lottery in 2005.

5. Angrist, Imbens, and Rubin 1996.

6. Studying a single summary outcome variable reduces to a minimum the number of hypotheses we need to test. This helps ensure that our significance tests are accurate.

7. We reanalyzed the data conditioning on key covariates, including a measure of the social disadvantage of the census block group in which the child resided and a measure of the educational and occupational attainment of persons living in that block group. We also analyzed the data using all students on whom we had lottery and covariate information, even if the reading or math test score was missing. For this purpose we used multiple model-based imputation, an approach that is comparatively robust in the presence of missing data because it uses all available information in the data to impute missing values. These analyses produced results that are very similar to those described here. This is not surprising: lottery winners were closely balanced on the covariates of interest, and there was no evidence of differential missing data. Moreover, the fraction of missing data was small: 50 out of 488 students did not produce at least one reading and one math test score.

8. This is our estimate of the "control complier mean" ($\hat{\mu}_{c0}$) and is computed as $\hat{\mu}_{c0} = (\hat{\mu}_c - \hat{\pi}_{AT}\hat{\mu}_{AT} - \hat{\pi}_{NT}\hat{\mu}_{NT})/\hat{\pi}_c$, where $\hat{\mu}_c$ is the mean of the control group (those who lost the lottery), $\hat{\mu}_{AT}$ is the mean of the "always-takers" (estimated by the sample average outcome of those assigned to the control who attended the charter school), $\hat{\pi}_{AT}$ is the fraction of always-takers (estimated by the proportion of control group members who attended the charter school), $\hat{\mu}_{NT}$ is the mean of the "never-takers" (estimated by the sample average outcome of those who won the lottery but did not

attend the charter school), and $\hat{\pi}_{NT}$ is the fraction of never-takers (estimated by the proportion of winners who did not attended the charter school). Interestingly, the never-takers score significantly higher than do the always-takers, as one would predict based on the assumption that the never-takers have a greater variety of schooling options than do the always-takers, and the assumption that families with greater options are more advantaged with respect to resources needed for cognitive development. Based on the relatively small samples of always- and never-takers, our estimate of 0.09 is quite uncertain, with a 95 percent confidence interval ranging from −0.08 to 0.24.

9. We use the 2011 data because the average test year in our sample is almost exactly 2011.

10. Deming 2009; Barnett 2011.

Chapter 9

1. We don't mean to imply that policies designed to reduce inequality have had no impact. After all, we don't know how severe inequality would be had those policies not been implemented.

2. Kardos, Johnson, et al. 2001; Kardos and Johnson 2007.

3. Lortie's (1975) widely cited book analyzes this organization of instruction. Kardos, Johnson, et al. (2001) and Johnson (2015) report on its continued relevance.

4. Among the most notable efforts to orchestrate an interplay between scholars and practitioners for the purpose of increasing and using knowledge about teaching is the professional development school, a project akin to the university teaching hospital in medicine. See Darling-Hammond 1994 for a cogent set of reflections on this strategy.

5. The Urban Teacher Education Program at the University of Chicago works according to this model.

6. At the high school level, the "Small Schools of Choice" movement has recently created over one hundred new public schools that are, on average, remarkably effective in promoting educational attainment among low-income youth (Bloom and Unterman 2014). Cohen and Moffitt (2009) provide examples of similarly effective networks of public elementary schools.

7. See our review in ch. 1, notes 1 and 2 of that chapter, and our results in ch. 8.

8. Gleason et al. 2010.

9. Neal 2002.

10. Cohen and Moffitt 2009.

Abdulkadiroglu, A., J. Angrist, S. Dynarski, T. Kane, and P. Pathak. 2011. "Accountability and Flexibility in Public Schools: Evidence from Boston's Charters and Pilots." *Quarterly Journal of Economics* 126 (2): 699–748.

Abdulkadiroglu, A., J. Angrist, S. Cohodes, S. Dynarski, J. Fullerton, T. Kane, and P. Pathak. 2009. "Informing the Debate: Comparing Boston's Charter, Pilot and Traditional Schools." Boston Foundation, Boston.

Adelman, C. 1995. "The New College Course Map and Transcript Files: Changes in Course-Taking and Achievement, 1972–1993." NCES PE 95-800. National Center for Education Statistics, US Department of Education, Washington, DC.

Alexander, K. L., D. R. Entwisle, and L. S. Olson. 2001. "Schools, Achievement, and Inequality: A Seasonal Perspective." *Educational Evaluation and Policy Analysis* 23 (2): 171–91.

———. 2007a. "Lasting Consequences of the Summer Learning Gap." *American Sociological Review* 72 (2): 167–80.

———. 2007b. "Summer Learning and Its Implications: Insights from the Beginning School Study." *New Directions for Youth Development* 114:11–32.

Allensworth, E., N. Takato, C. Durwood, E. Krone, and C. Mazzeo. 2010a. "Are Two Algebra Classes Better Than One? The Effects of Double-Dose Instruction in Chicago." Consortium on School Research, University of Chicago.

———. 2010b. "College Prep for All? What We've Learned from Chicago's Efforts." Consortium on School Research, University of Chicago.

Allington, R. L., A. McGill-Franzen, G. Camilli, L. Williams, J. Graff, J. Zeig, C. Zmach, and R. Nowak. 2010. "Addressing Summer Reading Setback among Economically Disadvantaged Elementary Students." *Reading Psychology* 31:411–27.

Angrist, J. D., S. M. Dynarski, T. J. Kane, P. A. Pathak, and C. R. Walters. 2010. "Inputs and Impacts in Charter Schools: KIPP Lynn." *American Economic Review* 100 (2): 239–43.

———. 2012. "Who Benefits from KIPP?" *Journal of Policy Analysis and Management* 31 (4): 837–60.

Angrist, J. D., G. W. Imbens, and D. B. Rubin. 1996. "Identification of Causal Effects Using Instrumental Variables." *Journal of the American Statistical Association* 91 (434): 444–55.

Angrist, J. D., P. A. Pathak, and C. R. Walters. 2013. "Explaining Charter School Effectiveness." *American Economic Journal: Applied Economics* 5 (4): 1–27.

Anyon, J. 1995. "Race, Social Class, and Educational Reform in an Inner-City School." *Teachers College Record* 97: 69–94.

Aronson, J., J. Zimmerman, and L. Carlos. 1999. *Improving Student Achievement by Extending School: Is It Just a Matter of Time?* San Francisco: WestEd.

Azevedo, R. 2007. "Understanding the Complex Nature of Self-Regulatory Processes in Learning with Computer-Based Learning Environments: An Introduction." *Metacognition and Learning* 2: 57–65.

Baker, D. P., and D. L. Carlos. 1986. "Mothers' Strategies for Children's School Achievement: Managing the Transition to High School." *Sociology of Education* 59 (3): 156–66.

Balfanz, R., N. Legters, and W. Jordan. 2004. *Catching Up: Impact of the Talent Development Ninth Grade Interventions in Reading and Mathematics in High-Poverty High Schools.* Baltimore: Johns Hopkins University, Center for Research on the Education of Students Placed at Risk.

Ball, D. L. 1990. "The Mathematical Understandings That Prospective Teachers Bring to Teacher Education." *Elementary School Journal* 90:449–66.

———. 2000. "Bridging Practices: Intertwining Content and Pedagogy in Teaching and Learning to Teach." *Journal of Teacher Education* 51: 241–47.

Ball, D. L., H. C. Hill, and H. Bass. 2005. "Knowing Mathematics for Teaching: Who Knows Mathematics Well Enough to Teach Third Grade, and How Can We Decide?" *American Educator* 29 (1): 14–17.

Ball, D. L., M. Thames, and G. Phelps. 2008. "Content Knowledge for Teaching: What Makes It Special?" *Journal of Teacher Education* 59 (5): 389–407.

Barbarin, O., D. Bryant, T. McCandies, M. Burchinal, D. Early, R. Clifford, R. Pianta, and C. Howes. 2006. "Children Enrolled in Public Pre-K: The Relation of Family Life, Neighborhood Quality, and Socioeconomic Resources to Early Competence." *American Journal of Orthopsychiatry* 76 (2): 265–76.

Barnett, W. S. 2011. "Effectiveness of Early Educational Intervention." *Science* 333 (6045): 975–78.

Barr, R., and Dreeben, R. 1991. "Grouping Students for Reading Instruction." *Handbook of Reading Research*, vol. 2, edited by R. Barr, M. L. Kamil, P. Mosenthal, and P. D. Pearson, 885–910.

Beilock, S. 2010. *Choke: What the Secrets of the Brain Reveal about Getting It Right When You Have To.* New York: Simon and Schuster.

Bidwell, C. 1965. "The School as a Formal Organization." In *Handbook of Organizations*, edited by J. March. Chicago: Rand McNally.

Blair, C., and K. G. Scott. 2002. "Proportion of Learning Disabilities Placements Associated with Low Socioeconomic Status: Evidence for a Gradient?" *Journal of Special Education* 36:14–22.

Bloom, H., and R. Unterman. 2014. "Can Small High Schools of Choice Improve Educational Prospects for Disadvantaged Students?" *Journal of Policy Analysis and Management* 33 (2): 290–319.

Bodovski, K., and G. Farkas. 2007. "Mathematics Growth in Early Elementary School: The Roles of Beginning Knowledge, Student Engagement and Instruction." *Elementary School Journal* 108 (2): 115–30.

Borg, S. 2003. "Teacher Cognition in Language Teaching: A Review of Research on What Language Teachers Think, Know, Believe, and Do." *Language Teaching* 36 (2): 81–109.

Borman, G. D., and M. Boulay. 2004. *Summer Learning: Research, Policies, and Programs.* Mahwah, NJ: Lawrence Erlbaum Associates.

Borman, G. D., and G. M. Hewes. 2002. "The Long-Term Effects and Cost-Effectiveness of Success for All." *Educational Evaluation and Policy Analysis* (4): 243–66.

Borman, G. D., G. M. Hewes, L. T. Overman, and S. Brown. 2003. "Comprehensive School Reform and Achievement: A Meta-analysis." *Review of Educational Research* 73 (2): 125–230.

Borman, G. D., R. E. Slavin, A. C. K. Cheung, A. M. Chamberlain, N. A. Madden, and B. Chambers. 2007. "Final Reading Outcomes of the National Randomized Field Trial of 'Success for All.'" *American Educational Research Journal* 44 (3): 701–31.

Boulay, B., A. Robertson, K. Maree, and L. Fox. 2010. *Evaluation of the Expanded Learning Time Initiative: Year 3 Outcomes Report*. Cambridge, MA: Abt Associates.

Bowey, J. A. 1995. "Socioeconomic Status Differences in Preschool Phonological Sensitivity and First-Grade Reading Achievement." *Journal of Educational Psychology* 87 (3): 476–87.

Bowles, S., H. Gintis, and M. Osborne. 2000. "The Determinants of Earnings: Skills, Preferences, and Schooling." Economics Department Working Paper Series No. 87. University of Massachusetts, Amherst.

Brener, N., J. Martindale, and M. Weist. 2001. "Mental Health and Social Services: Results from the School Health Policies and Programs Study." *Journal of School Health* 71 (7): 305–12.

Bryk, A., L. Gomez, D. Joseph, N. Pinkard, L. Rosen, and L. Walker. 2005. "The Conceptual Framework for the Information Infrastructure System." Unpublished manuscript.

Bryk, A., and D. Kerbow. 2006. "Developmental Map of Students' Growth." In *Strategic Teaching and Evaluation of Progress: A Manual to Guide Assessment*, 9. Chicago: Urban Education Institute.

Bryk, A., J. Nagaoka, and F. Newmann. 2000. "Chicago Classroom Demands for Authentic Intellectual Work: Trends from 1997–1999." Consortium on School Research, University of Chicago. https://consortium.uchicago.edu/publications/chicago-classroom -demands-authentic-intellectual-work-trends-1997-1999.

Bryk, A. S., and S. W. Raudenbush. 1988. "Toward a More Appropriate Conceptualization of Research on School Effects: A Three-Level Hierarchical Linear Model." *American Journal of Education* 97 (1): 65–108.

Bryk, A., S. Rollow, and G. Pinnell. 1996. "Urban School Development: Literacy as a Lever for Change." *Education Policy* 10:172–201.

Bryk, A. S., and B. Schneider. 2002. *Relational Trust: A Core Resource in Schools*. New York: Sage Publications.

Bryk, A. S., P. B. Sebring, E. Allensworth, J. Q. Easton, and S. Luppescu. 2010. *Organizing Schools for Improvement: Lessons from Chicago*. Chicago: University of Chicago Press.

Bryk, A. S., P. Sebring, D. Kerbow, S. Rollow, and J. Q. Easton. 1998. *Charting Chicago School Reform: Democratic Localism as a Lever for Change*. Boulder, CO: Westview Press.

Bryk, A. S., and U. Treisman. 2010. "Make Math a Gateway, Not a Gatekeeper." *Chronicle of Higher Education*, April 18. Retrieved from http://chronicle.com/article/Make-Math-a -Gateway-Not-a/65056.

Camilli, G., S. Vargas, S. Ryan, and W. S. Barnett. 2010. "Meta-analysis of the Effects of Early Education Interventions on Cognitive and Social Development." *Teachers College Record* 112 (3): 579–620.

Carnegie Forum on Education and the Economy. 1986. "A Nation Prepared: Teachers for the 21st Century." Report for the Task Force on Teaching as a Profession. Carnegie Corporation of New York.

Carneiro, P., and J. Heckman. 2003. "Human Capital Policy." In *Inequality in America: What*

Role for Human Capital Policies?, edited by A. Krueger and J. Heckman, 77–239. Cambridge, MA: MIT Press.

Carnoy, M., and R. Rothstein. 2013. *What Do International Tests Really Show about American Student Performance?* Washington, DC: Economic Policy Institute.

Chalfant, J., M. Pysh, and R. Moultrie. 1979. "Teacher Assistance Teams: A Model for Within-Building Problem Solving." *Learning Disability Quarterly* 2:85–96.

Chall, J. S. 1983a. *Learning to Read: The Great Debate.* New York: John Wiley.

———. 1983b. *Stages of Reading Development.* New York: McGraw-Hill.

Chetty, R., J. Friedman, and J. Rockoff. 2014. "Measuring the Impacts of Teachers II: Teacher Value-Added and Student Outcomes in Adulthood." *American Economic Review* 104 (9): 2633–79.

Chetty, R., J. Friedman, N. Hilger, E. Saez, D. W. Schanzenbach, and D. Yagan. 2011. "How Does Your Kindergarten Classroom Affect Your Earnings? Evidence from Project Star." *Quarterly Journal of Economics* 126 (4): 1593–660.

Chubb, J. E., and T. M. Moe. 1990. *Politics, Markets, and America's Schools.* Washington, DC: Brookings Institution Press.

Clark, C., and A. Foster. 2005. *Children's and Young People's Reading Habits and Preferences: The Who, What, Why, Where and When.* London: National Literacy Trust.

Clark, D., and M. C. Linn. 2003. "Designing for Knowledge Integration: The Impact of Instructional Time." *Journal of the Learning Sciences* 12 (4): 451–93.

Clay, M. M. 1987. "Learning to Be Disabled." *New Zealand Journal of Educational Studies* 22 (2): 155–73.

———. 1991. *Becoming Literate: The Construction of Inner Control.* Portsmouth, NH: Heinemann.

———. 2001. *Change over Time in Children's Literacy Development.* Portsmouth, NH: Heinemann.

———. 2005a. *Literacy Lessons Designed for Individuals, Part One: Why? When? And How?* Portsmouth, NH: Heinemann.

———. 2005b. *Literacy Lessons Designed for Individuals, Part Two: Teaching Procedures.* Portsmouth, NH: Heinemann.

Clotfelter, C. T., H. F. Ladd, and J. Vigdor. 2005. "Who Teaches Whom? Race and the Distribution of Novice Teachers." *Economics of Education Review* 24 (4): 377–92.

Cohen, D. K., M. McLaughlin, and J. Talbert. 1993. *Teaching for Understanding: Challenges for Practice, Research and Policy.* San Francisco: Jossey-Bass.

Cohen, D. K., and S. L. Moffitt. 2009. *The Ordeal of Equality: Did Federal Regulation Fix the Schools?* Cambridge, MA: Harvard University Press.

Cohen, D. K., S. W. Raudenbush, and D. L. Ball. 2003. "Resources, Instruction, and Research." *Educational Evaluation and Policy Analysis* 25 (2): 119–42.

Coleman, J. S. 1988. "Social Capital and the Creation of Human Capital." *American Journal of Sociology* 94:95–120.

Coleman, J. S., E. Q. Campbell, C. J. Hobson, J. McPartland, A. J. Mood, F. D. Weinfeld, and R. L. York. 1966. *Equality of Educational Opportunity.* Washington, DC: US Department of Health, Education, and Welfare.

Colvin, C. R. 1993. "Childhood Antecedents of Young-Adult Judgability." *Journal of Personality* 61 (4): 611–35.

Comer, J. P. 1980. *School Power: Implications of an Intervention Project.* New York: Free Press.

———. 1992. "Educational Accountability: Shared Responsibility between Parents and Schools." *Stanford Law and Policy Review* 4:113–22.

Connor, C. M., F. J. Morrison, B. J. Fishman, C. Schatschneider, and P. Underwood. 2007. "Algorithm-Guided Individualized Reading Instruction." *Science* 315 (5811): 464.

Connor, C. M., S. B. Piasta, B. Fishman, S. Glasney, C. Schatschneider, E. Crowe, P. Underwood, and F. J. Morrison. 2009. "Individualizing Student Instruction Precisely: Effects of Child × Instruction Interactions on First Graders' Literacy Development." *Child Development* 80 (1): 77–100.

Cooper, H., B. Nye, K. Charlton, J. Lindsay, and S. Greathouse. 1996. "The Effects of Summer Vacation on Achievement Test Scores: A Narrative and Meta-analytic Review." *Review of Educational Research* 66 (3): 227–68.

Cornman, S., P. Keaton, and M. Glander. 2013. "Revenues and Expenditures for Public Elementary and Secondary School Districts: School Year 2010–11 (Fiscal Year 2011)." NCES 2013-44. National Center for Education Statistics, US Department of Education, Washington, DC.

Cuban, L. 1988. *The Managerial Imperative and the Practice of Leadership in School.* Albany: University of New York Press.

Cucchiara, M. B., and E. M. Horvat. 2009. "Perils and Promises: Middle-Class Parental Involvement in Urban Schools." *American Educational Research Journal* 46 (4): 974–1004.

Darling-Hammond, L. 1994. *Professional Development Schools: Schools for Developing a Profession.* New York: Teachers College Press.

Datnow, A. 1998. *The Gender Politics of Educational Change.* London: Falmer Press.

Datnow, A., L. Hubbard, and H. Mehan. 2002. *Extending Educational Reform: From One School to Many.* London: Routledge.

De la Fuente, A., and A. Ciccone. 2003. *Human Capital and Growth in a Global and Knowledge-Based Economy.* Luxembourg City: European Commission, European Social Fund.

Deming, D. 2009. "Early Childhood Intervention and Life-Cycle Skill Development: Evidence from Head Start." *American Economic Journal: Applied Economics,* 1 (3): 111–34.

Dickens, W. T., and J. R. Flynn. 2006. "Black Americans Reduce the Racial IQ Gap: Evidence from Standardization Samples." *Psychological Science* 17 (10): 913–20.

Dobbie, W., and R. G. Fryer Jr. 2009. "Are High Quality Schools Enough to Close the Achievement Gap? Evidence from a Social Experiment in Harlem." NBER Working Paper No. 15473. National Bureau of Economic Research, Cambridge, MA. Retrieved from http://www.nber.org/papers/w15473.

———. 2011. "Getting beneath the Veil of Effective Schools: Evidence from New York City." *American Economic Journal: Applied Economics* 5 (4): 28–60.

Downey, D. B., Paul T. von Hippel, and B. A. Broh. 2004. "Are Schools the Great Equalizer? Cognitive Inequality during the Summer Months and the School Year." *American Sociological Review* (5): 613–35.

Dreeben, R. 1971. *The Nature of Teaching.* Glenview, IL: Scott Foresman.

Dreeben, R., and R. Barr. 1988. "The Formation and Instruction of Ability Groups." *American Journal of Education* 97 (1): 34–64.

Duncan, A. 2013. *The Threat of Educational Stagnation and Complacency: Remarks of U.S. Secretary of Education Arne Duncan at the Release of the 2012 Program for International Student Assessment (PISA).* December 3. Retrieved from http://www.ed.gov/news/speeches/threat-educational-stagnation-and-complacency.

Duncan, G. J., C. J. Dowsett, A. Claessens, K. Magnuson, A. C. Huston, P. Klebanov, L. S. Pagani, L. Feinstein, M. Engel, J. Brooks-Gunn, H. Sexton, K. Duckworth, and C. Japel. 2007. "School Readiness and Later Achievement." *Developmental Psychology* 43 (6): 1428–46.

Duncan, G. J., and K. A. Magnuson. 2011 "The Nature and Impact of Early Achievement Skills, Attention Skills, and Behavior Problems." In *Whither Opportunity? Rising Inequality, Schools, and Children's Life Chances*, edited by G. J. Duncan and R. J. Murnane, 47–69. New York: Russell Sage Foundation.

Duncan, G. J., and R. J. Murnane. 2014. *Restoring Opportunity: The Crisis of Inequality and the Challenge for American Education*. Cambridge, MA: Harvard Education Press.

Ehri, L. C. 1997. "Learning to Read and Learning to Spell Are One and the Same, Almost." In *Learning to Spell: Research, Theory, and Practice across Languages*, edited by C. A. Perfetti, L. Rieben, and M. Fayol, 237–69. Mahwah, NJ: Erlbaum.

Elmore, R. F. 2000. "Building a New Structure for School Leadership." Albert Shanker Institute, New York.

———. 2002. "Bridging the Gap between Standards and Achievement: The Imperative for Professional Development in Education." In *Secondary Lenses on Learning Participant Book: Team Leadership for Mathematics in Middle and High Schools*, edited by C. M. Grant, V. L. Mills, M. Bouack, E. Davidson, B. S. Nelson, and S. Benson, 313–44. Thousand Oaks, CA: Corwin.

———. 2004. *School Reform from the Inside Out: Policy, Practice, and Performance*. Cambridge, MA: Harvard Education Press.

———. 2005a. "Agency, Reciprocity, and Accountability in Democratic Education." In *The Institutions of American Democracy: The Public Schools*, edited by S. H. Fuhrman and M. Lazerson, 277–301. New York: Oxford University Press.

———. 2005b. "Accountable Leadership." *Educational Forum* 69 (2): 134–42.

Elmore, R. F., and D. Burney. 1997. *Investing in Teacher Learning. Staff Development and Instructional Improvement, Community School District 2, New York City*. New York: National Commission on Teaching & America's Future.

Engel, Mimi, A. Claessens, and M. Finch. 2013. "Teaching Students What They Already Know? The (Mis)Alignment between Mathematics Instructional Content and Student Knowledge in Kindergarten." *Educational Evaluation and Policy Analysis* 35 (2): 157–78.

Entwisle, D. R., and K. L. Alexander. 1992. "Summer Setback: Race, Poverty, School Composition, and Mathematics Achievement in the First Two Years of School." *American Sociological Review* 57 (1): 72–84.

Farmer-Hinton, R. L. 2002. *When Time Matters: Examining the Impact and Distribution of Extra Instructional Time*. Chicago: University of Chicago. ERIC Document Reproduction Service No. ED479926.

Feagin, J. R., and V. Hernan. 2000. *White Racism: The Basics*. New York: Routledge.

Fink, E., and L. B. Resnick. 2001. "Developing Principals as Instructional Leaders." *Phi Delta Kappan* 82 (8): 598–606.

Finn, J. D., and C. M. Achilles. 1990. "Answers and Questions about Class Size: A Statewide Experiment." *American Educational Research Journal* 27 (3): 557–77.

Flores, A. 2007. "Examining Disparities in Mathematics Education: Achievement Gap or Opportunity Gap?" *High School Journal* 91 (1): 29–42.

Fountas, I. C., and G. S. Pinnell. 1996. *Guided Reading: Good First Teaching for All Children*. Portsmouth, NH: Heinemann.

——. 2001. *Guiding Readers and Writers Grades 3–6: Teaching Comprehension, Genre, and Content Literacy.* Portsmouth, NH: Heinemann.

——. 2009. *When Readers Struggle: Teaching That Works.* Portsmouth, NH: Heinemann.

——. 2010. *The Fountas & Pinnell Leveled Book List, K–8+.* 2010–12 edition. Portsmouth, NH: Heinemann.

Frazier, Julie A., and F. J. Morrison. 1998. "The Influence of Extended-Year Schooling on Growth of Achievement and Perceived Competence in Early Elementary School." *Child Development* 69 (2): 495–517.

Fryer, R. G., and S. D. Levitt. 2006. "The Black-White Test Score Gap through Third Grade." *American Law and Economics Review* (2): 249–81.

Fullan, M. 1999. *Change Forces: The Sequel.* Abington: Routledge.

Gamoran, A., and T. Loveless. 2003. "Robert Dreeben's Contributions to the Sociology of Education." In *Stability and Change in American Education: Structure, Process, and Outcomes,* edited by M. T. Hallinan, A. Gamoran, W. Kubitschek, and T. Loveless, 3–14. Clinton Corners, NY: Eliot Werner Publications.

Gamoran, A., and R. D. Mare. 1989. "Secondary School Tracking and Educational Inequality: Compensation, Reinforcement, or Neutrality?" *American Journal of Sociology* 94:1146–83.

Gamoran, A., M. Nystrand, M. Berends, and P. C. LePore. 1995. "An Organizational Analysis of the Effects of Ability Grouping." *American Educational Research Journal* 32: 687–715.

Gay, G. 2000. *Culturally Responsive Teaching: Theory, Research, and Practice.* New York: Teachers College Press.

Gettinger, M. 1984. "Achievement as a Function of Time Spent in Learning and Time Needed for Learning." *American Educational Research Journal* 21 (3): 617–28.

Gibbs, C. H. 2010. "Measuring the Impact of Full-Day Kindergarten: Experimental and Quasi-experimental Evidence." PhD diss., University of Chicago.

Gill, B., P. M. Timpane, K. E. Ross, D. J. Brewer, and K. Booker 2007. *Rhetoric versus Reality: What We Know and What We Need to Know about Vouchers and Charter Schools.* Santa Monica, CA: Rand Corporation.

Ginder, S. A., J. E. Kelly-Reid, and F. B. Mann. 2015. "Graduation Rates for Selected Cohorts, 2006–11; Student Financial Aid, Academic Year 2013–14; and Admissions in Postsecondary Institutions, Fall 2014." Institute for Education Sciences, US Department of Education, National Center for Education Statistics.

Gleason, P., M. Clark, C. C. Tuttle, and E. Dwoyer. 2010. *The Evaluation of Charter School Impacts: Final Report.* NCEE 2010–4029. Washington, DC: US Department of Education, National Center for Education Evaluation and Regional Assistance.

Goddard, R. D., and R. J. Miller. 2010. "The Conceptualization, Measurement, and Effects of School Leadership: Introduction to the Special Issue." *Elementary School Journal* 111 (2): 219–25.

Goldberg, A. E. 1989. "A Unified Account of the Semantics of the Ditransitive." In *Annual Meeting of the Berkeley Linguistic Society* 15, 79–90.

Goldhaber, D. D., and D. J. Brewer. 1997. "Why Don't Schools and Teachers Seem to Matter? Assessing the Impact of Unobservables on Educational Productivity." *Journal of Human Resources* 32 (3): 505–23.

Gordon, R., T. Kane, and D. O. Staiger. 2006. "Identifying Effective Teachers Using Performance on the Job." In *Path to Prosperity: Hamilton Project Ideas on Income Security,*

Education, and Taxes, edited by J. Furman and J. Bordoff, 189–225. Washington, DC: Brookings Institution Press.

Griffith, A. I., and D. E. Smith. 2005. *Mothering for Schooling.* Hove: Psychology Press.

Gunderson, E. A., G. Ramirez, S. C. Levine, and S. L. Beilock. 2012. "The Role of Parents and Teachers in the Development of Gender-Related Math Attitudes." *Sex Roles* 66 (3–4): 153–66.

Gunderson, E. A., G. Ramirez, S. L. Beilock, and S. C. Levine. 2013. "Teachers' Spatial Anxiety Relates to 1st- and 2nd-graders' Spatial Learning." *Mind, Brain, and Education* 7 (3): 196–99.

Guthrie, J. T., A. Wigfield, and K. C. Percenevich. 2004. *Motivating Reading Comprehension: Concept-Oriented Reading Instruction.* Mahwah, NJ: Lawrence Erlbaum.

Haden, C. A., R. A. Haine, and R. Fivush. 1997. "Developing Narrative Structure in Parent-Child Reminiscing across the Preschool Years." *Developmental Psychology* 33 (2): 295–307.

Hallinger, P. 1992. "The Evolving Role of American Principals: From Managerial to Instructional to Transformational Leaders." *Journal of Educational Administration* 30 (3): 35–48.

Hallinan, M. T., and A. B. Sorensen. 1983. "The Formation and Stability of Instructional Groups." *American Sociological Review* 48:838–51.

Hanushek, E. A., P. E. Peterson, and L. Woessmann. 2013. *Endangering Prosperity: A Global View of the American School.* Washington, DC: Brookings Institution Press.

Hargreaves, A. 1994. *Changing Teachers, Changing Times: Teachers' Work and Culture in the Postmodern Age.* New York: Teachers College Press.

Hart, B., and T. Risley. 1995. *Meaningful Differences in the Everyday Experience of Young American Children.* Baltimore: P. H. Brookes.

Haslem, M. B., B. Pringle, and N. Adelman. 1996. *The Uses of Time for Teaching and Learning.* Washington, DC: US Department of Education, Office of Educational Research and Improvement.

Heath, S. B. 1983. *Ways with Words: Language, Life, and Work in Communities and Schools.* Cambridge: Cambridge University Press.

Heck, R. H., and P. Hallinger. 2010. "Collaborative Leadership Effects on School Improvement: Integrating Unidirectional- and Reciprocal-Effects Models." *Elementary School Journal* 111 (2): 226–52.

Heckman, J. J., and T. Kautz. 2012. "Hard Evidence on Soft Skills." *Labour Economics* 19 (4): 451–64.

Heckman, J. J., and A. B. Krueger, eds. 2003. *Inequality in America: What Role for Human Capital Policy?* Cambridge, MA: MIT Press.

Heckman, J. J., and P. A. LaFontaine. 2010. "The American High School Graduation Rate: Trends and Levels." *Review of Economics and Statistics* 92 (2): 244–62.

Henig, J. 2008. *Spin Cycle: How Research Gets Used in Policy Debates: The Case of Charter Schools.* New York: Russell Sage Foundation.

Hernstein, R. J., and C. Murray. 1994. *The Bell Curve: Intelligence and Class Structure in American Life.* New York: Free Press.

Hess, G. A., Jr. 1991. *School Restructuring, Chicago Style.* Thousand Oaks, CA: Corwin Press.

———. 1995. *Restructuring Urban Schools: A Chicago Perspective.* New York: Teachers College Press.

Hibel, J., S. C. Faircloth, and G. Farkas. 2008. "Unpacking the Placement of American Indian and Alaska Native Students in Special Education Programs and Services in the

Early Grades: School Readiness as a Predictive Variable." *Harvard Educational Review* 78 (3): 498–528.

Hill, H. C., D. L. Ball, and S. G. Schilling. 2008. "Unpacking Pedagogical Content Knowledge: Conceptualizing and Measuring Teachers' Topic-Specific Knowledge of Students." *Journal for Research in Mathematics Education* 39 (4): 372–400.

Hill, H. C., B. Rowan, and D. L. Ball. 2005. "Effects of Teachers' Mathematical Knowledge for Teaching on Student Achievement." *American Educational Research Journal* 42 (2): 371–406.

Hoff-Ginsberg, E. 1991. "Mother-Child Conversation in Different Social Classes and Communicative Settings." *Child Development* 62 (4): 782–96.

Holmes Group. 1986. "Tomorrow's Teachers." Holmes Group, East Lansing, MI.

Hong, G., and Y. Hong. 2009. "Reading Instruction Time and Homogeneous Grouping in Kindergarten: An Application of Marginal Mean Weighting through Stratification." *Educational Evaluation and Policy Analysis* 31 (1): 54–81.

Horn, L., and L. K. Kojaku. 2001. "High School Academic Curriculum and the Persistence Path through College: Persistence and Transfer Behavior of Undergraduates 3 Years after Entering 4-Year Institutions." NCES 2001-163. National Center for Education Statistics, Washington, DC.

Horvat, E. M., E. B. Weininger, and A. Lareau. 2003. "From Social Ties to Social Capital: Class Differences in the Relations between Schools and Parent Networks. *American Educational Research Journal* 40 (2): 319–51.

Hubbard, L., H. Mehan, and M. K. Stein. 2006. *Reform as Learning: School Reform, Organizational Culture, and Community Politics in San Diego.* New York: Routledge / Taylor & Francis Group.

Huttenlocher, J., W. Haight, A. Bryk, M. Seltzer, and T. Lyons. 1991. "Early Vocabulary Growth: Relation to Language Input and Gender." *Developmental Psychology* 27 (2): 236–48.

Huttenlocher, J., M. Vasilyeva, E. Cymerman, and S. Levine. 2002. "Language Input and Child Syntax." *Cognitive Psychology* 45 (3): 337–74.

Jackson, C. K., and E. Bruegmann. 2009. "Teaching Students and Teaching Each Other: The Importance of Peer Learning for Teachers." *American Economic Journal: Applied Economics* 1 (4): 85–108.

Jacob, B. A., and L. Lefgren. 2004. "Remedial Education and Student Achievement: A Regression-Discontinuity Analysis." *Review of Economics and Statistics* 86 (1): 226–44.

Jordan, N. C, J. Huttenlocher, and S. C. Levine. 1992. "Differential Calculation Abilities in Young Children from Middle- and Low-Income Families." *Developmental Psychology* 28:644–53.

Johnson, S. M. 2015. "Will VAMS Reinforce the Walls of the Egg-Crate School?" *Educational Researcher* 44:117–26.

Kuhn, M., and K. Dempsey. 2011. "End the Math Wars." *Learning & Leading with Technology* 39 (3): 18–21. ERIC Document Reproduction Service No. EJ954321.

Jones, L. V., N. Burton, and E. Davenport. 1982. "Mathematics Achievement Levels of Black and White Youth." L. L. Thurstone Psychometric Laboratory, University of North Carolina at Chapel Hill.

Kardos, S. M., and S. M. Johnson. 2007. "On Their Own and Presumed Expert: New Teachers' Experience with Their Colleagues." *Teachers College Record* 109 (9): 2083–106.

Kardos, S. M., S. M. Johnson, H. G. Peske, D. Kauffman, and E. Liu. 2001. "Counting on

Colleagues: New Teachers Encounter the Professional Cultures of Their Schools." *Educational Administration Quarterly* 37 (2): 250–90.

Karweit, N. 1984. "Time-on-Task Reconsidered: Synthesis of Research on Time and Learning." *Educational Leadership* 41 (8): 32.

Kane, T. J., D. F. McCaffrey, T. Miller, and D. O. Staiger. 2013. *Have We Identified Effective Teachers? Validating Measures of Effective Teaching Using Random Assignment*. Seattle: Bill & Melinda Gates Foundation.

Kerbow, D., and S. Bryk. 2005. "STEP Literacy Assessment: Technical Report of Validity." Retrieved from https://www.researchgate.net/publication/265040072_STEP_Literacy _Assessment_Technical_Report_of_Validity_and_Reliability.

Kerbow, D., J. Gwynne, and B. Jacob. 1999. "Implementation of a Balanced Literacy Framework and Student Learning: Implications for Program Development." University of Chicago Center for School Improvement. Retrieved from http://usi.uchicago.edu /research.html.

Kilpatrick, J., J. Swafford, and B. Findell, eds. 2001. *Adding It Up: Helping Children Learn Mathematics*. Washington, DC: National Academies Press.

Klibanoff, R. S., S. C. Levine, J. Huttenlocher, M. Vasilyeva, and L. V. Hedges. 2006. "Preschool Children's Mathematical Knowledge: The Effect of Teacher 'Math Talk.'" *Developmental Psychology* 42 (1): 59–69.

Kolbe, T., M. Partridge, and F. O'Reilly. 2012. "Time and Learning in Schools: A National Profile." National Center on Time & Learning, Boston. Retrieved from http://www .timeandlearning.org/publications/time-and-learning-schools-national-profile.

Krueger, A. B. 2003. "Inequality: Too Much of a Good Thing." In *Inequality in America: What Role for Human Capital Policies?*, edited by A. B. Krueger and J. J. Heckman, 1–76. Cambridge, MA: MIT Press.

Krueger, A. B., and D. M. Whitmore. 2001. "The Effect of Attending a Small Class in the Early Grades on College-Test Taking and Middle School Test Results: Evidence from Project STAR." *Economic Journal* 111 (468): 1–28.

Kuhn, M., and K. Dempsey. 2011. "End the Math Wars." *Learning & Leading with Technology* 39 (3): 18–21. ERIC Document Reproduction Service No. EJ954321.

Ladson-Billings, G. 1994. *The Dreamkeepers: Successful Teachers of African American Children*. San Francisco: Jossey-Bass.

Lampert, M., H. Beasley, H. Ghousseini, E. Kazemi, and M. Franke. 2010. "Using Designed Instructional Activities to Enable Novices to Manage Ambitious Mathematics Teaching. *Instructional Explanations in the Disciplines* 2:129–41.

Lareau, A. 1989. *Home Advantage*. New York: Falmer.

———. 2003. *Unequal Childhoods*. Berkeley: University of California Press.

Lareau, A., and W. Shumar. 1996. "The Problem of Individualism in Family-School Policies." Special issue. *Sociology of Education* 69:24–39.

Le Corre, M., and S. Carey. 2007. "One, Two, Three, Four, Nothing More: An Investigation of the Conceptual Sources of the Verbal Counting Principles." *Cognition* 105 (2): 395–438.

Le Corre, M., G. Van de Walle, E. M. Brannon, and S. Carey. 2006. "Re-visiting the Competence/Performance Debate in the Acquisition of the Counting Principles." *Cognitive Psychology* 52 (2): 130–69.

Lee, C. 2007. *The Role of Culture in Academic Literacies: Conducting Our Blooming in the Midst of the Whirlwind*. New York: Teachers College Press.

Lee, V. E., and D. T. Burkam. 2002. *Inequality at the Starting Gate: Social Background Differences in Achievement as Children Begin School.* Washington, DC: Economic Policy Institute.

Lesnick, J., B. Hart, and J. Spielberger. 2011. "More Time for Learning: Student Participation in Extended Day Programming at the UCCS Donoghue Campus during the 2009–10 School Year." Chapin Hall, University of Chicago.

Levine, S. C., K. R. Ratliff, J. Huttenlocher, and J. Cannon. 2012. "Early Puzzle Play: A Predictor of Preschoolers' Spatial Transformation Skill." *Developmental Psychology* 48 (2): 530–42.

Levine, S. C., L. W. Suriyakham, M. L. Rowe, J. Huttenlocher, and E. A. Gunderson. 2010. "What Counts in the Development of Young Children's Number Knowledge?" *Developmental Psychology* 46 (5): 1309–19.

Levy, F., and R. J. Murnane. 2004. *The New Division of Labor: How Computers Are Creating the Next Job Market.* New York: Russell Sage Foundation.

Liberman, I. Y., and D. Shankweiler. 1985. "Phonology and the Problems of Learning to Read and Write." *RASE: Remedial & Special Education* 6 (6): 8–17.

Lightfoot, S. L. 1981. "Toward Conflict and Resolution: Relationships between Families and Schools." *Theory into Practice* 20 (2): 97–104.

Lipman, P. 1998. *Race, Class, and Power in School Restructuring.* Albany: State University of New York Press.

———. 2002. "Making the Global City, Making Inequality: The Political Economy and Cultural Politics of Chicago School Policy." *American Educational Research Journal* 39 (2): 379–419.

———. 2004. *High Stakes Education: Inequality, Globalization, and School Reform.* New York: Routledge.

Little, J. W. 1990. "The Persistence of Privacy: Autonomy and Initiative in Teachers' Professional Relations." *Teachers College Record* 91 (4): 509–36.

Lortie, D. 1975. *Schoolteacher: A Sociological Study.* Chicago: University of Chicago Press.

Louis, K. S. 2007. "Changing the Culture of Schools: Professional Community, Organizational Learning, and Trust." *Journal of School Leadership* 16:477–87.

Louis, K. S., S. D. Kruse, and A. S. Bryk. 1995. "Professionalism and Community: What Is It and Why Is It Important in Urban Schools?" In *Professionalism and Community: Perspectives on Reforming Urban Schools,* edited by K. S. Louis and S. D. Kruse, 3–24. Thousand Oaks, CA: Corwin.

Loury, Glenn. 2002. *The Anatomy of Racial Inequality.* Cambridge, MA: Harvard University Press.

Loveless, T. 2013. "PISA's China Problem." Brookings Institution, Brown Center Chalkboard series, October 9. Retrieved from http://www.brookings.edu/research/papers/2013/10/09-pisa-china-problem-loveless.

———. 2014. "Lessons from the PISA-Shanghai Controversy." Brookings Institution, Brown Center Report on American Education, March 18. Retrieved from http://www.brookings.edu/research/reports/2014/03/18-pisa-shanghai-loveless.

Lubienski, S. T. 2002. "Research, Reform, and Equity in U.S. Mathematics Education." *Mathematical Thinking and Learning* 4:103–25.

Lundberg, I., J. Frost, and O. Petersen. 1988. "Effects of an Extensive Program for Stimulating Phonological Awareness in Preschool Children." *Reading Research Quarterly* 23:263–84.

Ma, L. 1999. *Knowing and Teaching Elementary Mathematics: Teachers' Understanding of Fundamental Mathematics in China and the United States.* Mahwah, NJ: Lawrence Erlbaum.

MacIntyre, H., and J. Ireson. 2002. "Within-Class Ability Grouping: Placement of Pupils in Groups and Self-Concept." *British Educational Research Journal* 28:249–63.

Maloney, E., G. Ramirez, E. Gunderson, S. Levine, and S. Beilock. 2015. "Intergenerational Effects of Parents' Math Anxiety on Children's Math Achievement and Anxiety." *Psychological Science* 26 (9): 1–9.

Massachusetts 2020. 2011. "Massachusetts Expanded Learning Time Initiative, 2010–2011 Update." Retrieved from www.mass2020.org/sites/default/files/2011_ma_update.pdf.

McCarton, C. M., J. Brooks-Gunn, I. F. Wallace, and C. R. Bauer. 1997. "Results at Age 8 Years of Early Intervention for Low-Birth-Weight Premature Infants: The Infant Health and Development Program." *JAMA: Journal of the American Medical Association* 277 (2): 126–32.

McFarland, D. 2001. "Student Resistance: How the Formal and Informal Organization of Classrooms Facilitate Everyday Forms of Student Defiance." *American Journal of Sociology* 107 (3): 612–78.

McGhee Hassrick, E. 2007. "Organizational Inequalities: The Social Production of Parent Pressures in Urban Schools." PhD diss., University of Chicago. ProQuest AAT 3287063.

McGhee Hassrick, E., and B. Schneider. 2009. "Parent Surveillance in Schools: A Question of Social Class. *American Journal of Education* 115 (2): 195–225.

McLoyd, V. C. 1998. "Socioeconomic Disadvantage and Child Development." *American Psychologist* 53 (2): 185–204.

Mehan, H., A. Herweck, and J. Meihls. 1986. *Handicapping the Handicapped: Decision Making in Students' Educational Careers.* Stanford, CA: Stanford University Press.

Mehta. 2013. "How Paradigms Create Politics: The Transformation of American Educational Policy, 1980–2001." *American Educational Research Journal* 50 (2): 285–324.

Merseth, K. 2009. *Inside Urban Charter Schools: Promising Practices and Strategies in Five High-Performing Schools.* With K. Cooper, J. Roberts, M. C. Tieken, J. Valant, and C. Wynne. Cambridge, MA: Harvard Education Press.

Meyer, J. W., and B. Rowan. 1977. "Institutionalized Organizations: Formal Structure as Myth and Ceremony." *American Journal of Sociology* 83 (2): 340–63.

Miles, K. H., and S. Frank. 2008. *The Strategic School.* Thousand Oaks, CA: Corwin.

Miller, L. 1998. "Redefining Teachers, Reculturing Schools: Connections, Commitments and Challenges." In *International Handbook of Educational Change*, edited by A. Hargreaves, A. Lieberman, M. Fullan, and D. Hopkins, 529–43. Dordrecht: Springer Netherlands.

Milner, H. R. 2013. "Scripted and Narrowed Curriculum Reform in Urban Schools." *Urban Education* 48 (2): 163–70.

Mix, K. S. 2008. "Surface Similarity and Label Knowledge Impact Early Numerical Comparisons." *British Journal of Developmental Psychology* 26:13–32.

Mix, K. S., J. Huttenlocher, and S. C. Levine. 2002. "Multiple Cues for Quantification in Infancy: Is Number One of Them?" *Psychological Bulletin* 128 (2): 278–94.

Moll, L. C., C. Amanti, D. Neff, and N. Gonzalez. 1992. "Funds of Knowledge for Teaching: Using a Qualitative Approach to Connect Homes and Classrooms." Special issue. *Theory into Practice* 31 (2): 132–41.

Mooney, M. 1990. *Reading to, with, and by Children.* Katonah, NY: Richard C. Owen.

Morris, D. 1993. "The Relationship between Children's Concept of Word in Text and Phoneme Awareness in Learning to Read: A Longitudinal Study." *Research in the Teaching of English* 27 (2): 133–54.

Morrison, F. 2000. "Specificity in the Nature and Timing of Cognitive Growth in Kindergarten and First Grade." *Journal of Cognitive Development* 1 (4): 429–48.

Morrison, F. J., and C. M. Connor. 2002. "Understanding Schooling Effects on Early Literacy: A Working Research Strategy." *Journal of School Psychology* 40 (6): 493–500.

Moultrie, L. 1992. "The School Reform Left Behind." Master's thesis, University of Chicago.

Mour, S. 1977. "Do Teachers Read?" *Reading Teacher* 30 (4): 397–401.

Muller, C., and D. Kerbow. 1993. "Parent Involvement in the Home, School, and Community." In *Parents, Their Children, and Schools*, edited by B. Schneider and J. S. Coleman, 13–42. Boulder, CO: Westview.

Muncey, D., and P. McQuillan. 1996. *Reform and Resistance in Schools and Classrooms: An Ethnographic View of the Coalition of Essential Schools*. New Haven, CT: Yale University Press.

Murnane, R. J. 2013. "U.S. High School Graduation Rates: Patterns and Explanations." *Journal of Economic Literature* 51 (2): 370–422.

Murnane, R. J., and F. Levy. 1996. *Teaching the New Basic Skills: Principles for Educating Children to Thrive in a Changing Economy*. New York: Free Press.

National Commission on Excellence in Education. 1983. "A Nation at Risk: The Imperative for Educational Reform." Washington, DC: US Government Printing Office.

National Council of Teachers of Mathematics, Commission on Standards for School Mathematics. 1989. "Curriculum and Evaluation Standards for School Mathematics." The Council, Reston, VA.

National Reading Panel. 2000. "Teaching Children to Read: An Evidence-Based Assessment of the Scientific Research Literature on Reading and Its Implications for Reading Instruction." Report of the National Reading Panel. Washington, DC: National Institute of Child Health and Human Development.

National Research Council. 2004. *On Evaluating Curricular Effectiveness: Judging the Quality of K–12 Mathematics Evaluations*. Washington, DC: National Academy Press.

———. 2009. *Mathematics Learning in Early Childhood: Paths toward Excellence and Equity*. Washington, DC: National Academy Press.

Neal, D. 2002. "How Vouchers Could Change the Market for Education." *Journal of Economic Perspectives* 16 (4): 25–44, doi:10.1257/089533002320950966.

———. 2006. "Why Has Black-White Skill Convergence Stopped?" In *Handbook of Economics of Education*, edited by E. Hanushek and F. Welch, 511–76. Amsterdam: Elsevier.

Newmann, F., B. King, and M. Rigdon. 1997. "Accountability and School Performance: Implications from Restructuring Schools." *Harvard Educational Review* 67 (1): 41–74.

Newmann, F., and G. Wehlage. 1995. *Successful School Restructuring: A Report to the Public and Educators by the Center on Organization and Restructuring of Schools*. Washington, DC: American Federation of Teachers.

New Zealand Ministry of Education. 1996. "Te Whāriki: He Zhāriki Mātauranga mō ngā Mokopuna o Aotearoa: Early Childhood Curriculum." Wellington: Learning Media. http://www.education.govt.nz/assets/Documents/Early-Childhood/te-whariki.pdf.

Nisbett, R. 1998. "Race, Genetics and IQ." In *The Black-White Test Score Gap*, edited by C. Jencks and M. Phillips, 86–102. Washington, DC: Brookings Institution Press.

Noguera, P. 2003. *City Schools and the American Dream: Reclaiming the Promise of Public Education*. New York: Teachers College Press.

Nomi, T., and E. Allensworth. 2008. "'Double-Dose' Algebra as an Alternative Strategy to Remediation: Effects on Students' Academic Outcomes." Consortium on Chicago School Research, University of Chicago.

Nomi, T., and E. M. Allensworth. 2010. "The Effects of Tracking with Supports on Instructional Climate and Student Outcomes in High School Algebra." Consortium on School Research, University of Chicago.

Nomi, T., and S. Raudenbush. 2016. "Making a Success of Algebra for All." *Educational Evaluation and Policy Analysis.*

Nye, B., S. Konstantopoulos, and L. V. Hedges. 2004. "How Large Are Teacher Effects?" *Educational Evaluation and Policy Analysis* 26 (3): 237–57.

Oakes, J., A. Gamoran, and R. N. Page. 1992. "Curriculum Differentiation: Opportunities, Outcomes, and Meanings." In *Handbook of Research on Curriculum*, edited by P. Jackson, 570–608.

Ogbu, J. U. 1999. "Beyond Language: Ebonics, Proper English, and Identity in a Black-American Speech Community." *American Educational Research Journal* 36 (2): 147–84.

Oreopoulos, P. 2006. "Estimating Average and Local Average Treatment Effects of Education When Compulsory Schooling Laws Really Matter." *American Economic Review* 96 (1): 152–75.

Park, H. 2013. *Re-examining Education in Japan and Korea: Demystifying Stereotypes.* New York: Routledge.

Parrila, R., J. R. Kirby, and L. McQuarrie. 2004. "Articulation Rate, Naming Speed, Verbal Short-Term Memory, and Phonological Awareness: Longitudinal Predictors of Early Reading Development?" *Scientific Studies of Reading* 8 (1): 3–26.

Parsons, T. 1959. "The School Class as a Social System." *Harvard Educational Review* 29: 297–318.

Payne, C. M. 2005. "Still Crazy after All These Years: Race in the Chicago School System." Seminar presentation at the Consortium for Chicago School Research, Chicago, April 22.

———. 2008. *So Much Reform, So Little Change: The Persistence of Failure in Urban Schools.* Cambridge, MA: Harvard Education Press.

Pearson, P. D., and L. Fielding. 1991. *Comprehension Instruction.* White Plains, NY: Longman.

Perry, T. 2003. *Young, Gifted and Black: Promoting High Achievement among African-American Students.* Boston: Beacon.

Peterson, C., and A. McCabe. 1992. "Parental Styles of Narrative Elicitation: Effect on Children's Narrative Structure and Content. *First Language* 12 (36): 299–321.

Phillips, M. 2000. "Understanding Ethnic Differences in Academic Achievement: Empirical Lessons from National Data." In *Analytic Issues in the Assessment of Student Achievement*, edited by David Grissmer and Michael Ross, 103–32. Washington DC: US Department of Education, National Center for Education Statistics.

Phillips, M., J. Crouse, and J. Ralph. 1998. "Does the Black-White Test Score Gap Widen After Children Enter School?" In *The Black-White Test Score Gap*, edited by Christopher Jencks and Meredith Phillips, 229–72. Washington, DC: Brookings Institution Press.

Pinnell, G. S. 1989. "Reading Recovery: Helping At-Risk Children Learn to Read." *Elementary School Journal* 90:161–83.

Pinnell, G. S., J. J. Pikulski, K. K. Wixson, J. R. Campbell, P. B. Gough, and A. S. Beatty. 1995. "Listening to Children Read Aloud: Data from NAEP's Integrated Reading Performance Record (IRPR) at Grade 4." NCES 95-726. US Department of Education. Office of Educational Research and Improvement, Washington, DC. ERIC No. ED378550.

Planty, M., W. Hussar, T. Snyder, G. Kena, A. Kewal Ramani, J. Kemp, K. Bianco, and R. Dinkes. 2009. "The Condition of Education." NCES 2009-082. Institute of Education Sciences, National Center for Education Statistics, US Department of Education, Washington, DC.

Porter, W., R. Riley, L. Towne, A. M. Hightower, S. C. Lloyd, K. L. Sellers, and C. B. Swanson. 2012. "Preparing for Change: A National Perspective on the Common Core State Standards Implementation Planning." Seattle: Education First and Editorial Projects in Education.

Programme for International Student Assessment. 2012. "Snapshot of Student Performance in Mathematics, Reading, and Science." Retrieved from http://www.oecd.org /pisa/keyfindings/PISA-2012-results-snapshot-Volume-I-ENG.pdf.

Puma, M., S. Bell, R. Cook, C. Heid, and M. Lopez. 2005. "Head Start Impact Study: First Year Findings." Administration for Children & Families, Washington, DC.

Pressley, M. 1998. Reading Instruction That Works: The Case for Balanced Teaching. New York: Guilford.

Pressley, M., L. Raphael, J. D. Gallagher, and J. DiBella. 2004. "Providence-St. Mel School: How a School That Works for African-American Students Works." Journal of Educational Psychology 96:216–35.

Ramani, G. B., and R. S. Siegler. 2008. "Promoting Broad and Stable Improvements in Low-Income Children's Numerical Knowledge through Playing Number Board Games." Child Development 79 (2): 375–94.

Rampey, B. D., G. S. Dion, and P. L. Donahue. 2009. "NAEP 2008 Trends in Academic Progress." NCES 2009–479. Institute of Education Sciences, National Center for Education Statistics, US Department of Education, Washington, DC.

Raudenbush, S. W. 2009. "The Brown Legacy and the O'Connor Challenge: Transforming Schools in the Images of Children's Potential." Educational Researcher 38 (3): 169–80.

Raudenbush, S. W., and R. Eschmann. 2015. "Does Schooling Increase or Reduce Social Inequality?" Annual Review of Sociology 41:443–70.

Raudenbush, S. W., R. P. Fotiu, and Y. F. Cheong. 1998. "Inequality of Access to Educational Resources: A National Report Card for Eighth-Grade Math." Educational Evaluation and Policy Analysis 20 (4): 253–67.

Raudenbush, S. W., and R. Kasim. 1998. "Cognitive Skill and Economic Inequality: Findings from the National Adult Literacy Survey." Harvard Educational Review 68 (1): 33–79.

Raudenbush, S. W., J. Marshall, and E. Art. 2011. "Year-by-Year Cumulative Impacts of Attending a High-Mobility Elementary School on Children's Mathematics Achievement in Chicago, 1995–2005." In Whither Opportunity? Rising Inequality, Schools, and Children's Life Chances, edited by G. J. Duncan and R. J. Murnane, 359–75. New York: Russell Sage Foundation.

Raudenbush, S. W., B. Rowan, and Y. F. Cheong. 1993. "Higher Order Instructional Goals in Secondary Schools: Class, Teacher, and School Influences." American Educational Research Journal 30 (3): 523–53.

Ravitch, D. 2001. Left Back: A Century of Battles over School Reform. New York: Touchstone Books.

Rayner, K., B. R. Foorman, C. A. Perfetti, D. Pesetsky, and M. S. Seidenberg. 2001. "How Psychological Science Informs the Teaching of Reading." Psychological Science in the Public Interest 2 (2): 31–74.

Raywid, M. 1995. "Professional Community and Its Yield at Metro Academy." In Profession-

alism and Community: Perspectives on Reforming Urban Schools, edited by K. S. Louis and S. D. Kruse, 45–75. Thousand Oaks, CA: Corwin.

Raz, I. S., and P. Bryant. 1990. "Social Background, Phonological Awareness and Children's Reading." *British Journal of Developmental Psychology* 8 (3): 209–25.

Reardon, S. F. 2011. "The Widening Academic Achievement Gap between the Rich and the Poor: New Evidence and Possible Explanations." In *Whither Opportunity? Rising Inequality, Schools, and Children's Life Chances*, edited by G. J. Duncan and R. J. Murnane, 91–116. New York: Russell Sage Foundation.

Reardon, S. F., and K. Bischoff. 2011. "Income Inequality and Income Segregation." *American Journal of Sociology* 116 (4): 1092–153.

Reay, D. 1998. *Class Work: Mothers' Involvement in the Children's Primary Schooling*. London: UCL Press.

Rivera-Batiz, F. L. 1992. "Quantitative Literacy and the Likelihood of Employment among Young Adults in the United States." *Journal of Human Resources* 27 (2): 313–28.

Roderick, M., B. Jacob, and A. Bryk. 2002. "Summer in the City: Achievement Gains in Chicago's Summer Bridge Program." In *Summer Learning: Research, Policies and Programs*, edited by G. D. Borman and M. Boulay, 73–102. Mahwah, NJ: Erlbaum.

Rollow, S. G. 1998. "Grounding a Theory of School Community Politics: Lessons from Chicago School Reform." PhD diss., University of Chicago.

Rollow, S. G., and A. S. Bryk. 1995. "Catalyzing Professional Community in a School Reform Left Behind." In *Professionalism and Community: Perspectives on Reforming Urban Schools*, edited by K. S. Louis and S. D. Kruse, 105–42. Thousand Oaks, CA: Corwin.

Romance, N. R., and M. R. Vitale. 2001. "Implementing an In-Depth, Expanded Science Model in Elementary Schools: Multiyear Findings, Research Issues, and Policy Implications." *International Journal of Science Education* 23:373–404.

Rothman, R. 2011. *Something in Common: The Common Core Standards and the Next Chapter in American Education*. Cambridge, MA: Harvard Education Press.

Rowan, B. 1990. "Commitment and Control: Alternative Strategies for the Organizational Design of Schools." *Review of Research in Education* 16:353–89.

Rowan, B., and S. W. Raudenbush. 2016. "Teacher Evaluation in American Schools." In *Handbook of Research on Teaching*, 5th ed., edited by Drew H. Gitomer and Courtney A. Bell, 1159–216. Washington, DC: American Education Research Association.

Rowan, B., S. Raudenbush, and Y. F. Cheong. 1993. "Teaching as a Nonroutine Task: Implications for the Management of Schools." *Educational Administration Quarterly* 29 (4): 479–500.

Rowe, M. L., S. C. Levine, J. A. Fisher, and S. Goldin-Meadow. 2009. "Does Linguistic Input Play the Same Role in Language Learning for Children with and without Early Brain Injury?" *Developmental Psychology* 45 (1): 90–102.

Rosenholtz, S. 1989. *Teachers' Workplace: The Social Organization of Schools*. New York: Longman.

Rumelhart, D. E., and A. Ortony. 1977. "The Representation of Knowledge in Memory." In *Schooling and the Acquisition of Knowledge*, edited by R. C. Anderson, R. J. Spiro, and W. E. Montague, 99–135. Hillsdale, NJ: Erlbaum.

Sarason, S. 1996. *Revisiting "The Culture of the School and the Problem of Change."* New York: Teachers College Press.

Sarnecka, B. W., and M. D. Lee. 2009. "Levels of Number Knowledge during Early Childhood." *Journal of Experimental Child Psychology* 103:325–37.

Saxe, G. B., S. R. Guberman, and M. Gearhart. 1987. "Goals and Contexts: A Reply to the Commentaries." Reply to commentaries of "Social Processes in Early Number Development." *Monographs for the Society for Researching Child Development* 52 (2): 160–63.

Schmidt, W. H., C. C. McKnight, and S. Raizen, eds. 2007. *A Splintered Vision: An Investigation of US Science and Mathematics Education.* Vol. 3. New York: Springer Science & Business Media.

Schoenfeld, A. H. 2004. "The Math Wars." *Educational Policy* 18:253–86.

Schrag, J., and K. Henderson. 1996. *School-Based Intervention Assistance Teams and Their Impact on Special Education.* Alexandria, VA: National Association of State Directors of Special Education. ERIC Document Reproduction Service No. ED392196.

Schwartz, A. E., and L. Stiefel. 2011. "Immigrants and Inequality in Public Schools." In *Whither Opportunity? Rising Inequality, Schools, and Children's Life Chances*, edited by G. J. Duncan and R. J. Murnane, 419–42. New York: Russell Sage Foundation.

Schweinhart, L., H. Barnes, and D. Weikart. 1993. *Significant Benefits: The High/Scope Perry Preschool Study through Age 27.* Ypsilanti, MI: High/Scope Educational Research Foundation.

Sergiovanni, T. J. 2000. *The Lifeworld of Leadership.* San Francisco: Jossey-Bass.

Slavin, R. E., and N. A. Madden. 2006. "Success for All, Roots and Wings: 2006 Summary of Research on Achievement Outcomes." Johns Hopkins University, Center for Research and Reform in Education, Baltimore.

Small, M. 2009. *Unanticipated Gains: Origins of Network Inequality in Everyday Life.* Oxford: Oxford University Press.

Smith, J., V. Lee, and F. Newmann. 2001. "Instruction and Achievement in Chicago Elementary Schools." Consortium on School Research, University of Chicago. https://consortium.uchicago.edu/publications/instruction-and-achievement-chicago-elementary-schools.

Snow, C. E. 2010. "Academic Language and the Challenge of Reading." *Science* 450:328.

Snow, C. E., M. S. Burns, and P. Griffin. 1998. *Preventing Reading Difficulties in Young Children.* Washington, DC: National Academy Press.

Snow, D. A. 2001. "Extending and Broadening Blumer's Conceptualization of Symbolic Interactionism." *Symbolic Interaction* 24 (3): 367–77.

Snyder, T. D., and S. A. Dillow. 2011. "Digest of Education Statistics, 2010." National Center for Education Statistics, US Department of Education, Washington, DC. Retrieved from https://nces.ed.gov/pubsearch/pubsinfo.asp?pubid=2011015.

Sorenson, A. B., and M. T. Hallinan. 1986. "Effects of Ability Grouping on Academic Achievement." *American Educational Research Journal* 23 (5): 519–42.

Stecher, B., G. Bohrnstedt, M. Kirst, J. McRobbie, and T. Williams. 2001. "Class-Size Reduction in California: A Story of Hope, Promise, and Unintended Consequences." *Phi Delta Kappan* 82 (9): 670–74.

Stein, M. K., L. Hubbard, and H. Mehan. 2004. "Reform Ideas That Travel Far Afield: The Two Cultures of Reform in New York City's District# 2 and San Diego." *Journal of Educational Change* 5 (2): 161–97.

Stein, N. L., M. W. Hernandez, and F. K. Angorro. 2011. "A Theory of Coherence and Complex Learning in the Physical Sciences: What Works (and What Doesn't)." In *Developmental Cognitive Science Goes to School*, edited by N. L. Stein and S. Raudenbush, 75–112. New York: Taylor and Francis.

Stigler, J. W. 1990. *Mathematical Knowledge of Japanese, Chinese, and American Elementary School Children*. Reston, VA: National Council of Teachers of Mathematics.

Stigler, J. W., and J. Hiebert. 2009. *The Teaching Gap: Best Ideas from the World's Teachers for Improving Education in the Classroom*. New York: Simon and Schuster.

Stoll, L., and L. K. S. Louis, eds. 2007. *Professional Learning Communities*. Maidenhead: Open University Press.

Stone, S. I., M. Engel, and J. Nagaoka. 2005. "Getting It the Second Time Around: Student Classroom Experience in Chicago's Summer Bridge Program." *Teachers College Record* 107 (5): 935–57.

Sulzby, E., and W. H. Teale. 1987. "Young Children's Storybook Reading: Longitudinal Study of Parent Child Interaction and Children's Independent Functioning." Ann Arbor: University of Michigan Press.

Tach, L., and G. Farkas. 2006. "Learning-Related Behaviors, Cognitive Skills, and Ability Grouping When Schooling Begins." *Social Science Research* 35 (4): 1048–79.

Tatum, B. D. 1997. *Why Are All the Black Kids Sitting Together in the Cafeteria? And Other Conversations about Race*. New York: Basic Books.

Taylor, D., and D. Strickland. 1986. *Family Storybook Reading*. Portsmouth, NH: Heinemann.

Teale, W. H., and E. Sulzby. 1987. "Literacy Acquisition in Early Childhood: The Roles of Access and Mediation in Storybook Reading." In *The Future of Literacy in a Changing World*, edited by D. Wagner, 111–30. New York: Pergamon.

Tivnan, T., and L. Hemphill. 2005. "Comparing Four Literacy Reform Models in High-Poverty Schools: Patterns of First-Grade Achievement." *Elementary School Journal* 105 (5): 419–41.

Tomlinson, S. 1982. *A Sociology of Special Education*. London: Routledge.

Tracy, D. M. 1987. "Toys, Spatial Ability, and Science and Mathematics Achievement: Are They Related?" *Sex Roles* 17:115–38.

Tyack, D. 1974. *The One Best System: A History of American Urban Education*. Cambridge, MA: Harvard University Press.

Useem, E. L. 1992. "Middle Schools and Math Groups: Parents' Involvement in Children's Placement." *Sociology of Education* 65 (4): 263–79.

Useem, E. L., J. B Christman, E. Gold, and E. Simon. 1997. "Reforming Alone: Barriers to Organizational Learning in Urban School Change Initiatives." *Journal for Education for Students Placed at Risk* 2 (1): 55–78.

Valle, J. W., and E. Aponte. 2002. "IDEA and Collaboration: A Bakhtinian Perspective on Parent and Professional Discourse." *Journal of Learning Disabilities* 35 (5): 470–80.

Vanneman, A., L. Hamilton, J. B. Anderson, and T. Rahman. 2009. "Achievement Gaps: How Black and White Students in Public Schools Perform in Mathematics and Reading on the National Assessment of Educational Progress." NCES 2009–455. National Center for Education Statistics, Washington, DC.

Vellutino, F. R., and D. M. Scanlon. 1987. "Phonological Coding, Phonological Awareness and Reading Ability: Evidence from a Longitudinal and Experimental Study." *Merrill-Palmer Quarterly* 33:321–63.

Velting, O. N., and G. J. Whitehurst. 1997. "Inattention-Hyperactivity and Reading Achievement in Children from Low-Income Families: A Longitudinal Model." Special issue, *Journal of Abnormal Child Psychology* 25 (4): 321–31.

Vincent, D. 2000. *The Rise of Mass Literacy: Reading and Writing in Modern Europe*. Oxford: Blackwell.

Waite, R. D. 2000. "A Study of the Effects of Everyday Mathematics on Student Achievement of Third-, Fourth-, and Fifth-Grade Students in a Large North Texas Urban School District." PhD diss., University of North Texas. Dissertation Abstracts International, 61(10), 3933A. UMI No. 9992659.

Walker, J. M. T., A. S. Wilkins, J. R. Dallaire, H. M. Sandler, and K. V. Hoover-Dempsey. 2005. "Parent Involvement: Model Revision through Scale Development." *Elementary School Journal* 106 (2): 85–104.

Waller, W. 1932. *The Sociology of Teaching*. Hoboken, NJ: Wiley.

Weick, K. E. 1976. "Educational Organizations as Loosely Coupled Systems." *Administrative Science Quarterly* 21 (1): 1–19.

Wellman, H. M. 1993. "Early Understanding of Mind: The Normal Case." In *Understanding Other Minds: Perspectives from Autism*, edited by S. Baron-Cohen, H. Tager-Flusberg, and D. Cohen. Oxford: Oxford University Press.

Weizman, Z. O., and C. E. Snow. 2001. "Lexical Output as Related to Children's Vocabulary Acquisition: Effects of Sophisticated Exposure and Support for Meaning." *Developmental Psychology* 37 (2): 265–79.

Wells, G. 1985. *Language Development in the Preschool Years*. Cambridge: Cambridge University Press.

Wharton-McDonald, R., M. Pressley, and J. M. Hampston. 1998. "Literacy Instruction in Nine First-Grade Classrooms: Teacher Characteristics and Student Achievement." *Elementary School Journal* 99 (2): 101–28.

White, K. R. 1982. "The Relation between Socioeconomic Status and Academic Achievement." *Psychological Bulletin* 91 (3): 461–81.

Wick, Tom. 2009. "The Chicago Elementary School Model." Harper Society Founders Circle Forum 2009. Urban Education Institute.

Wilkening, F. 2011. "Children's Cognitive Algebra and Intuitive Physics as Foundations of Early Learning in the Sciences." In *Developmental Cognitive Science Goes to School*, edited by N. L. Stein and S. W. Raudenbush, 143–56. New York: Routledge.

Wilson, V. L., and W. H. Rupley. 1997. "A Structural Equation Model for Reading Comprehension Based on Background, Phonemic, and Strategy Knowledge." *Scientific Studies of Reading* 1 (1): 45–63.

Wilson, W. J. 1987. *The Truly Disadvantaged*. Chicago: University of Chicago Press.

Woodworth, K. R., J. L. David, R. Guha, H. Wang, and A. Lopez-Torkos. 2008. "San Francisco Bay Area KIPP Schools: A Study of Early Implementation and Achievement." SRI International, Menlo Park, CA.

Wu, H. 2011. "The Mis-education of Mathematics Teachers." *Notices of the American Mathematical Society* 58 (3): 372–84.

Wynn, K. 1990. "Children's Understanding of Counting." *Cognition* 36:155–93.

———. 1992. "Children's Acquisition of the Number Words and the Counting System." *Cognitive Psychology* 24:220–51.

Zeuli, J. S. 1994. "How Do Teachers Understand Research When They Read It?" *Teaching and Teacher Education* 10 (1): 39–55.

INDEX

Note: Page numbers in *italic* indicate figures and tables.